SUPER POWERS
AND WORLD ORDER

SUPER POWERS AND WORLD ORDER

CARSTEN HOLBRAAD

EDITOR

AUSTRALIAN NATIONAL UNIVERSITY PRESS
CANBERRA 1971

CONTENTS

v

PREFACE

At the height of the Cold War, an outbreak of open hostilities between the Eastern and the Western bloc may sometimes have seemed rather more likely than perhaps it actually was. The intense heat generated by political rivalry and ideological conflict in that period made it difficult to realise that the opponents were fast reaching deadlock in their power relations and to appreciate that both protagonists were exercising considerable restraint in crisis situations. If, in the late 1940s and most of the 1950s, there may have been a tendency to exaggerate fear, in the earlier 1960s the inclination rather seemed to be to go to the opposite extreme and expect too much in the way of great power co-operation. As the balance of power between the United States and the Soviet Union was revealing itself more clearly and a certain harmony of interests between them becoming more apparent, tension between the camps was relaxing and a new situation taking shape. While a number of joint Russo-American efforts in international politics led some sharp-sighted observers to detect the emergence of an informal condominium of super powers, the tension arising between the United States and France and the break-up of the alliance between the Soviet Union and China encouraged speculation about a future multilateral concert of nuclear great powers.

If, during the Cold War, it was easy to overlook those elements of the relationship between East and West which restrained the opponents from entering into general war and, in the early years of the détente, it was tempting to ignore those elements which still divided the parties, now it may be possible to take a more balanced view of what passes between the United States and the Soviet Union. Perhaps, in the first years of the 1970s, we may reach a more realistic basis for speculating about the future pattern of international politics. Will the two super powers be joined rather in hostile rivalry than in limited co-operation? Will other major powers oppose attempts at joint super power control or take a place alongside the two dominant powers to form a multilateral concert of the world? Are we moving towards unmitigated international anarchy or witnessing the founding of a more solid world order? These are some of the more important questions dealt with in this book.

In September, October, and November of 1969, the Department of International Relations in the Research School of Pacific Studies at the

Australian National University arranged a series of seminars, of which the initial aim was to examine tendencies towards a condominium of super powers and explore the idea of a concert of several great powers. With reference to some Western writings of the earlier 1960s, I discussed in the introductory paper the nature of condominium and the conditions for concert, basing the analysis on historical cases of such great power arrangements. Other contributors, each from a different angle, surveyed the recent history of the relations of the powers, analysed the existing situation and speculated about the future. Dr Coral Bell, then a Visiting Fellow in the Department, discussed the nature of the political relationship between the dominant powers. Dr Ian Bellany and Dr T. B. Millar dealt with the arms issues, the former concentrating on the central balance of nuclear forces and the latter examining the attempt of the principal nuclear powers to prevent proliferation. Professor C. P. FitzGerald presented the reactions of China to tendencies towards Russo-American collusion. Mr J. L. Richardson, a member of the Department of Government at the University of Sydney, addressed himself to the past, present, and future roles in international politics of the secondary powers in Western Europe and Asia. Finally, Professor Sisir Gupta prepared a paper in which he viewed the pattern of great power relations and the problems of world order from the angle of the Third World. When it was decided to revise and expand the seven papers for publication, Professor Hedley Bull, who had been overseas during the period of the seminars, undertook to write a concluding chapter about world order and super powers. Finally, Professor Arthur Burns, who is a member of the Department of Political Science in the Research School of Social Sciences at this university, provided the Introduction to the symposium.

Though the chapters of this volume were finished during the earlier half of 1970, each author had an opportunity to revise briefly as late as November of that year.

Canberra
November 1970

CARSTEN HOLBRAAD

ABBREVIATIONS

ABM	Anti-Ballistic Missile
EEC	European Economic Community
FOBS	Fractional Orbital Bombardment System
GNP	Gross National Product
IAEA	International Atomic Energy Agency
ICBM	Inter-Continental Ballistic Missile
ISS	Institute for Strategic Studies
MIRV	Multiple Independently-targetable Re-entry Vehicle
SALT	Strategic Arms Limitation Talks
SLBM	Submarine Launched Ballistic Missile
UNCTAD	United Nations Conference on Trade and Development

A. L. BURNS

INTRODUCTION

A super power is one able to wreck half the world, and committed upon conditions to do so. Also, it must command the technology and economy to maintain into the foreseeable future the strategic forces needed for that destructive capacity. Australia would not become a super power merely by purchasing twenty-five nuclear submarines and four hundred Polaris missiles. But even the nuclear-strategic potential, though necessary, will not suffice; for the United Kingdom could sustain by an effort much greater strategic forces than at present, yet not the other dimensions of military potential which the ambiguous usage of 'super power' requires.

Those further 'dimensions' seem to include the potential to issue to one's chief opponents a conventional military threat at a level which before the nuclear era would have been apt to set off a major war if carried out. The threat may be presented, as by both the United States and the Soviet Union, from the territories of one's reliable allies or satellites. Some commentators have grounded their assertion that the United States is the only super power on the fact that the Soviet Union cannot yet deploy such vast conventional forces world wide: i.e., 'super power' entails 'naval power'. The latter implicitly suggested criterion looks stronger, but is actually weaker (Britain of the early 1960s would have been a super power) than the requirement that major war *conventional* forces be deployable against one's chief opponents. That requirement cannot now be met by the United Kingdom, and even Japan, more populous and situated close to China and the Soviet Union, may never come to meet it. Japan's is the borderline case; despite the talent, the education, and the present militarily favourable profile of her population, one hundred million islanders may be too few again to confront China conventionally, let alone the Soviet Union; yet one would be a bold man to assert that it *could* not suffice. The concept of a super power gains all its interest from such doubts about future applicability, for example to Japan and to Western Europe. The word's primary use, however, is not as a general concept (cf. the truly general 'Great Power') but as a collective proper noun (cf. 'the Seven Wonders of the World'; 'the Cabal'; also 'the

European System', of which it could be asked whether the Ottoman Empire were a member).

Indeed the primary usage of 'super powers' involves the suggestion, not of a mere collective, but of an interrelated one, as can be seen from the requirement about major conventional forces; for if a very strong power existed which had no chief opponent actually in view, but maintained forces as an insurance against unknown contingencies, I have a notion that the plural 'super powers' would drop out of use and some such phrase as 'the central powers' (excluding the power without opponents) take its place. As things are, the questions whether China is, or is about to become, a super power hang not only or mainly upon China's current military potential (though her development of thermonuclear weapons was a *sine qua non*), but also upon her inextricable relations with the Soviet Union and the United States.

Again, the nature of those relations affects the usage of the expression: they must be susceptible, over the years, to drastic change between hostility and the closest co-operation. One of the terminological difficulties about a united Western Europe's coming to be called a super power is the implicit restriction upon the range of relations it might have with the United States; they would be unlikely to become warlike, as have Sino-Soviet relations. If two thermonuclear and conventional powers were to co-operate in indissoluble amity, we would probably revert to the term 'blocs'.

A counter-example to the above analysis may seem to be afforded by the mid-1960s' contention that because of its strategic, economic, and technical pre-eminence, the United States was the sole super power. Though that appears to intend 'sole member of the super power class', I think it should rather be understood as a forecast (mistaken as it turned out) of change toward a hegemonial world order.

If 'super powers' is a tacitly relational expression, then we have already implied something about our other debatable expression, 'world order', which of course means something very much like 'the interrelations of all the powers'. Apparently our world order includes the relations, from 'hostile' to 'co-operative', between powers capable of deploying major-war conventional forces against each other, and of supporting the technological economy to produce strategic forces which might kill hundreds of millions, and which are targeted to do so, given the worst contingency.

This is sober fact. It is our over-willing reassurance by the phenomena of détente, of the Non-Proliferation Treaty, of the Strategic Arms Limitation Talks, that is intoxicated complacency. Our present situation contains the possibility of nuclear disaster, and therefore of a post-disaster world. Certainly, the disaster is quite unlikely in the short run: if it were even a little more likely, the powers would now be taking steps that would make it likelier still—conditions for outbreak of war pass instantaneously from the rather unlikely to the almost irresistible. But the notion of likelihood (or 'personal probability') loses sense the longer the run. To ask how probable is the outbreak of nuclear war during or before the year 1990 is absurd; we cannot even tell whether the likelihood will grow or shrink year by year. But we can say that disaster is quite possible, so that it and its possible aftermaths are contingencies to be considered, not only by the civil defence co-ordinator but by the social scientist. The great discontinuity that nuclear war would make may exceed the grasp of our methodology, but it would be a kind of experience not unfamiliar to earlier societies: to primitives confronted by developed cultures, to the prophets and peoples of the Old Testament. Most of their known world could be wiped out, as could most of our nuclear world order.

The order of the super powers contained in our world order is also one which speeds but neither checks nor guides the process of developing strategic weapons nor, except in the case of the Non-Proliferation Treaty's non-nuclear adherents, that of acquiring weapons nor, unless the SALT succeed beyond expectations, that of deploying and targeting them. But, as Dr Ian Bellany points out below, the prospects of war and peace depend partly upon the nature and quantity of the forces deployed and about to be deployed. So the super powers may well arm themselves into reciprocal and fatal dilemma, unrestrained by external institutions or by an immanent balancing mechanism, a hidden hand. Thus in complement, security from major and especially from nuclear war depends too much upon what Dr Coral Bell calls 'crisis management' (in contrast with 'crisis avoidance' which she too deems to be beyond the present super powers) that is, upon the wisdom, foresight, and self-discipline of the super powers' rulers. We shall glance later at the evidence for their having those essential qualities.

Two features of our present world order that fundamentally distinguish it from all previous ones are (1) the suddenly great scale of its leading societies, both in population and in social organisation (to which also we refer below) and (2) the new effects of standing conditions, especially of geography. All parts of the globe are within an hour's or less missile distance from anywhere else, but conventional forces must still be flown across or sailed across oceans. The tasks of the nuclear deterrent strategist remain far simpler if his is an islanded power than if it also has frontiers with or land approaches to its nuclear opponents. The latter impose a direct connection between conventional and nuclear security, and leave India, China, the Soviet Union, and Continental Europe in long-run situations much more drastic than those of oceanic and even of narrow-sea powers. By itself the Sino-Soviet geopolitics (see Professor C. P. FitzGerald's contribution) makes the hope of a generally disarmed and co-operating world chimerical, and nuclear holocaust a distinct possibility for many decades to come. The contrast with present relations amongst advanced Western societies, discussed below, is remarkable.

A final point about the interrelations of the super powers in our present world order: what appeared, misleadingly, to be a bilateral (two party) relation between the Americans and the Russians is now a multilateral (several party) relation. That will seem to be a numerical platitude; the case is, nevertheless, that several party relations differ in kind from two party relations, and cannot be reduced to or analysed into them (moreover, every addition of a party creates a new state of affairs, requiring a new diagnosis). Suppose, as a fanciful instance, that there really were a Russian-American condominium, whichever of Dr Holbraad's acute explications of that term one chooses: then if China were to join the condominium, it would necessarily become a different system. By the same token, a three party deterrent relation between the United States, the Soviet Union, and China is quite a different matter from one between Russians and Americans alone, or from one between them and the British and the French; it differs even from the previous three party nuclear relation which in the early 1960s obtained between the United Kingdom and the other two, since the United Kingdom was in as close a combination with the United States as it is possible for a sovereign but lesser nuclear power to be.

Those earlier several party relations are worth discussing. Despite the special nuclear relationship, Britain was (and, unobtrusively, still is) genuinely a third independent party: she could be secure against a selectively anti-British attack by the Soviet Union, not only because of passive elements (e.g. joint early warning with the United States), but because of her capacity to retaliate devastatingly against Russia with weapons under her sovereign control. The case of the French is even clearer: United States policy in the early 1960s was bent upon denying France an independent deterrent because, as an eminent American strategist put it, the Americans could think of no acceptable way of starting World War III, and to be 'triggered' by the Europeans was about the worst.

In essence, the several party nuclear situation is that a quite weak nuclear power can hope to benefit from the awesome two party deterrent relation between the Russians and the Americans if it has evidently some prospect, directly or indirectly, of seriously damaging either or both of them no matter what either or both of them have done. If a third party is thus hooked onto the Russian-American balance, a fourth party can hook, if not onto the major two, at least onto the third; and so on. Remember that every addition of a new party, and any substantial change in the abstractable strategic relation between any pair or more, will always require a new analysis from the fundamentals. These topics have been expounded elsewhere at what must be tiresome length;[1] all that needs to be laboured here is that China, if threatened by the United States, could counter-threaten the Soviet Union; or, if threatened by the Soviet Union, could counter-threaten Western Europe, Japan, or other non-American interests of the United States. Such a policy will not deter as effectively as that of reciprocal and equivalent threat, which Moscow and Washington now present to each other, and so nuclear powers will be apt to aim at the latter, as the Soviet Union has done since the late 1950s, when it too made hostages of Western European states against the ominous American threat. Yet China, for example, for a long time to come will not be able to deter the United States principally by what she might deliver on the North American continent, but rather by the destruction she is already capable of wreaking in the Soviet Union. China's present and long-run strategic situations are desperate, and the Peking régime, though by no means reckless (see FitzGerald), is totalitarian and considers its own possible fall the ultimate disaster. By contrast Britain and France, though they may be prepared to force Washington's hand in the extremely remote event of a major Russian attack on Western Europe, would certainly not attempt to do so by threatening *American* cities directly: Western powers for the last twenty years have flinched from the final rigour of nuclear deterrent logic. Several party relations between nuclear states, in this matter, like two party relations need not be wholly hostile or egotistic.

It is mainly in that light that Russian-American *rapprochement,* détente, co-operation, condominium is to be understood at the nuclear level: their paramount interest is to avoid being set upon each other. Their other interests, of great strength in themselves, as Dr T. B. Millar points out, are to increase their control over their allies and their client states—in the Soviet's case, the Non-Proliferation Treaty was directed at their Eastern European empire, perhaps as much as at Western Germany. On the other hand that empire is not only of exploitative but even more of long-run strategic importance to Moscow, for the reasons of deterrent security on its Western margins already mentioned. This is not to say that for instance Czechoslovakia, August 1968, was strategically unavoidable by the Soviet Union, any more than that Vietnam was by Presidents Kennedy and Johnson: alarmed and brutal tyranny in the one case, false strategic doctrine, false geopolitics, and presidential fantasy in the other, are needed for their explanation. Contingent malice and folly add their measure of evil to the apparently necessary horrors of the nuclear deterrent system, which seem to have come to stay.

That system, however, is by no means all there is to the present world order, even though one must begin, as Professor Bull implies, from the

[1] A. L. Burns, *Of Powers and Their Politics.* Englewood Cliffs, N.J.: Prentice-Hall, 1968.

super powers, the other nuclear powers, and their several party relations. In this book, Mr James Richardson considers the situations and responses of non-nuclear or not-yet-nuclear states among the 'secondary' powers, notably Japan and most of Western Europe. Professor Gupta's profound, realistically subtle and moving contribution traces the story of the 'Third World's' part in the universal process. Dr Bell and Dr Millar deal indirectly with related themes. Practising no particular expertise, I can inject here only an impression: that parts of the world may be turning away from the nuclear concerns that cannot but obsess the super powers, and be showing evidence of a new kind of power-political behaviour which may begin to modify the current order. Japan and a number of Latin American states have recently engaged in it, but the chief exemplars are the Western Europeans. For at least twenty years several of the Western states on the Continent, and the United Kingdom, have practised the arts of statecraft with and against each other; they have formed, maintained or dissolved, joined or stayed out of, many political institutions, several of them of a new kind. They have enriched and impoverished each other, devalued and revalued against each other, abetted and opposed each others' policies. And in that time none of them has moved a battalion against another. Clearly it is possible, as the Europeans have demonstrated, to be powers and practise power politics, and yet to do so without the sanction of force. With the exception of Western Germany during the next twenty years or so, it would not matter if every Western European country including Spain and Portugal were nuclearly armed to the teeth: that would probably immobilise their military forces even more than now.

The one qualification to the above is whether this benign state of affairs would survive the disappearance of the Iron Curtain, which was a necessary and, some would argue, nearly a sufficient condition for the emergence on the Western side of it of forceless power politics. Are the *Eastern* European states interlinked and immobilised to anything like the extent that the Western are? Would power be balanced among them if the Soviet empire withdrew? Or would the example of a once-murderous Western system now reformed by change of environment entice the Easterner as well? However we answer those questions, the phenomena of intra-Western forcelessness, and the possibility that Japan may remain content merely to go on enriching herself and to forgo the status of super power,[2] cast a few rays of hope into this gloomy introduction.

Whether or not the gloom really shadows our world order, it is in any case produced by the writer's interpretation of international politics. All powers by their nature appear to me morally ambiguous, with evil aspect

[2] Both the European and the Japanese prospects are canvassed in A. L. Burns, 'Military-Technological Models and World Order'. *International Journal*, vol. XXIV, 1968-9, p. 790.

prevailing. Though greater powers need not be by that token greater evils, the criteria suggested in the first few pages above for the status of super power indicate that in the peculiar circumstances of the post-nuclear age the greater are in fact likelier to be the worse. With the prospect of unlikely thermonuclear destruction, super powers combine that of all-too-possible killing by conventional forces on a scale otherwise practised of late chiefly in the larger newly-emerged states. But the weakness distinctive of super powers is a consequence of the scale of social and economic organisation and of the size of population required to meet all the criteria. Tasks of rule, of administration, of government never before set the human race are prescribed to the super powers' rulers, not least of them the oversight of unpredictable research and development of new weapons apt to change the working of the international order. There is now evidence that in the last year or so the United States has begun to develop procedures and instrumentalities that at least establish the executive's grip upon the military-technological processes, though not enough (so far as the writer can tell) to have reasserted an assured political capacity to direct them. Ungoverned or inadequately governed, the best of super powers present to the world a danger as terrible in effect as did the pre-nuclear totalitarian powers of the 1930s, though in the last resort less horrifying because not purposefully diabolical. But the totalitarian super powers not only are blindly dangerous, but apt as well to deliberate and ruthless tyranny.

Every contribution to this volume reveals, as it was bound to reveal, its author's evaluations, that is, how he stands towards the super powers and the lesser powers, towards the world-political process and to the world order; what he fears and what he hopes will come. The very ideas are value-laden, 'order' favourably, 'powers' ambivalently. Moreover, one cannot discuss or even apprehend the subject matter except by employing such ideas or their equivalents. Nor are ideals, types of world order, kinds of situation, the only objects one values: particular societies, nations, and peoples are admired and despised, loved and hated for themselves. None of the contributors to this volume is a citizen of or adheres to either of the two evident super powers; but amongst us there is a certain variety of patterns of attachment to the several nations of the non-communist world, as well of course as to a greater variety of ideals and political values. Since the evidence needs illumination from different points of view, I consider that variety an advantage.

Conversely, one's system of values is to some extent put to the test by comparing the tracts of the subject illuminated from its point of view with the areas thrown light on by the others'. From which angle is the widest range of possibilities discerned?—from which are their permutations most subtly analysed, their outcomes most realistically foreseen? Much of this 'testing' must wait upon the future, and that tends to make the study of

B

world politics thankless work, for it will be looked back on, if at all, for its errors. But since most of the analysis in this volume concerns recent history, the criterion of comprehensiveness can be used by the reader in assessing the validity of our conclusions and, more importantly, the significance of the questions raised here about the present world order.

The questions raised by Dr Carsten Holbraad arise, as do the senses he assigns to the terms 'condominium' and 'concert', out of his comparative historical analysis. But that is far from committing him to the proposition that a condominium of super powers leading a concert of other nuclear powers would be the same species of animal as the historic condominia and concerts he has referred to. Rather can he inquire, for instance, whether the conditions for concert exist today, without a major war having preceded, without ideological and cultural unity of the kind that made possible the Concert of Europe. He understands the latter too well to have any great hope that a contemporary concert led by a super power condominium would be sure of coping with the late-twentieth-century situation.

Dr Bell's questions are about the most decisive of all international trans-actions. She is concerned, as were the observers of power politics in the nineteenth century, with the 'small group at the top of each society, who shared a considerable stock of common precepts and values with their opposite numbers in the other dominant powers'. Part of the justification for this concern is that lesser powers in the last twenty years have feared too little co-operation rather than too much between the super powers. I share with Dr Bellany a doubt whether the Soviet Union really is of the same mind with the United States on matters of strategic doctrine; and I wonder whether Dr Bell's theme of 'crisis management' can be sustained if the Russians and even more the Chinese have such different conceptions of the nature of international order from the highly distinctive Western concep-tions. Dr Bell's sharp query as to how little the super powers *need* to do to maintain their present prominence seems to me exactly the kind of question that a volume such as this should raise, and her interest in what the Chinese might do a necessary corrective to the reassuring impressions that SALT and other Russian-American partnerships convey. Yet by indicating the considerable diplomatic resources of the super powers in crisis management, she gives us rational ground for a moderate hope, and, as often before, introduces us to a well-considered yet a new concept of statecraft just as it begins to emerge in practice.

Dr Bellany is in some ways the odd man out in this book. Though he is concerned hardheadedly with what is called hardware, he opens up ranges of political issues that the rest of our deliberately political contributions miss, and puts matters we do touch upon into their complicated strategic context. In particular, the narrow domain he foresees for any super power agreement on strategic arms limitation diminishes the hopes of others that

Russian-American condominium would turn out quite benign; and his recognition of the cheapening and accessibility of nuclear deterrents, especially of the unorthodox varieties, raises acutely the question whether the two will continue to predominate beyond the 1970s. In retrospect also, his citing of D. J. Fink's article deflates those accounts of purposive and prudent development of American strategic doctrine in the late 1960s which the present writer, for one, had accepted: the change to 'assured destruction' and to 'parity' now seems to have been *faute de mieux*.

Dr Millar also poses embarrassing questions about the beneficence of super power agreement, while reminding us that alternate scenarios for a nuclear world order are no more encouraging. By implication, too, he points out elements of a contemporary power base neglected in the earlier pages of this introduction, and suggests how condominium is likely to be reinforced by restrictions upon the non-nuclear states' access to civilian nuclear technology.

Professor FitzGerald's salutary warning against the assumption that both the policies and the categories of Western and Soviet governments, differing as they do amongst themselves, are likely to be acceptable to China or to hundreds of millions in the non-European countries, may be read together with Professor Gupta's essay so as to help us use more critically the idea of a *world* order. If indeed China can take or leave alone the possibility that she join a condominium, and if Mao's successors escape as Professor Fitz-Gerald says they will the simplicities of their own propaganda, then our preoccupation with Russian-American relations may quite soon appear shortsighted and parochial, and the centre of international concern may shift quickly to the Chinese-Japanese-Russian triangle.

Nevertheless our present international agenda are overloaded with unre-solved items apt to busy us for the next few years. Mr James Richardson deals with many of these, as well as with the case of re-emerged Japan. He wisely rejects the possibility of *all* secondary powers combining against condominium, but refers us to the currently undecided question whether Europe's several divisions, or Eastern and Western Europe together, might assert more independent roles against the super powers. While he has stressed how foreshadowed American troop withdrawals from Western Europe are already tending to liquidate the post-1945 situation, does he perhaps make too little of the possibility of dangerous explosion in Eastern Europe, no matter by what means the post-war bonds are loosened?

To pick out salient questions from the intricate web of Professor Gupta's analysis would distort its fabric; so one may do no more than point to the grave difficulties it raises for many authoritative approaches to international affairs. The neo-classical doctrine that might is right, that the world goes best when it exempts leading powers from too close a moral criticism of their conduct, is put in question by Professor Gupta's observation that although the relations between the super powers have been stabilised, there has been a perceptible rise in the level of permissibility of chaos, conflict, and violence in those regions of the world which are peripheral for the purposes of the central power balance.

At the opposite extreme, the behaviouralist therapy of controlled communication must seem, in that shadow, to be at best of marginal use. Crisis management also (challenged by Mr Richardson as well) begins to look like an overloaded program. Lastly, Professor Gupta in effect reminds us of the conventional and the sub-military violence actually afflicting the Third World, whereas the nuclear threat that concerns Dr Millar, Dr Bellany, and the present writer may never be implemented; similarly the world-wide system of power that *we* emphasise appears less unifying in its effect when, as he indicates, China's and France's reassertions have incidentally down-graded the Third to the fifth or sixth world.

Where Professor Gupta foresees decline, frustration, and worse for much of the world order Professor Bull can contemplate its future as well as its recent past with a certain equanimity, also emphasising the unification and simplification which super powers have effected in it. These differences between their prognoses are caused by their attending in analysis to somewhat different features of the situation, which in turn is caused by differences in their fundamental evaluations: Professor Bull is a leading exponent of the classical doctrines of international order, and particularly of the variant that characterises the present political organisation of mankind as a 'society' of sovereign states. Now, though in the last analysis he sees international order as only a means of sustaining that world order which is a pattern of activity drawn so as to promote the primary social goals—of security against violence, enforcement of contracts, and stable possession of property—yet his insistence that sovereign states still form a *society*, and not for instance an anarchy, suggests both a favourable valuation of inter-power relations and also a judgment that the quality of present world politics is much the same as that of the comity of nineteenth-century Europe.

Moreover, he sees the United States and the Soviet Union, as super powers, continuing to play the role evolved within the European system to befit the European great powers; nor does he suppose that the possible future emergence of China as a super power will significantly change the nature of the leading powers' role, though it may well 'signify the transformation of the Soviet-American *world order*' (my emphasis) 'into something quite new'. He is far from endorsing all of the super powers' works; but he suggests that on the whole they are effective and make *for* world order, normatively as he conceives it, and that they should be given that kind of benefit of the doubt which is the due of those cast in a perennial and indispensable role.

Professor Bull's conception of the society of states, and his persuasion of continuity in the nature of its interrelations, help him illuminate features of the real world that tend to escape contrary interpreters: those who like the present writer rather see *dis*continuity after 1945 between the previous European-centred order of great and lesser powers and the present system, dominated—and, one would agree with him, simplified—by the thermo-nuclear, populous, and continent-based super powers; indeed a change in the very nature both of the system itself and of the powers foremost in it. *We* incline to think the Soviet Union and the United States alike ineffectual: unable except sometimes by main force to prevail while others go under to see to it that only certain conflicts will form the essential theme of inter-national politics, impotent above all to preserve that international order which Professor Bull requires to include 'immunity for envoys, the keeping of agreements and mutual respect for sovereign jurisdiction' and which the imperialist powers of the late nineteenth and the twentieth centuries man-aged fairly well to universalise. Despite the preference for the *status quo* which the super powers share, *we* see them as sources, however unequally, of *dis*order, for example, the manner and the means if not the original objectives of American intervention in Indo-China; both the objectives and the manner of Soviet intervention in Czechoslovakia.

Again, disagreements in perception and judgment arise from even slight differences in philosophy and valuation; amongst the primary ends of social, international, and world order Professor Bull does not include (consist-ently, since they are not universally valued) political liberty or protection of the weak and poor; nor has he the Augustinian's radical misgivings about all worldly powers. But such variation of perspectives brings this volume's subjects into a clearer view than a unified method and approach would have done.

A question about world order hardly noticed in this work concerns the interaction of internal, socio-political dynamics with the external system. Few at the beginning of the 1960s foresaw how first the advanced Western societies and then others would turn in on themselves and at least interrupt processes of trans-national integration. Perhaps we should hope for a com-panion volume of speculations on internal developments for the 1970s, to qualify our extrapolations of trends in world order.

CONDOMINIUM
AND CONCERT

When Cold War between the Soviet Union and the United States developed into détente, new terms and concepts came to the forefront in the vocabulary and thinking of students of international politics. In the 1960s, words and ideas which in the late 1940s and throughout the 1950s, when first Joseph Stalin had directed the policies of the Soviet Union and then John Foster Dulles had dominated the foreign policy of the United States, had nearly fallen into desuetude were revived by Western writers. Prominent in the new terminology were 'condominium' and 'concert'.

Condominium was used not only by some of those British and American writers who hoped that a high degree of co-operation between the super powers might secure world order, but also by some of those Europeans who feared that too much collaboration between the dominant powers would reduce the freedom of the other members of the states-system. In some ways it was an unfortunate choice of term. Condominium belongs to the terminology of international law. It is Latin for joint lordship, and refers to a concept which reached the modern world from the feudal system of mediaeval Europe. Particularly the old German *Reich* produced many condominial arrangements, a large number of which survived till the nineteenth century. Condominium was the subject of several Latin treatises which appeared in the seventeenth and eighteenth centuries, most of them written by Germans. In the nineteenth century a number of condominia were created in Europe, the best known being that of Prussia and Austria over Schleswig-Holstein and Lauenburg. It was established by the Vienna peace treaty of 1864 after the war with Denmark and lasted only till 1866, when the Austrian Emperor after military defeat transferred his rights over the duchies to the King of Prussia. Other examples of some historical interest include the arrangement between Austria-Hungary and Turkey over Bosnia and Herzegovina from 1879 till 1908 and that between

For my account of the earlier use of the term 'concert' and my survey of the history of the Concert of Europe in the second section of this chapter, I have drawn on the introduction to my book *The Concert of Europe: A Study in German and British International Theory, 1815-1914*, London: Longman, 1970.

Britain and France over the colony of the New Hebrides, which rests on a treaty of 1906 and a protocol of 1914 and survives as a reminder of the Anglo-French *entente* before World War I.

Writing in 1926,[1] the German international lawyer Verdross made a distinction between condominium and coimperium, which has since been accepted by other lawyers.[2] While condominium, according to him, means joint rule over territory belonging to the partners, coimperium is joint rule over somebody else's territory. In the latter type of arrangement the partners do not exercise full sovereign rights over the territory in question. The most prominent recent example of coimperium given by the writers who follow this distinction is that of the allied powers over Germany after 1945. Though Germany had lost the war and had surrendered unconditionally, she had not given up her status as a subject of international law. So the Big Four were occupying foreign territory and, therefore, were parties to a coimperium, not a condominium.

When used by international lawyers, both terms denote a type of arrangement which is composed of two elements, namely a formal association of two or more subjects of international law and a joint exercise of authority within a particular territory. Both of the component parts are defined by treaty. The partners are tied to each other by contractual bonds and are exercising treaty rights. In recent writings on international relations the word 'condominium' has been used rather differently. Those who have detected, urged, or opposed the development of a condominium of the Soviet Union and the United States in world politics have not generally had in mind an arrangement in which the relationship between the partners is set out in a treaty and their joint authority defined in legal terms. Though they have usually emphasised the need to express agreements to control the arms race in treaties, most of them have conceived of the partnership of super powers as resting on an informal understanding, and of the joint authority as being self-assumed and uncircumscribed. Rarely have they thought even of geographical limits to the exercise of this authority. While the condominia of international law are formal arrangements between any two or more subjects and are confined to particular territories, the condominium of these writers is a loose association of the world's most dominant powers and is global in principle. While the former may play only a minor

---

[1] Alfred Verdross, 'Staatsgebiet, Staatengemeinschaftsgebiet und Staatengebiet', *Zeitschrift für internationales Recht*, vol. 37, 1926, p. 293.

[2] See, e.g., *Wörterbuch des Völkerrechts*, Hans-Jürgen Schlochauer (ed.). Berlin: Gruyter, 1960-2, vol. I, 'Coimperium' and 'Condominium' (by P. Schneider), and Georg Schwarzenberger, *A Manual of International Law*. London: Stevens and Sons, 1967, pp. 58 and 628-9. Schwarzenberger defines condominium as 'joint exercise of sovereignty over territory by two or more subjects of international law' and coimperium as 'joint exercise of supreme jurisdiction by two or more subjects of international law over territory which they refrain from subjecting to their own territory' (pp. 628-9).

role in the political and diplomatic relations of the participants, the latter is the essence of the relationship of the partners.

Few of those who have speculated about such a world condominium seem to have had precise notions of the nature of the joint functions of the partners. Neither the idea of complete and effective government of the world, which might be described as the maximum function, nor the idea of a control strictly limited to the use and spread of nuclear weapons, which presumably would be the minimum function, has found many advocates among those in the habit of using the term 'condominium'. Most have taken intermediate positions, arguing that a successful exercise of control in a limited sphere or over particular issues might be a step towards a more general management of the affairs of the world. Among the earlier writers to take this line were Coral Bell in England and Herman Kahn in America. Writing in 1962, Kahn advocated a 'condominium on world affairs' between the United States and the Soviet Union based on a 'Hague' convention against the use of nuclear weapons. Such a convention, he thought, if effective, not only might be useful in discouraging the diffusion and controlling the use of nuclear weapons but also would be a major precedent for the creation of 'a very limited but possibly adequate "world government" '.[3] Two years later Coral Bell argued that it had become very difficult to avoid viewing world politics in terms of what she called 'the shadow condominium'. The basic function of the emergent condominium, in her view, was 'joint management of the central power-balance'. But in the joint resolution of the Cuban missile crisis she saw also elements of government.[4] In the thought of such writers two ideas may be distinguished: one which presents the condominium as an instrument for managing the balance of power and one which holds it up as a step towards world government. However, whether the emphasis is on balancing power or whether it is on governing the world, the modern notion of condominium generally implies a high degree of joint control over the major issues of international politics.

Since it is not suggested that the partners in the condominium should enjoy sovereign rights over the rest of the world, or over the regions within their joint control, the term 'coimperium' would be more consistent with current legal usage than 'condominium'. Though this term has been used occasionally, most of the synonyms that have gained some currency have not come from legal terminology. 'Joint hegemony', an expression frequently employed by John Strachey, and 'partnership', used by Arnold Toynbee, are in a way more suitable for describing a political relationship

[3] Herman Kahn, 'The Arms Race and World Order', Morton A. Kaplan (ed.), *The Revolution in World Politics*. New York and London: John Wiley and Sons, 1962, p. 350.

[4] Coral Bell, *The Debatable Alliance. An Essay in Anglo-American Relations*. Chatham House Essays: London, New York, and Toronto: Oxford University Press, 1964, p. 111.

than words borrowed from international law; but they fail to convey the element of government, which both Strachey and Toynbee had in mind when speculating about world order. On the other hand, 'duopoly' and 'diarchy', though they certainly bring out the elements of domination and rule, tend perhaps to lay even greater stress on them than intended by the writers using these terms. Duopoly, borrowed from economics, exaggerates the concentration of power and, therefore, conjures up a lop-sided picture of the system it is meant to describe. Diarchy, though it has a nice parallel in 'pentarchy'—a term which in the nineteenth century was widely used as a synonym for the Concert of Europe—brings to mind British rule in India. Yet, whatever the advantages and disadvantages of the various synonyms, and whatever the difficulties of using a word which in international law enjoys a much more precise meaning, condominium seems to be the most widely preferred word for describing joint super power control in international politics.

There is no linguistic reason why condominium should be restricted to apply to arrangements involving only two partners. Indeed, some of the writers who have speculated about the possibility of China at some future date joining the Soviet Union and the United States have used the term to refer also to an association of three parties. But the fact that there are no more than two super powers in the world today has made it more common to apply the word to a dualistic relationship only. This usage I shall follow here.

Looking to history for instruction about the nature of such condominia, one does not find a host of examples. Cases of dualistic situations are numerous, but generally characterised by rivalry between the two dominant powers. Yet, both ancient and modern history provide some examples of two great powers swallowing their differences and attempting together to govern or control a large part of the political world. In an interesting analysis of inter-empire relations, George Liska draws attention to the alliance of Egypt and Hatti in the thirteenth century B.C., the earliest case of condominium recorded in some detail.[5] It was the result of long years of war between the two empires, the battle fought at Kadesh in the fifth year of Rameses II being particularly important. In the year 21 of Rameses II, he and Khattusilis, the Hittite king, put an end to their hostility in Asia Minor and concluded a treaty of alliance, the text of which has survived. The two rulers not only renounced all projects of conquest against the other and pledged mutual assistance in the case of attack from any third quarter but also undertook to co-operate in the chastisement of delinquent subjects, probably in Syria in particular, and made provisions for extra-

---

[5] George Liska, *Imperial America: The International Politics of Primacy*, Studies in International Affairs, no. 2. Baltimore: The Johns Hopkins Press, 1967, pp. 13-14. Liska gives a few more examples of condominial arrangements in antiquity.

dition of refugees in either direction. The friendship between the two great powers of the time was cemented in the following years by a lively correspondence between the two courts and by a marriage of a daughter of the Hittite king to the Pharaoh. It lasted throughout the long reign of Rameses II and into that of his successor Merenptah, perhaps fifty years.[6]

Modern European history presents a number of dualistic situations with elements of condominium. The rather shortlived alliance between Russia and France, which began with Napoleon's defeat of the Tzar's army at Friedland in 1807 and ended with his invasion of Russia in 1812, was clearly an attempt to co-ordinate the policies and concert the efforts of the two empires. After the meeting of Napoleon and Alexander I on the river Niemen, a treaty was signed at Tilsit in 1807, in which the Emperor and the Tzar rearranged and divided the territories of central and eastern Europe and promised to support each other against Britain and Turkey. At Erfurt the following year the two rulers met again. Napoleon, having held out the prospect of a joint enterprise in the Near East and a partition of Turkey, now requested a pledge of Russian support against the various movements that threatened him in central Europe. None of these efforts at co-operation was successful. While Napoleon disappointed the Russian ruler in relations with Turkey and over the Polish question, Alexander I failed to stand by the French emperor against Britain and in Germany. Yet, the idea of joint domination was not absent from this alliance.

The Russo-French alliance has some sort of parallel in the relationship between Soviet Russia and Nazi Germany in the first two years of World War II. In both alliances Russia's partner was a rival in the west who was straining to defeat Britain and gain world hegemony; and in both situations Russia started as the weaker party and ended up joining forces with other powers and crushing her partner. The treaty of Tilsit rested on a division of territory; and the non-aggression pact of 1939 was accompanied by a secret protocol which defined German and Russian spheres of influence in the Baltic States, Poland, and Bessarabia. (At meetings between Molotov and Ribbentrop and Hitler in Berlin in November 1940 the Germans attempted, without much success, to interest the Russians in a delimitation of territorial interests on a world-wide scale in preparation for the projected liquidation of the British Empire.) But, while the Russo-French alliance aimed at active co-operation, the Russo-German did not. The pact between Hitler and Stalin was simply an agreement not to enter into hostilities with each other. The positive element of joint control, in terms of which condominium is defined, was not conspicuous in this relationship.

[6] James Henry Breasted, *A History of Egypt from the Earliest Times to the Persian Conquest.* New York: Charles Scribner's Sons, 1916, ch. XXI, and Alan Gardiner, *Egypt of the Pharaohs: An Introduction.* Oxford: Clarendon Press, 1961, ch. X.

Though on a smaller scale, one of the best examples of a dualistic situation with pronounced elements of condominium may be seen in nineteenth-century German politics. The Confederation inaugurated in 1816 consisted of two great powers, Austria and Prussia, a small group of 'middle states', including Bavaria, Württemberg, Baden, and Hanover, and nearly thirty small states and city republics. Throughout its fifty years of existence the affairs of the Confederation were dominated by Austria and Prussia, who were also European great powers. Their relationship varied from close co-operation, at times amounting in effect to joint government, to open competition, eventually leading to war. The high point of condominium was reached in the first decade of the restoration period, when Metternich pursued the policy of 'peaceful dualism' and the Prussian government leaned on him for support against the revolutionary movements. But the idea of dual government cropped up again in the 1850s, when Rechberg was Austrian minister to the Confederation and President of the Federal Diet at Frankfurt and Bismarck represented Prussia. After 1848, however, the relationship between the two powers was predominantly one of intense rivalry. First the Austrian Empire, under Schwarzenberg's leadership, set out to gain dominance over all of Germany. Later Prussia, guided by Bismarck, succeeded in defeating Austria and uniting the rest of Germany under the Hohenzollern throne.

None of the dualistic situations outlined here is analogous to the world condominium that some recent writers have had in mind. Each was formal in character, resting on either a treaty or a constitution, and limited in scope, extending only to the territories between, or in the vicinity of, the partners. Above all, the element of co-operation present in most of the four peaceful relationships rarely amounted to condominium, even in the less strict sense of the term. The degree of joint control exercised by Hatti and Egypt in parts of Asia Minor is difficult to establish from the scanty sources. While co-operative efforts in the Russo-French alliance were largely abortive, in the Russo-German relationship they were practically non-existent. 'Peaceful dualism' in the German Confederation was only periodically translated into joint government. Yet, an examination of such historical situations gives rise to a number of questions pertinent to the modern idea of condominium.

Do condominia owe their existence to shared danger? Of the four relationships considered here, the one that most fully satisfied the requirements of condominium is also the one in which the partners were most conscious of being exposed to the same danger. In the restoration period the governments of Austria and Prussia were more afraid of revolution than of anything else, and reached their highest degree of solidarity in opposition to radical movements. Though it has been argued that the long alliance of Egypt and Hatti served to resist the rise of Assyria, it is doubtful that the friendship of the two empires was largely a product of common fear of the Assyrians. Rather it may have been brought about through common exhaustion after many years of war in the disputed territories of Asia Minor and been kept up by separate involvement elsewhere. While the Hittites, already moving towards their decline, were facing threats on their western frontier, the Egyptians, having exhausted their military aggressiveness, were becoming absorbed in the domestic affairs of the empire. In the Russo-French alliance, too, separate absorption seems to have been a more powerful motivation than common danger. While Napoleon was challenging England, the Tzar was involved with Turkey. In this relationship, however, a third motivation, namely mutual fear, played perhaps an even greater role. As was the case in the alliance with Nazi Germany, Russia had more reason to fear her partner than her partner's enemy, and accepted the alliance, partly at least, to strengthen her position against the aggressor. Napoleon, on his side, having defeated Russia, concluded the alliance in order to be able to concentrate on England with a united Continent behind him. Similarly, Stalin probably accepted the non-aggression pact largely to gain time for preparing his country for war with the partner (though he did not overlook the advantages of the secret protocol, which satisfied certain Russian nationalist aspirations and provided the Soviet Union with a buffer zone), while Hitler proposed the pact in order to gain freedom to act against the Western powers. In certain circumstances, mutual fear, it seems, may be a powerful factor in bringing about and maintaining, for a time at least, a relationship of peaceful co-existence between two dominant powers. In some situations, separate, and mutually reconcilable, involvement may encourage such powers to engage in limited co-operation. But the exercise of joint control in international politics, these examples suggest, may require the presence of a substantial threat aimed at both parties. While mutual fear and separate concerns, whether or not they are necessary, do not seem to be sufficient motivations, shared fear, whether or not it is sufficient, seems to be a necessary motivation for entering into condominial arrangements.

How important is doctrinal agreement between the parties? In the partnership of Austria and Prussia in Germany the conservative ideology was clearly an important bond. Both in Metternich's time and in later years, shared faith in the monarchical principle and the existing order served to unite the two governments in their opposition to the new political movements and social forces. However, when political rivalry between the two powers became intense, doctrinal agreement was not enough to prevent a breakdown of the partnership. In the other alliances the harmony of interests was not strengthened by a community of ideas. Egypt and Hatti, like most empires which are far removed from each other, could have few cultural and ideological ties. Nor was doctrinal agreement conspicuous be-

tween Napoleonic France and Tzarist Russia. And the relationship between
Soviet Russia and Nazi Germany was marked not only by a complete
absence of such agreement but also by an open conflict of ideas. When
even so few examples show that doctrinal consonance does not always
prevent the collapse of a condominium and that doctrinal conflict does not
always prevent peaceful co-existence, one is led to infer that a community
of opinion is a less important bond than harmony of interests. But the
fact that doctrinal agreement was pronounced only in the German partnership, the most developed of the condominial arrangements considered here,
leaves the query whether this bond may not be necessary for creating and
sustaining a condominium.

Does condominium presuppose a division of spheres of influence between the partners? Though no record of an agreement to define the boundaries separating the regions in Asia Minor subject to Egyptian sway
from those under Hittite domination was found together with the text of
the treaty of alliance, it may be assumed that the two empires drew up a
dividing line somewhere in Syria.[7] A division of spheres of interest was the
basis of the Franco-Russian and the essence of the German-Russian
alliance. And when Hardenberg and Humboldt in the negotiations preceding the establishment of the German Confederation supported the policy of
joint Prusso-Austrian hegemony, they were aiming at the extension of Prussian superiority in the north of Germany, expecting Austria to take a
similar line in the south.[8] Two dominant powers in the process of entering
into a peaceful relationship with each other and securing joint control over
others are likely, it seems, at an early stage to come to an agreement,
explicit or implicit, about the limits of their spheres of predominant influence. In a situation of this kind, such an agreement may become the basis
of a division of labour between the partners in a condominium. In different
circumstances, however, a division of spheres of influence may be an end
in itself. Sometimes great powers carry co-operation no further than agreeing to divide the territories in which they are interested.

Are condominia usually marked by inequality and instability? In none of
the three dual relationships taken from modern history was there equality
of power at the outset. In the German Confederation, the weakest of the
five members of the European congress system of the restoration period
sought protection in a partnership with the strongest power in central
Europe. In 1807 and in 1939, a defeated or unprepared Russia attempted
to improve her position by coming to terms with the most powerful and
aggressive nation on the Continent. Yet all three alliances ended in military
defeat of the dominant partner. While Austria was forced out of Germany by

[7] Breasted, pp. 438-9.
[8] Hajo Holborn, *A History of Modern Germany, 1648-1840*. London: Eyre and
Spottiswoode, 1965, p. 444.

Prussia, Napoleonic France and Hitlerite Germany were crushed by coalitions in which Russia played an important part. This paradox might be seen as indicating a tendency for the scales of power within a condominial arrangement to tip in favour of the initially weaker partner, whether through a relative increase in its own strength or as a result of support from other powers, and for this reversal of the power relationship to lead to a collapse of the partnership. However, it was not—at least not in the first place—a Prussian challenge to Austria which brought the German condominium down, but Austrian efforts to outrival Prussia and gain dominance over Germany. Similarly, it was not a Russian challenge to her partners which destroyed the other peaceful relationships, but Napoleon's and Hitler's invasions of Russia in their attempts to subdue Europe. So an unstable partnership of two dominant but unequal powers, which seems to be the typical form of condominium, is perhaps more likely to break down through a bid by the stronger partner for universal dominion than as a result of an attempt by the weaker partner to gain equality or supremacy.

Does a condominium supersede the balance of power? The four cases used here were arrangements between two dominant powers to stabilise their relations with each other and strengthen their control over others. Those in which Russia participated were also attempts by the leading partners, Napoleonic France and Nazi Germany, to prevent the establishment of European coalitions strong enough to stand in the way of their aggressive designs. While condominial arrangements, from one point of view, consolidate dual balances, from another point of view they may be obstacles to the smooth operation of multiple balances of power. It may well be true that the partners to such an arrangement, conscious not only of controlling the simple balance between themselves but also of interfering with a complex balance involving third parties, easily come to believe that they stand above the balance of power.

The temptation to entertain this belief is particularly great for the dominant partner. Yet, no sooner had Napoleon and Hitler broken through their alliances with Russia than they found themselves at war with a coalition of most of the great powers of the world. Their bids for universal dominion destroyed the dual and geographically limited balances and brought them up against multiple and more universal forms of the balance of power. Their defeats led in each case to a consolidation of the multiple power balance, in the congress system of the European Concert and in the Security Council of the United Nations. Though condominia are instruments for controlling the balance of power, in the long run they are themselves subject to the operation of this system.

How promising is condominium as a means of securing international order? In the past, condominia have been so rare and generally so short-lived that one is tempted to describe them as unnatural relationships. Since dominant powers in dualistic situations generally are bent on securing supremacy rather than on reaching compromise, they more often develop relations of tension and conflict than of harmony and co-operation, more often find themselves at war than in partnership with each other. The condominial relationships which from time to time have occurred have, as a rule, either sprung from or petered out in war between the parties. Some, indeed, have been little more than truces. Of the four examples of peaceful co-existence brought up here, three of which had elements of condominium, two—that between Egypt and Hatti and that between the French Empire and Tzarist Russia—resulted from war, while three—all the modern ones—ended in violent hostilities between the partners. What is more, during their existence condominial arrangements have often been marred by mutual suspicion and disturbed by difficulties of agreeing on the lines of territorial division and the terms of co-operation. In particular the alliance of Russia and France during the Napoleonic War suffered from strain and tension of this kind. An exceptional relationship which, as a rule, either issues from or ends in war and, in its typical form, is not only brief and unstable but also marked by tension and rivalry does not seem a particularly suitable instrument for controlling the relations of nations and ordering the affairs of the world.

For the more optimistic notions of condominium as a source of order in international society history may provide little support. However, while it is dangerous to ignore the lessons of the past, it is a mistake to assume that they can be applied automatically to the present. The existing international situation, though in its basic features not without interesting parallels in the history of Europe and other parts of the world, has some novel elements of which account must be taken in any analysis. With the introduction of nuclear weapons in a global political system it may well have become more necessary for the dominant powers to restrict their rivalry with each other and to exercise some joint control over others in the interest of international order. Other contributors to this volume will discuss whether it also has become more possible.

In the 1960s the term 'concert' appeared frequently in the works of those Western writers who, in their speculations about the future order of international society, went beyond the idea of a condominium of two super powers and envisioned a group of perhaps half a dozen great powers jointly managing international politics. Like 'condominium', 'concert' has a long history. Originating from the Italian verb 'concertare', which means to accord together, it reached the English language from the French 'concerter'. At its adoption it was confounded with 'consort', which prevailed at least till the Restoration of 1660.[9] Though it occasionally turned up in

9 *The Oxford English Dictionary*, 'Concert'.

diplomatic language earlier in the eighteenth century, it did not gain currency there till the early 1790s, when Continental statesmen were also using it.[10] In the terminology of diplomacy and politics it generally meant either *ad hoc* diplomatic co-operation or temporary political agreement between two or more states, usages which outlasted the nineteenth century and still are quite common.

After 1815, however, the word acquired another meaning as well. To the extent that it became associated with the congress system—the European political system introduced by the Congresses of Vienna and Paris, developed by the Congress of Aix-la-Chapelle and continued in the Congresses of Troppau, Laibach, and Verona—it came to refer to an established diplomatic arrangement. Both Castlereagh and Metternich, who played the major parts in founding and shaping the new system, occasionally used the term in this sense.[11]

It was only later that 'concert' became linked with 'Europe', to form the phrase 'the Concert of Europe'. This expression—of which the French equivalent, 'le concert européen', was used in the Paris peace treaty of 1856 —became common in the English language in the second half of the nineteenth century. At the time of the Crimean War, Queen Victoria employed it in a sense which already had acquired institutional overtones.[12] But it was not till the great crisis in the Eastern question in the late 1870s that the phrase became widely used. In Gladstone's speeches and writings of the two years preceding the Congress of Berlin 'the European Concert' clearly had a quasi-institutional meaning. This it has retained till today. 'The Concert of Europe' still stands for a loose association of those European great powers whose practice of habitually consulting each other and occasionally acting together distinguished the international politics of the nineteenth century.

The writers who in recent years have explored the idea of a 'concert' of

[10] While Kaunitz employed the term on 21 December 1791 (Albert Sorel, *L'Europe et la Révolution Française*. Paris: Plon, 1887, vol. II, p. 345), Grenville used it in December 1792, when he suggested 'a concert between other Gov[ernmen]ts to provide for their own security'. (*Foundations of British Foreign Policy from Pitt (1792) to Salisbury (1902)*, H. Temperley and L. M. Penson (eds.). Cambridge: Cambridge University Press, 1938, p. 9).

[11] See, e.g., *Memoirs and Correspondence of Viscount Castlereagh, Second Marquess of Londonderry*, C. Vane (ed.). London: Murray, 1848-53, vol. XI, p. 105; *Despatches, Correspondence, and Memoranda of Field Marshal Arthur Duke of Wellington*, ed. his son. London: Murray, 1867-80, vol. VII, p. 168 (for Castlereagh); and *Mémoires, Documents et Ecrits divers laissés par le prince de Metternich*, M. A. de Klinkowstroem (ed.). Paris: Plon, 1880-4, vol. III, p. 168.

[12] In a letter of 11 January 1855, Victoria reminded Frederick William IV that she had warned him repeatedly of the dangers of 'separating from the Concert of Europe'. *Further Letters of Queen Victoria. From the Archives of the House of Brandenburg-Prussia*, H. Bolitho (ed.). London: Thornton Butterworth, 1938, p. 53; see also Bolitho, p. 62.

C

several nuclear powers have used the term in much the same sense as it acquired in the terminology of European politics before 1914. Whether, as John Strachey, they have thought of such a concert as a step towards world government or whether, as George Liska, they have seen it mainly as a means of managing the balance of power, what these writers have had in mind is an association of half a dozen or more great powers co-operating in the management of the international politics of the world as the European great powers did in Europe in long periods of the last century. Indeed, it has been rather more common for such writers to point to the Concert of Europe than to the Council of the League of Nations, or even to the original Security Council of the United Nations, when explaining their ideas. While Strachey and Liska have held up the old Concert as an example for the future, F. H. Hinsley has predicted that the position in the world in the last third of the twentieth century will be not very different from that which prevailed in Europe in the first half of the nineteenth century.[13] In view of this tendency to draw inspiration from European history of the last century, it may be worth surveying the record of the Concert of Europe and considering some of the circumstances which gave rise to it.

The Concert of Europe, like its successors the League of Nations and the United Nations, sprang from war. The Revolutionary and Napoleonic Wars affected the European states-system in two distinct ways. On the one hand, revolution and invasion put an end to the tranquillity and security of all states and encouraged the powers to make common cause. On the other hand, the prolonged struggle with France tested the strength of each state and separated the stronger powers from the rest. The product of this duality of unifying and separating influences was the wartime coalition of Austria, Prussia, Russia, and Britain. When the allies had defeated Napoleon, they retained the special position they had acquired in Europe. At the Congress of Vienna, they took charge of negotiations, redrew the political map of Europe, concluded the peace treaties and, finally, renewed their alliance. On 20 November 1815 they signed the treaty of the Quadruple Alliance at Paris. Though the primary aim of this treaty was to provide against the dangers of a return of a Napoleonic régime in France, the treaty also made provisions for the conduct of European politics in general. In its sixth article the parties agreed to meet periodically 'for the purpose of consulting upon their common interests, and for the consideration of the measures which at each of these periods shall be considered the most salutary for the repose and prosperity of nations and for the maintenance of the peace

---

[13] John Strachey, *On the Prevention of War*. London: Macmillan, 1962, pp. 296-7; Liska, *Imperial America*, pp. 89-90; and F. H. Hinsley, *Power and the Pursuit of Peace: Theory and Practice in the History of Relations between States*. Cambridge: Cambridge University Press, 1963, p. 356.

of Europe'. It was on the basis of this article that the great powers managed the affairs of Europe in the post-war period.

Already at the Congress of Aix-la-Chapelle in 1818, a fundamental disagreement arose between Britain and her allies. While Castlereagh saw the new system of politics primarily as a guarantee for the territorial settlement of 1815, Metternich and other Continental statesmen wanted to use it as an instrument for suppressing revolutionary movements throughout Europe. In the following years the chasm widened. The British, favoured by stability in their social and political structure and protected by the Channel against revolutionary infection from abroad, could afford to concentrate on preventing aggression and maintaining the established balance of power. The Continentals, exposed to the pressures of democratic and nationalist movements, found it more urgent to take measures to uphold the existing dynastic structure of the society of Europe. While the former thought of the congress system as an association of sovereign states for mutual security, the latter tended to see it as a union of monarchs in defence of the social order. The two attitudes could not be reconciled, and finally the system broke down. After 1822, when Canning took charge of British foreign policy, it was no longer possible to arrange regular or frequent meetings of the five great powers. Yet the practice of consulting and co-operating survived. Though it never became a regular habit, the great powers resorted to it so often throughout the century that together they almost acquired the character of a European institution.

Contrary to the League and the United Nations, the Concert of Europe was not an orderly organisation with a permanent structure. At its best, it might be described as an informal institution; at its worst, as non-existent. Till the middle of the nineteenth century, the four founders of the congress system and France, the defeated power who had been admitted at the Congress of Aix-la-Chapelle, were the only members. At the Congress of Paris in 1856 the Ottoman Empire was formally accepted as a partner in the Concert, though in reality only admitted as a member of the European international society. At the London Conference of 1867 on Luxembourg, united Italy joined. And in 1871 the German *Reich* took Prussia's place. Finally, in the last decades of the century a few non-European great powers, the United States in particular, associated themselves for some purposes with the Concert of Europe.

The greater part of the work carried out by the Concert was done in congresses of sovereigns or their ministers, or in conferences of ambassadors presided over by the foreign minister of the country in which the meeting was taking place. One historian has counted eight of the former and eighteen of the latter type of meeting.[14] They were distributed irregularly

[14] Charles Webster, *The Art and Practice of Diplomacy*. London: Chatto and Windus, 1961, pp. 59 and 69.

throughout the century, far more falling before the year in which Bismarck founded the German *Reich* than after. Except for the early congresses, which were based on article VI of the treaty of the Quadruple Alliance, all the meetings were *ad hoc*. In many cases their subject was some aspect or other of the Eastern question, which the Congress of Vienna had largely ignored; but the representatives of the great powers also handled a considerable number of other issues, which ranged from the Belgian question in the early 1830s to African affairs in the middle 1880s. The last meeting was in London in 1912 and 1913, when the Eastern question once more was on the agenda. After a final attempt to bring the powers together and preserve peace, the Concert of Europe dissolved in World War I.

In the acts and declarations that issued from the congresses and conferences, as well as in statements by individual participants, it was often asserted that the aim of the great powers was to maintain the peace of Europe. It is true that the assembled statesmen sometimes succeeded in settling through negotiation issues which might have led to war and in localising wars which could have become general. But the century of the European Concert was not the golden age of peace that it is sometimes made out to have been. Indeed, in several ways this institution was closely associated with war. It was not only that the Concert sprang from the Napoleonic Wars and petered out in World War I, but also that its record in between was far from peaceful. Though the forty years after the Congress of Vienna were remarkable for peaceful relations among the members of the Concert, the next two decades saw each of them go to war with another great power. In the Crimean War Britain and France, together with Turkey, fought Russia. In 1859 France went to war with Austria on behalf of Italy. In 1866 Prussia fought Austria. And four years later war broke out between Prussia and France. The 1870s and 1880s were relatively calm but not marked by a high degree of solidarity among the great powers. The last decades before 1914 were dominated by intensified rivalry between hostile alliances. What is more, frequently throughout the century great powers involved themselves in wars with small states or engaged in hostilities beyond Europe, especially in Asia and Africa. The Concert of Europe clearly did not succeed in banishing war from European politics.

In this respect, the most interesting of the major wars of the nineteenth century was the Crimean. From one point of view, this war might be seen as signalling the breakdown of the system of the Concert. But a number of contemporary statesmen as well as some modern historians have regarded it, on the contrary, as a manifestation of this system. Gladstone, for example, always maintained that it was not an ordinary war between great powers, but a war fought by the European Concert—with Britain and France taking an active part and Austria and Prussia giving passive support —in the name of international law. The allied powers were not just fighting

Russia to defend or further their interests in the Near East; they were imposing established principles of international conduct on a recalcitrant member of the European society of nations.[15] According to this view, the occurrence of even a major war is not necessarily incompatible with the existence of a concert. If a great power challenges the accepted principles of law and order, the other members of the concert may have to go to war to uphold them. In the last resort, a concert is concerned with maintaining and extending international order rather than with preserving peace, with correcting the crime of aggression rather than with preventing the evil of war. In the extreme situation, the price of order may be war.

The particular circumstances which gave rise to the Concert of Europe and shaped its development are well known, having been studied by both historians and political scientists.[16] Firstly, the Concert rested on a stable balance of power. The equilibrium of Europe, which had been upset by France, was restored through the defeat of Napoleon and consolidated in the peace treaties. For many years the territorial settlement of 1815 remained a solid basis for the political system of Europe. This system consisted of five more or less comparable great powers, who towered over a larger number of small states of varying strength. One of the great powers, Britain, was rather stronger than the others, and isolated by water from the rest of Europe. For historical and geographical reasons, she was not inclined to use her predominance to subdue the Continent, but content to keep the other powers divided and in check. By playing the crucial part of the balancer in the system, she helped it to perform its function of maintaining, through crises and wars, the balance of power in Europe. Till well into the century, maintaining the power balance meant, in the first place, upholding the Vienna order. Thus, the territorial settlement of 1815 was not only the foundation but also, to some extent, the *raison d'être* of the Concert of Europe.

The second important condition for the establishment and maintenance of the Concert was the consciousness of shared danger. The statesmen of

---

[15] *Hansard's Parliamentary Debates*, 3rd ser., vol. CXXXVIII, col. 1071, 24 May 1855; see also W. E. Gladstone, *Gleanings of Past Years, 1843-78*. London: Murray, 1879, vol. I, 'Life of the Prince Consort' (1877), pp. 103-4. F. H. Hinsley's view of the Crimean War is rather similar to Gladstone's. He points out that it was in the name of Europe that the other powers went to war and in the cause of the Concert of Europe that Russia was constrained (Hinsley, *Power and the Pursuit of Peace*, p. 230), and draws attention to the parallel between the Crimean War and the war fought in Korea nearly a hundred years later 'by Powers determined to uphold and vindicate one conception of the Charter of the United Nations' (p. 227).

[16] See especially Hinsley, *Power and the Pursuit of Peace*; George Liska, *Europe Ascendant: The International Politics of Unification*. Baltimore: The Johns Hopkins Press, 1964; Stanley Hoffmann, *Organisations internationales et pouvoirs politiques des Etats*, Cahiers de la Fondation Nationale des Sciences Politiques, No. 52. Paris: Armand Colin, 1954; and R. N. Rosecrance, *Action and Reaction in World Politics. International Systems in Perspective*. Boston: Little, Brown and Co., 1963.

the restoration had two great fears: war and revolution. From the history of the French Revolution and the Napoleonic Wars they had learned that these evils were closely related. While domestic revolution might lead to foreign aggression and European war, invasion by foreign armies could prepare the way for revolution. Their fear of European war was largely a fear of French aggression. For half a century after 1815 France was regarded as the potential enemy of Europe, any serious disturbance of her internal tranquillity being treated as an emergency which might have incalculable consequences for her neighbours in particular and Europe in general. Only after the Franco-Prussian War did it become clear that the country which had produced Napoleon was no longer the principal threat to peace. The fear of revolution, too, turned the eyes of European statesmen towards the country of the Great Revolution. Metternich and Frederick William IV, together with so many other adherents of the conspiracy theory of revolution, were convinced that Paris was the centre of an international network of subversion. After 1818, when revolutions began to break out in the various parts of Europe once occupied by Napoleon, the Continental governments found it necessary not only to heed the indirect threat from Paris but also to deal with the direct danger that the new forces within every country seemed to present to the entire structure of European society. The revolutionary threat retained its credibility till 1848.

Common fear of war and revolution made for solidarity among the governments. Though most of the time the great powers were engaged in rivalry with each other, they generally were careful to keep tension below the level where disunity might give an aggressor a chance to overthrow the states-system or the revolutionaries an opportunity to destroy the social order. After the middle of the century the situation changed. With the memory of general war fading and the threat of France and the danger of revolution proving exaggerated, the reasons for restraint gradually disappeared. In some countries, Germany after 1866 being the principal example, the governments joined forces with the nationalist and liberal movements, by which the governments received fresh energies and the one-time revolutionary forces gained respectable spearheads. This increase in national unity went hand in hand with an intensification of international rivalry and a decline in European solidarity. Long before the end of the century, the divisions in European politics were again, as they had been before the French Revolution, almost entirely vertical. The bonds that had united the statesmen of the restoration against international Jacobinism were no longer there.

The fact, too, that the great powers had outlets for energy other than rivalry and war in Europe played an important part in maintaining the Concert. One outlet was internal. The industrial revolution, by presenting each power with an opportunity to develop its resources and strengthen its economy, opened up new paths of self-aggrandisement. The quest for economic power, being largely self-absorbing, tended to reduce the craving for territorial expansion in Europe, though not in the world beyond. By drawing energy away from aggressive pursuits on the Continent and reducing the pressure on the frontiers within Europe, it served to curb the tension in the states-system and to facilitate co-operation among the great powers.

The other outlet was external. Hand in hand with industrial progress and economic expansion went colonisation. In the nineteenth century the great powers situated on the fringes of Europe, especially Britain and Russia but also France, were able to subdue peoples and acquire territories in the world beyond, particularly in Africa and Asia. Though the expansionist pursuits of these powers led them into some rivalry on other continents, their involvement on the periphery of the political world often helped to reduce competition and control tension nearer the centre. Till late in the century, the relative concord in Europe prevailed over the conflict in the world, as at the Berlin Conference of 1884-5, where the powers succeeded in reaching some agreement on African affairs. Eventually, however, rivalry in the world exacerbated tension in Europe. When the power that occupied the central position on the Continent became aware of having been left behind in the race for colonies, it decided to seek a place in the world, even if it meant destroying the political system of Europe. The imperialist rivalry of the last decades before 1914 culminated in World War I.

Finally, the influence of a high degree of cultural affinity and some measure of ideological agreement among the powers is worth noting. The geographical contiguity and common cultural heritage, the continuous relations and parallel development of the great European nations had produced a fairly homogeneous society. Despite its history of persistent rivalry and frequent wars, nineteenth-century Europe constituted a family of nations. In a way, even the wars, as Dostoievsky and Treitschke pointed out, were an integrating force in the international society of Europe. Like family quarrels, they not only divided the members but also, by teaching them to know and to respect each other's peculiarities, brought them closer together. The bonds between the nations were sealed by intricate dynastic blood relationships, the results of generations of intermarriage. The supreme manifestation of the cultural and ideological ties and the dynastic links was the Holy Alliance of 1815. Shocked by the French Revolution and the long wars, all the Christian sovereigns in Europe, except the King of England and the Pope, put their names to the declaration of principles drawn up by Tzar Alexander. But the Concert of Europe, too, was to some extent a product of a common outlook. Shared values and ideas not only facilitated consultations and co-operation among the sovereigns and ministers of the great powers but also imposed a framework on their altercations and rivalries. Though hardly the most important factors, cultural similarity and ideological compatibility complemented the more substantial forces of cohesion and helped the Concert of Europe to survive.

The conditions for concert were interdependent. Fear of war and concern with economic expansion were closely linked. Similarly, dread of revolution and awareness of a European society based on common values and ideas fortified each other. The connection between balance of power in Europe and territorial expansion beyond is another example. While balance at the centre encouraged expansion on the periphery, the quest for new territories in the world facilitated stability and repose in Europe. Such interdependence tended to make the existence of the Concert of Europe more precarious. A reversal of any one set of the circumstances favouring the Concert could undermine the whole basis for the solidarity and co-operation of the great powers.

If these were the circumstances that allowed the Concert of Europe to come into being and sometimes to dominate European international politics, the question that now arises is whether the conditions for concert exist today. First of all, is it possible to establish a concert of the world without going through another world war? The great concerts of the past, of 1815, 1919, and 1945, all originated in major wars. In each case, it was a certain degree of unity among the victorious allies, forged in wartime coalition, together with a common determination to maintain peace, a reaction to the suffering and exhaustion caused by a general war, which made it possible for statesmen to respond to the need for a reorganisation of international society by setting up a formal concert of the principal powers. The tasks of controlling the ex-enemy and implementing the peace treaties served to maintain the concert in the first post-war years. Whether the alarming effect of a series of major crises more dangerous than any experienced so far, or even the shock of a limited nuclear war, would be enough to produce the unity and determination that seem necessary to bring great powers into formal concert is a matter for speculation.

The failure of the attempt to revive the Concert of Europe shortly before the outbreak of World War I suggests that the definite prospect of a major war is a much weaker impetus to concert than the recent experience of such a war. Even the danger of a major nuclear war may not frighten the powers into solidarity. No doubt, the fear of general war is greater in this age of nuclear weapons than in earlier times. Though to each of the governments of the principal powers the threat of nuclear war is still among the means of its foreign policy, to every one of them the avoidance of just such a war is all but the most important end of policy. The existence of a common interest in averting or limiting war is as obvious today as in any period of the last century, including the post-Napoleonic age of restoration, when all of Europe was weary of warfare and determined to preserve peace.

But as a bond of union this community of interest has some weaknesses. First, it rests not on experience and memory but on foresight and imagination. Though there is abundant material to indicate the horrors of nuclear warfare on a major scale, nobody so far has actually endured them. The somewhat theoretical nature of the basis for the community of interest tends to give a slightly unreal quality to the solidarity of the governments. Second, if one or more of the great powers feared, or—like China before she acquired significant nuclear capacity—more or less successfully pretended to fear, nuclear war less than the others did, the mutuality of fear might be breached. This would tend to undermine the community of interest and to loosen the solidarity of the powers. An outbreak of nuclear war on a major scale could be expected to change the situation in both respects. The shock and exhaustion caused by such an experience would add new depth to the fears of those who survived and might make the governments more keenly aware of their common interest in preventing similar catastrophes in the future. Such an event would also disturb the insouciance, or call the bluff, of those governments which previously might have appeared less concerned than others about the dangers of nuclear war. A few days of warfare of this type might prove a greater impulse to solidarity than many years of traditional war, assuming that international society survived the cataclysm.

Could shared fear of subversion and aggression by one of the powers give rise to a concert of the world? If, for example, Communist China chose to pursue a decidedly expansionist policy, it would clearly be a matter of serious concern to her immediate great power neighbours, Russia, India, and Japan, as well as to America, and even to Europe. Even so, the powers of the world would be quite unable to treat China the way the European powers sometimes treated France in the age of Metternich. It is not only that the 'revisionist' and the 'capitalist' powers lack a common ideological foundation for a joint confrontation with China, but also that this power, contrary to post-Revolutionary France, has provided little evidence that any aggressiveness on her part would present an extreme danger to the states-system in general, as distinct from her closest neighbours. The history of both the Revolutionary and Napoleonic Wars and World War II suggests that nothing less than an open and forceful challenge to the international system as a whole is capable of bringing the other powers into coalition, and then only after great difficulties about the terms of alliance. China, it seems, not only would have to go a good deal further than pursuing her present policy, of giving mainly moral support to revolutionary movements abroad and directing largely verbal abuse at her rivals, but also would have to improve her nuclear capability considerably, and might even have to prove through major hostilities her intention and ability to upset the international order, before the other powers of the world felt threatened enough to join each other in an anti-Chinese concert. This would apply also to any other great power who might decide to challenge the international system and, through subversion and aggression, attempt to bring about a new world order.

Will the balance of power remain stable enough to support a world concert of nuclear powers? It is probably true that the central balance has been stabler in the 1950s and 1960s than in any other period of this century. In a predominantly dualistic situation of international politics, nuclear parity between the Soviet Union and the United States has consolidated the balance between East and West and perhaps secured it for years to come. It is not impossible that equilibrium can be maintained also if the secondary nuclear powers increase their stocks of arms and improve their means of delivery, and if other powers join the nuclear club. It is even arguable that a multiple balance which arises from competition in nuclear armaments is inherently stabler than one which, like that of nineteenth-century Europe, is a product of rivalry for territory. On the other hand, it is possible that the existing system proves unable to absorb the impact of new super powers and incapable of transforming itself from an essentially dual into a truly multiple balance of power. In any case, the present inequality between super powers and potential super powers is so great that it would be a long time before a concert of the world could be achieved which, like the Concert of Europe, would be composed of a group of more or less comparable great powers. Perhaps even more important, it is very doubtful that there would be any power in such a concert which would be likely to play the part of the balancer as well as Britain did in the last century. Even George Liska, who cast the United States in this role, wondered whether she would have the necessary detachment to act as concert leader.[17] So even if it did prove possible to establish through nuclear arms a foundation as stable as that provided by the Vienna settlement, it would still be uncertain whether a modern multiple balance of power could be operated nearly as successfully as was the old European system.

Are there adequate alternative outlets for the energies of the great powers? For the two super powers, the economic growth race and scientific competition are strong encouragements to self-absorption, especially in the case of the Soviet Union. Both have also serious immediate or long-term domestic political problems to occupy them. China and other developing major powers in Asia and South America will for many decades have to devote large proportions of their energies to economic development and social improvement. Neither Britain nor France has finally overcome the economic difficulties that have faced them since World War II. And a united Europe would for many years have to concentrate a good deal of

[17] Liska, *Imperial America*, pp. 89-90.

attention on organisational problems. But, though domestic challenges to the great powers of the future are likely to be both plentiful and demanding, they may not play quite the same role as they did in the nineteenth century. Contrary to the old European powers, who were at more or less the same stage of economic development, with Britain a little more industrially advanced than the rest, the potential members of a concert of the world are sharply divided into 'have' and 'have-not' states. Self-involvement, in such circumstances, is likely to make nations more aware of the economic inequality of international society, more conscious of belonging either to the rich or to the poor countries. Rather than reducing the general level of international tension, it may shift friction from the political to the economic sphere. Among the results that might be expected from such a change would be a reduction in tension between the Soviet Union and the United States, both have states, and an increase in tension between, for example, the Soviet Union and China or Japan and India. The ultimate imaginable effect of a tendency to play down political conflicts and ideological issues and to concentrate on the economic inequalities and social injustices of international society would be a confrontation between the advanced and the less-developed nations, a situation which could hardly be conducive to the formation of a concert of the world. That the great economic have states, with the exception of Japan, are also have states in military terms enhances the inequality between the rich and the poor powers and makes it even more difficult to establish and maintain a concert of more or less comparable great powers.

While the net effect of the internal outlets for energy and ambition may be to transfer international conflict to the economic sphere, the difficulty about external outlets is that they are nearly closed in the modern world. In a global political system the powers obviously have a much narrower geographical scope for expansion than the members of the old European system had. Neo-colonial activities in the less advanced regions of the world, like competition for spheres of influence in areas adjacent to two or more great powers, are more likely to increase than to reduce tension among potential members of a concert of the world. Exploration and colonisation of space do not yet offer an opportunity of re-establishing the nineteenth-century concord between relative restraint and stability along the internal boundaries between the powers and expansion and rivalry in the less sensitive regions beyond the geographical limits of the states-system. The idea of a political and strategic rivalry in space which eventually may help to reduce tension on earth so far belongs to science fiction rather than to practical politics.

Finally, will cultural differences and ideological conflicts stand in the way of a concert of the world? Clearly, the international society of the second half of the twentieth century, which is universal in principle, does not have the homogeneity of the European society of the nineteenth century. Modern means of transport and communication, a high degree of economic interdependence and the existence of formal international institutions do not make up for the absence of the centuries of shared history and dynastic intermarriage which linked the old European states. A concert which comprised not only the United States and a number of European nations but also China, Japan, and India could hardly be held together by cultural affinity and ideological agreement. However, these factors of cohesion may be the least important. If there were a number of other circumstances which favoured the development of a concert of the world, it might be possible to have it even in the absence of cultural and ideological harmony. The cause for pessimism is that also the more important conditions for concert, as derived from analysis of the Concert of Europe, seem to be unfulfilled, with the possible exception of common awareness of the dangers of general war. The best ground for hope then is that the fear of nuclear war may prove powerful enough to make up for the shortcomings of the existing situation, without this fear first having to be reinforced through experience.

The historical cases discussed in this chapter must be a warning against excessive optimism in thinking about the possibility of controlling nuclear weapons and managing international politics through either a condominium of two super powers or a concert of half a dozen great powers. A mixture of the two types of association, which was one of the possibilities considered by Strachey, would present a third prospect. A concert of several great powers under the joint presidency of two super powers might be a little easier to bring about than either a condominium or a concert alone. The element of condominium in such an arrangement would help to consolidate the military and economic superiority of the two super powers and, for that reason, would make a mixed system more attractive to the Soviet Union and the United States than a concert of equals. The element of concert, on the other hand, would ensure the secondary great powers some influence over the settlement of major issues of international politics and, hence, would make such a system more acceptable to the principal powers in Asia and Western Europe than a pure condominial arrangement. A condominium of two within a concert of several powers would be a compromise between those whose advantage lies in a simple condominium and those who have an interest in a simple concert.

But, though it might be the best solution to the problem arising from the clash of interests between the super powers and the secondary great powers, such a mixed system would nevertheless be extremely difficult to establish and maintain. Even if the global condominium of the two super powers operated through a wider concert of great powers, it would still be faced with some, if not all, of the difficulties that in the past have beset condominial arrangements. And even if the concert of the world were presided over by two super powers, its existence would still be subject to at least some of the conditions that have determined the fortunes of earlier concerts of great powers. So a mixture of the two types of association would encounter obstacles of a twofold nature.

If, nevertheless, the powers, acting in response to the need to control nuclear weapons and alleviate the worst effects of international anarchy, did find a way of overcoming all of these obstacles, and succeeded in setting up a mixed system of condominium and concert, there would still be grounds for scepticism. The first question worth asking is whether they would be able in the long run to maintain international order through such an arrangement without occasionally resorting to major war. From one point of view, the association of super powers and great powers would be a system of collective security, whether formal or informal. Whatever the details of the arrangement, it would include some provisions for dealing with threats of aggression by one or more of the great powers. Though the idea, of course, would be to deter the recalcitrant power, or powers, from disrupting the existing international order merely by *threatening* joint military action by the rest, in the last resort the sanction would have to be war. In a world of nuclear arms, this could mean nuclear war. So the possibility cannot be excluded that the powers might find themselves in a situation where they could defend the principles of the concert and uphold their conception of international order only by fighting a major war, a Crimean War of the nuclear age. Whether the system could survive a modern war of this type, as the European Concert survived the Crimean War, and perhaps even draw strength from the experience of catastrophe, or whether it would collapse in unmitigated anarchy is a subject for speculation.

If this difficulty, too, were overcome, and the powers of the concert found that they, in emergencies, could check a challenge merely by resolutely threatening joint action, with nuclear weapons if necessary—and thus be spared the dilemma of having to choose between upholding their principles of international order at the expense of peace and evading major war at the cost of international order—one question more would remain. It concerns relations between the partners in the mixed concert and the other members of the states-system. The most feasible arrangement imaginable in present circumstances is one in which the Soviet Union and the United States separately exercised hegemony in Eastern Europe and Latin America and jointly exerted overall control in the international politics of the rest of the world, while the principal powers in Western Europe joined them in the management of crises arising in the Middle East, Western Europe, the Atlantic region and perhaps Africa, and the leading powers in Asia participated in the concert for the purpose of helping to deal with international issues occurring in the Asian region. It is difficult to see how such a system could be successful in curbing international disorder without seriously curtailing the scope of most other states in the world. Certainly, on many occasions it was at the expense of smaller states that the Concert of Europe performed its functions in the European states-system. Though some countries, notably Greece and Belgium, owed their liberty to the joint intervention of the great powers, others repeatedly found their endeavours rebuffed and their interests ignored by the European Concert. Throughout the nineteenth century the loud self-praise of the great powers was accompanied by an often suppressed, but always indignant, protest from lesser states against selfish behaviour and high-handed attitude on the part of the powers of the 'Pentarchy'. Not only powers of second rank, such as Spain, Sweden, and the Netherlands, but also states of lower rank, Württemberg for example, were sufficiently provoked by what to them appeared as great power tutelage to join the chorus of protest. There is little reason to suppose that the partners in a world-wide system of joint super power control and concerted great power management would be less inclined than the old European great powers to override the rights and ignore the interests of individual smaller states. In any case, whatever their inclinations in this respect, it would be no more possible for them than it was for the powers of the European Concert efficiently to perform their function of maintaining international order without seriously encroaching upon many other states. Whether or not they used the United Nations as their instrument would probably make little difference in this regard.

While, in relations among the partners in a system of condominium and concert, the price of order could possibly be major war, in relations between them and others it would undoubtedly be a sharp curtailment of the independence of lesser states. If, in an age of nuclear weapons, the super powers and the great powers *were* able to give us a substantial measure of order, and perhaps also a long period of peace, would it be too ungrateful to ask, on behalf of the middle powers and the small states of the world, what about freedom?

THE ADVERSE PARTNERSHIP

The twenty-five years or so of the nuclear age to date have assumed a historical shape markedly unlike the expectations of those who first pre-occupied themselves with the impact of the new weapons on international politics. Armageddon has not yet arrived, but neither has the new order of peace and harmony among the nations that the more optimistic hoped for. What is lightly called 'the post-war period' has proved to be a period of limited and peripheral wars—and wars which have been *kept* limited and peripheral, I shall argue, by the operations of the central balance of power. If there is a sense of *déjà vu* in all this it is because that phrase might serve as a description also of large tracts of the nineteenth century. The phrase 'adverse partnership', which I owe to Professor Marshall Shulman, as a description of the evolving relationship between the Soviet Union and the United States, is an apt description also of the central balance of power in many earlier periods of history. There have been wide fluctuations of con-sciousness, among the powers making up this central balance at any par-ticular time, of the 'partnership' elements in their relationship as against the 'adversary' elements. Probably some stretches of the Concert of Europe period demonstrate the highest level of consciousness of common interest as between the dominant powers, and some stretches of the twentieth cen-tury represent a very low level indeed in this consciousness. But there is a case for saying that the central balance of power can always be described as an adverse partnership, and that to examine the way in which this ambi-valent relation has become understood in the post-war period is not to discern the emergence of a new pattern but rather the recognition of an old one. The weapons with which the pattern is maintained are different, certainly, but they have imposed less change than is often supposed on the pattern itself.

If one is looking for actual demonstrable evidence of the existence of any such sense of common interest between the present dominant powers, one has to confine oneself to the last eight years or so of the period under review, perhaps from the establishment of the 'hot line' in 1963 after the Cuban missile crisis, through the Partial Test-Ban Treaty, the 1967 crisis, and the Non-Proliferation Treaty to the SALT negotiations of 1970. However, I would argue that these developments represent visible signs above ground of a preliminary germination process which had been going on below the level of international visibility since about 1955, or even earlier. The often-derided business of international 'summitry' did produce its fruits, though belatedly enough.

To understand the history of the process concerned, one needs first to distinguish the elements from which this adverse partnership (suspending for a moment any disbelief in its reality) has been constructed. The basic stuff of the relationship seems to me to be simply two kinds of fear: a mutual fear by the United States and the Soviet Union of each other, and their common fear of China. The mutual fear of each other was certainly prior in time, and is still, I think, primary in importance, at least in 1970, though one's judgment on this might be different by 1980. The Chinese regard the adverse partnership as essentially just a collusion between 'the imperialists' (i.e. the Americans) and the 'social imperialists' (i.e. the Russians) to encircle China and defeat the rightful hopes of the 'revolutionary peoples of the world'. One might make quite a good case for this view if one looked only at the period since about 1964. Indeed, if one is considering chiefly changes in the Soviet position, one can make a case of sorts for dating preoccupation with dangers assumed to stem from Chinese policies from 1959. But even making this concession to Chinese insistence on their central role in the diplomatic evolution under examination one would still be left with the need to explain developments in the period 1949-59, when neither of the dominant powers had much real reason to be apprehensive of China. Perhaps it would appropriately indicate the historical progression of events to say that the basic structure of the adverse partnership was constructed in the earlier years, from the mutual fear generated between the United States and the Soviet Union during the first phase of their nuclear duopoly, but that the top storeys and roof of the structure show a clear Chinese inspiration.

Two kinds of fear—a mutual fear and a common fear—might seem a morally unsatisfactory basis for partnership even in international politics, where one cannot expect much. But in fact this substance of fear has shown itself in some ways more durable and more *workable* as a material than more amiable-sounding considerations. The conventions or modes of expression through which it has proved workable are four. I will call them the exchange of hostages, surveillance, a common strategic ideology, and a convention of crisis management. This essay will be devoted to consideration of the way these modes of relationship have evolved, and the degree of their interdependence.

The first element, the exchange of hostages, does not seem to require much examination since the idea is quite familiar to anyone acquainted with the general theory of deterrence. In an age of nuclear strike, obviously, almost all the urban populations of each of the dominant powers and their allies may be regarded as 'hostages' for the prudent decision-making of their respective governments, in the sense that those governments have no way of protecting their respective peoples from the military sanctions available to the adversary power. This has been the case in practical measure as the 'throw-power' of the potential adversary has grown for the populations of the Soviet Union and Western Europe since the late 1940s, and the United States since 1958 or so. The date in each case is rather nominal, giving the starting-point of a process rather than its point of true effectiveness.

Since the prospect of ABM systems began to look real in the mid-1960s, it has been argued that they might undermine this central prop of the deterrent system by allowing one side or the other to 'withdraw its hostages' through providing effective defence for its city populations. Possibly if a highly effective system were available to one side, and no equivalent to the other, ABMs could seriously modify the present symmetry of deterrence as between the United States and the Soviet Union. But this does not really seem likely, since the two adversaries seem to have evolved systems that are reasonably comparable. Given the level of research expenditure on each side and the diligence of intelligence services, some such comparability is perhaps probable in most kinds of advanced weapon systems. And provided that all that is in question is a reduction in the number of hostages on each side, no major modification of this element in the relationship seems likely. Seven million dead is probably as effectively deterring a prospect as seventy million. It may even be the case that this 'hostages' factor works without any necessary comparability in the degree of damage each adversary is able to do the other. This is of importance in determining the leverage of China, whose ability to inflict damage on the other two is certainly far less (and will remain far less, even in the mid-1970s) than their respective abilities to inflict reciprocal damages. That is, even while the number of 'hostages' held by China remains relatively low, the system may yet work for her as it does for the other two.

In the second relationship, surveillance, China is, as far as the available information goes, at a more complete disadvantage *vis-à-vis* the other two than in respect to the holding of hostages. But this is a field in which information is hard to come by, and it is possible that Western sources are under-estimating Chinese capacities. By 'surveillance' I mean simply the ability of the dominant powers to watch each other, to estimate each other's military capabilities, political intentions, and level of readiness. The traditional way of maintaining this watch has of course been by espionage. One would hesitate to assume that there has been any reduction in this branch

D

of international endeavour: on the indications, it flourishes as robustly as ever. But the larger proportion of the special material that comes in to the 'intelligence community' in the two dominant powers must certainly now be provided by the newer modes of scientific watching. (There is some slight indication that Britain and France also are beginning to operate in this field.) These systems rely on reconnaissance satellites, U-2 and similar aircraft, radar and sonar arrays, sensors on the seabed, upper-air analysis, seismographic monitoring of explosions, and techniques which are kept even more carefully secret than these. It is, of course, rather difficult to obtain firm information in this field, but one would assume that the whole land surface of each of the adversary powers is already under continuous weekly photo-surveillance to detect changes in military installations: China presumably receives this attention from each of the other two. The information so gathered relates primarily to capabilities, but some of it also says a good deal about intentions and 'readiness-posture', for instance the detected level of missile alert.

Intelligence services like the Central Intelligence Agency have had such a bad press in the Cold War period that it may be necessary to justify the implication that their peculiar contribution to the total flow of information that reaches decision makers is of special importance. Ninety per cent of this total flow undoubtedly comes from the sources called 'white' or legitimate. Governments deliberately convey to each other a great deal of perfectly genuine information about their respective capabilities and intentions. Speeches by political leaders: published arms budgets: parliamentary debates: demonstrations like the Soviet May Day reviews: official statistics: agreements on the presence of service attachés at embassies—all these provide a great deal of information deliberately made available to the adversary as well as allies and the home public. But since the relationship remains adverse, the very conveying of this information is within a framework which implies both the expectation and the reality of mistrust, deception, bluff, fraud, and guile. Each side must ask, totting-up, what has come in from these 'white' or legitimate sources, not only *what* has the other side told us about its capabilities, but *why* have they told us this? Have they shown us a Potemkin village? This was very much the reaction in Washington, for instance after the first fly-past in the Moscow May Day parade of 1954 of the Soviet long-range heavy bombers, the Badger and Bison models. The Russians frequently describe the sort of inspection procedures proposed for arms control agreements as 'licensed espionage'. One could more reasonably describe espionage as unlicensed inspection, and useful (i.e. convincing) precisely because it is unlicensed. It derives its authority, like that of a Customs 'random check', from the fact that no volunteering is involved on the part of those subject to check. (Detecting the cases where there is such a 'volunteering', for example through a double agent, is of course a notable element in the art of transmitting only authentic information to the chief decision makers.)

I have been speaking up to now of the gathering of information about weapons or forces actually in being, and of the necessity of a consciousness in the decision maker's mind not only of what information his intelligence community has communicated to him, on the capabilities, apparent intentions, and levels of readiness of the other side, but his consciousness that the adversary's intelligence community is probably in receipt of equivalent information concerning his own society. It is not only the knowledge that he has an effective surveillance over the adversary, but equally the assumption of a similar level of such knowledge on the other side, that permits the necessary confidence to grow in the *predictability* of the adversary and the reliability of his signals. If the decision makers of the United States, for instance, had to take into account the possibility that Soviet decision makers might be wildly wrong about American capabilities, it would add a destructive element of radical uncertainty to their calculations.

The other variety of information which has been the chief preoccupation of intelligence services in the nuclear age has been early warning of notable breakthrough in scientific research. Its transmission has had a quite different, but equally important function in the growth of the adverse partnership. It has helped account for the increasing symmetry of weapons systems on the two sides of the balance. I suppose this symmetry would in due course have emerged even without the services, to put it delicately, of people like Klaus Fuchs and the others, but it would not have begun to emerge as early as it actually did, that is by 1949, with the testing of the first Soviet atomic device.

It is this symmetry of the weapons structures of the two dominant powers which in turn permitted the evolution of the next factor in the adverse partnership, which I have called a common strategic ideology. I do not by this mean to imply that American and Soviet assessments and theories are alike on all points in the strategic field. On the contrary they have differed a good deal on various matters. What I mean is that their overall general appreciation of the nature of the new weapons has grown steadily more similar since 1953, when Stalin's death permitted the junking of his orthodoxy of the 'permanently operating factors'. If this proposition seems doubtful, consider what the intellectual basis of the strategic arms limitation talks could be if not a tacit consensus as to the meaning of these weapons.

The two parties have to assign roughly the same meaning to particular weapons, have to see the potential battle to some extent in the same terms to be able to negotiate meaningfully about it, or even to believe that negotiation between themselves is useful. The evidence that this is the case is not to be looked for in words: the 'declaratory policies' of the two adversaries may well remain quite distinctive, especially on points like whether limited war is possible, and the feasibility of use of tactical nuclear weapons. The evidence of the 'operational' strategic ideology, as against the declaratory one, is to be found in the structure of the armed forces which the decision makers have chosen to make available for their future selves. The reshaping of Soviet military programs since Khrushchev's time has patterned itself quite clearly on the American model, not only in the initial shift towards a nuclear deterrent force, but in the later emphasis on mobile forces suitable for use in local crises. Thus the build-up of Soviet naval forces, for instance, must undoubtedly be related to Soviet observation of how useful such forces were to the United States in the Lebanon-Jordan crisis of 1958 and the Cuba missile crisis of 1962.

It may be objected that this sort of tacit understanding within a limited specific field is not what most people mean by an ideology. The word usually is reserved in the loose Western usage for a system of general ideas about the political, cultural, and economic relationships of a society, or else, in the Marxist usage, for the 'false consciousness' of a particular group, rationalising the situation of advantage or disadvantage in which that group finds itself. From the point of view of the great nuclear dissident, China, the common American and Soviet system of ideas is of course seen in the latter fashion as a rationalisation of the situation of nuclear advantage in which the United States and the Soviet Union find themselves. But from a Western point of view it may be interpreted as a 'special ideology' as against a 'general ideology'—that is, an ideology special to a particular professional group. And here there is a striking parallel with the society of states of the nineteenth century. The differences in domestic political ideology between the powers of the Concert of Europe period seemed hardly less great to the men of that time than those between Brezhnev's Russia and Nixon's America do in 1970: perhaps less so. But the diplomatic relations of the epoch were controlled by a small group at the top of each society, who shared a considerable stock of common concepts and values with their opposite numbers in the other dominant powers. In fact this similarity was so great that individual members of those élites could transfer their professional services from one of the states involved to another: for instance, Nesselrode could be the chief foreign policy decision maker for Tzarist Russia. It will be a long time before there is any contemporary equivalent of this in terms of actual transfer of loyalty, aside of course from the defectors from either side. But there is a kind of intellectual analogy, in the sense that the strategic theorists of the nuclear age, practically all Americans, can provide their theoretical services equally to the adversary. Usually there is a lapse of five years or so in the transfer of ideas. But if you ask who is the Soviet version of Schelling or Kahn or Wohlstetter, the answer is probably—Schelling or Kahn or Wohlstetter, even though the doctrine may be mediated through Sokolovsky or Talensky or Rotmistrov.

Obviously this special professional ideology built around the military means of the nuclear age is never likely to extend much beyond a tiny élite of policy advisers. But probably international ideologies never *have* extended much beyond a very small minority. They remain effective so long as the decision makers share them, and as the Chinese are fond of pointing out, this has clearly been the case as between American and Russian decision makers in a number of crises since about 1958.

I will not deal with the present Chinese rejection of or exclusion from this strategic ideology, except to say that it may be related to, among other things, the Chinese disadvantage in the field of surveillance. If you look at the differences over strategy between China and the Soviet Union in a number of crises from 1958 to 1962 (differences which were great enough effectively to destroy the Sino-Soviet alliance) you can say that they comprised a number of different factors, including ideology and contrasts of national interest, but there is a perfectly clear element of lesser understanding on the Chinese side of the realities of American will and even perhaps capability. And this must be related to the Chinese disadvantage in surveillance techniques.

Finally, there remains for examination what I have called the convention of crisis management. This function, I would argue, is what justifies the adverse partnership, which otherwise might be potentially just an embryonic great power tyranny, a mutual benefit scheme for dividing the loot of the society of states between the dominant powers. In fact at some periods of diplomatic history one can argue that the central balance did become an adverse partnership of this sort: an agreement as to who should cut up the victims, as Professor Langer has said.

Minor powers must always to some extent look upon the co-operation of the dominant powers with a jaundiced and suspicious eye, bearing past instances of this tendency in mind. Yet if one examines the evolution of the contemporary system over the past twenty-five years, one is struck by how much it has been created by the opposite fear, of too little co-operation rather than too much. If the Azerbaijan crisis of 1946 is regarded as the first true adversary crisis of the post-war system, it was twenty-one years (to the Middle Eastern crisis of 1967) before the evolution of the system had made consultation between the dominant powers a first reaction in time of crisis. And in one phase of the evolution, roughly 1953-60, the dominant powers were very much in the situation of a reluctant pair being nudged together by over-anxious matchmakers, particularly Britain. The relationship only really became self-consciously accepted in Washington during Kennedy's presidency, and consciously maintained and developed (though less articulately) during Johnson's. It is rather ironic, considering his role in the Dulles epoch, that it should have fallen to Nixon to make it formally explicit, as he did in the 'State of the Union' message of 1970.

> If we are to have peace in the last third of the twentieth century, a major factor will be the development of a new relationship between the United States and the Soviet Union . . . we are moving with precision and purpose from an era of confrontation to an era of negotiation . . . Our negotiations on strategic arms limitations and in other areas will have far greater chance for success if both sides enter them motivated by mutual self-interest rather than naive sentimentality. It is with this same spirit that we have resumed discussions with communist China at Warsaw.[1]

There are clear reasons in the recent history and the ideologies of the United States and the Soviet Union why this evolution was comparatively slow, reluctant and attended by moral qualms on both sides. As far as Washington is concerned, the tradition of regarding the dominant members of the society of states as necessarily the managers of the system is far less well-rooted than it is in the Europeon chancelleries. The Europeans can always look back to the hundred years or so after 1815 as their classic period in this activity,[2] whereas the United States tended to see the potentially dangerous and sinister side of the European manager's role even at its better periods, as is quite clear for instance from the origins of the Monroe Doctrine. It remains relatively easy, even now, to imagine a repudiation of this role in Washington, if its costs became too high or the domestic troubles of American society became overwhelming. And the costs of Vietnam (which have really been the costs of a gross and disastrous *mismanagement*) may tend to be put down as the costs of normal management.

On the Russian side, the reasons for reluctance to acknowledge the role are of a different sort. Russia is still in theory and aspiration a revolutionary power, and she has had a genuine revolutionary power, China, at her elbow taunting her openly ever since 1963 with collusion with the imperialists. Nevertheless there was undoubtedly a very marked re-emergence of the traditions of Tzarist diplomacy in the Stalinist period (persisting since) and one can argue that Russian policy even before 1946 was in fact already suffused with the idea of the world being run by a great power directorate. This is quite clearly visible in Stalin's policy at Yalta and in Russian insistence on the powers of the permanent members of the Security Council, and in many other issues.

Some of the shrewdest analysts of power politics were so much impressed, during the bitter early years of the Cold War, with the obstacles to any

---

[1] *The Times*, 23 January 1970.

[2] Classic in the sense that the crises of this period (1815-1911) were usually so managed that war did not eventuate, and those wars that did (e.g. Crimean and Franco-Prussian) were prevented from becoming cataclysmic to the system as a whole.

consensus between the dominant powers (in contrast to the situation as between the European dominant powers of earlier systems) as to assume that no reversion towards the traditional pattern was possible. That it has in fact re-emerged is probably a testimony to its genuinely functional character, but the persuasions of the European allies of the dominant powers (particularly Britain) must be allowed a considerable part in the process.

The initial four years of the post-war era, to 1949, may be regarded as a period in which the new adversary coalitions were formed, and their territorial limits defined. The first Berlin crisis, 1948-9, operated (though it was probably not designed) as a test case to show how well these coalitions and limits would stand under pressure. The period from the beginning of this crisis to the Korean truce approach in 1951 was probably the single most dangerous stretch of the entire post-war period, not because Stalin was a particularly reckless decision maker (he was probably more cautious than Khrushchev, for instance) but because the conventions of the post-war system were as yet just emerging. For parts of this time the Central Intelligence Agency were refusing to forecast peace for more than sixty days ahead.

There succeeded, however, a period of détente enhanced but not really created by the death of Stalin. It is nowadays almost forgotten how suspicious American decision makers were of the notion of détente when it first clearly emerged in 1953 (with Churchill as its main proponent) and when it produced the first summit meeting of 1955. Dulles's fear was that détente would lead to the falling apart of the Western coalition so laboriously put together in 1948-9. In fact it proved far more dangerous to the adversary coalition, the Sino-Soviet alliance, which was probably split beyond repair by the time of Khrushchev's visit to America in 1959. So to the 1945-9 period of setting-up the adversary coalitions and delimiting their territories, we can add the 1949-62 period as the one in which the rules of the limited adversary relationship were worked out, sometimes through processes of great danger as in 1962.

The period since 1963 has been one in which the détente has established itself as being solidly based in a conviction of mutual interest and has shown this by surviving crises that would undoubtedly have been fatal to the more fragile détentes of earlier systems. Events such as Vietnam, the 1967 Middle Eastern crisis and the 1968 Czech crisis, have disturbed it astonishingly little. The 1967 crisis probably should be accounted the beginning of the period in which we still find ourselves, a period of conscious and explicit effort by the United States and the Soviet Union to 'de-couple' their relationship to each other from the crises of local balances. When the Middle East fighting began in June 1967 Moscow and Washington at once used the 'hot line' to exchange assurances that there would be no intervention from the one side if there was none from the other. Both powers, that is, were more anxious to obviate any risk of involvement with the other than to secure their respective friends and strategic interests in the Middle East.

This determination has shown itself since in other areas. Contrast the reaction of the dominant powers to the attempted Katanga secession of 1960, which was almost the occasion for a major adversary crisis of the central balance, with their comparative non-reaction to the attempted Biafra secession of 1966-9, which never looked in the least like precipitating crisis between the dominant powers. Yet Nigeria is a more important African state than the Congo, and the Soviet supply of arms to the Federal government has probably been more effective as a basis of future influence than the rather feeble and confused Soviet efforts to aid Mr Lumumba. What has changed in the period between the two attempted secessions is not Africa, but the relations between the two dominant powers. In the persistent climate of détente, they remain confident that they can de-couple the crises of the Third World from their power relationship with each other.

It will be objected, and rightly, that that was not the American reaction in Vietnam: that the 'domino theory' under which intervention was begun in that area is in fact a proclamation that local power relationships cannot be de-coupled from those of the central balance. This is true, but the basic political decision on Vietnam—the American decision to sustain the South Vietnamese government against its natural enemies, both within South Vietnam and in Hanoi—was taken in 1954, during a much earlier phase of this diplomatic evolution. And it was taken in the context of power relationships with China, not with the Soviet Union. There has unfortunately been only minimal progress as yet towards an evolution of American-Chinese relationships in the direction taken by American-Russian relationships. It would be too pessimistic to say *no* progress: actually if one classes 1965 as the point of sharpest recent crisis between the two powers, there has been quite perceptible improvement since then. But if one is looking hopefully for some route whereby China might be co-opted to the adverse partnership, the obstacles are a lot more visible than the ways round them.

One might perhaps argue that the best index of difference in the two stages of evolution is the difference in modes of communication. The establishment of a Washington-Peking 'hot line' would certainly be even more of a quantum jump in the level of communication between the United States and China than it was between the United States and the Soviet Union. (It might in fact be a more useful and less potentially embarrassing mode of communication than an American ambassador in Peking and a Chinese ambassador in Washington.) At any rate, the plenitude of means of communication as between American and Soviet policy makers compared with the exiguousness and infrequency of use of the one channel of American communication with Chinese policy makers (the Warsaw talks) offers a striking testimony of who is odd man out in the present central balance.

This is important from the point of view of what I have called the chief function of the adverse partnership, that of crisis management. The primary instrument of crisis management is the 'signal'—that is a threat or offer communicated to the adversary. Such signals are not necessarily verbal: some of the least ambiguous consist of changes in military deployment. When the Soviet Union moved thirteen extra divisions to the military districts facing China, that was as little ambiguous a signal as can well be imagined. Likewise when it appointed as Commander of its Far Eastern Military District Major-General Vladimir Tobulko, who has been second in command to the chief of the Soviet rocket forces, that also was generally accepted as a signal to the Chinese of what would probably be the nature of any future war between China and the Soviet Union: a signal that the Soviet Union did not intend to follow the Chinese rules for people's war.

Ambiguity in signalling between the powers has a bad name: it is generally assumed to lead to miscalculation, and thus to war. Dulles used to make a good deal of play with the 'war-by-miscalculation' thesis, and his diplomacy may be said to have been largely devoted to preventing it by drawing firm lines around particular areas, and erecting 'keep off' notices to allegedly predatory powers, like China, through the conclusion of mutual defence agreements with the minor powers concerned. It was long an article of faith among Republicans in America that the Korean War was precipitated by a Soviet miscalculation which stemmed from a misleading signal on the part of Dean Acheson when, as Secretary of State, he defined the defence perimeter in Asia in a speech of January 1960, and left South Korea clearly outside it.[3]

Perhaps it would have been as well not to define that perimeter. However, ambiguity in signalling is not always merely confusing and productive of miscalculation. It may be creative, if it allows the adversary to invent for himself options which will be useful to the preservation of peace. A good instance of this is the ambiguity of signalling, deliberate or accidental, on the part of Khrushchev which enabled the settlement of the Cuban missile crisis. This ambiguity consisted in the fact that Khrushchev sent two messages to President Kennedy, signalling quite contrasted attitudes. The first or 'dovelike' message (26 October) conveyed the sense of his being overwhelmed by the approach to the nuclear brink, and eager for a settlement on any reasonable terms. The second or 'hawklike' message (27 October) conveyed a toughminded determination on the part of the Praesidium to

---

[3] The speech was to the National Press Club in Washington. There is an inevitable tension between the demand of the analyst of policy (like journalists) for such definitions of national commitments, and the need of policy makers for a zone of manoeuvre.

extract any possible advantage from the situation, specifically the removal of the Thor missiles in Turkey. The response of the crisis managers round Kennedy to this ambiguity has become known as the Trollope ploy, which has been defined as 'the acceptance of an offer which has not really been made in order to induce the adversary to accept the acceptance'.[4] That is, they took the first or dovelike message as the definition of the Russian position, and simply ignored the more intransigent one, though it had been received second, and probably despatched second, and might logically have been presumed to be the most authoritative Russian definition of their position. This creative use of the ambiguity in the Russian signalling was the choice round which the crisis resolution turned.

Similarly, though Dulles spoke so darkly of the dangers of ambiguity, one could argue that one of the more notable of his successes (by his own calculation) in crisis management turned on an ambiguity in signalling. Again one cannot be certain whether this ambiguity was accidental or contrived: my judgment would favour regarding it as contrived. At any rate, it arose from the simultaneous sending of two sets of American signals on the situation concerning Quemoy and Matsu: tough and intransigent words from the part of Dulles, and much milder ones from the part of President Eisenhower. The success of this technique lay in its effect on the adversary coalition: it drove a wedge into the split which had just begun, at this time, to develop in the Sino-Soviet alliance. In effect the Russians 'chose' the intransigent strand in the signal, conveyed by the words of Dulles, as evidence that the Chinese strategy involved too many risks: the Chinese 'chose' the milder message, conveyed by the words of President Eisenhower, as evidence that the imperialists could be edged out of this fragment of Chinese territory, given a little boldness. Of course the respective choices made by the Russians and the Chinese were conditioned by the fact that Chinese national objectives (but not Russian) would have been advanced by the acquisition of Quemoy and Matsu. This is always to be expected: the psychologists have demonstrated that, exposed to a flow of communications, the individual 'selects' those items most congenial to previous thought-patterns. The principle is not new: what is interesting is its relevance to the beaming of diplomatic signals to an alliance whose separate decision élites will inevitably have different patterns of national objectives and experiences. In this case the ambiguous communication was undoubtedly more successful as a piece of crisis management than either a wholly intransigent or a wholly conciliatory set of signals would have been, in that it not only secured the optimum US objective in that particular crisis

[4] The reference is to Anthony Trollope, the Victorian novelist, whose heroines were given to interpreting a squeeze of the hand on the part of the hero as a full proposal of marriage.

(retaining the islands without a fight) but also the bonus of the entering wedge in the adversary coalition.

Clearly this is a technique which might equally be used against an alliance like NATO, and probably has been, though not with such success. The nearest approach to success may have been during the Czech crisis of 1968. No information is available on what signals the Russians sent to the NATO powers, especially the United States, on the eve of the invasion of Czechoslovakia, to assure them that nothing *more* than Czech territory was intended, but judging by the conspicuously relaxed posture of the NATO powers during these events, the signals were convincing—at any rate to Washington and London. Whether they were equally convincing to Bonn is a rather moot point. If one of the members of NATO, probably Germany, had maintained that the Russian intentions were ambiguous, and had for instance demanded a 'Stage one alert' in NATO, it would have presented the United States with a choice between an intramural crisis and a possible adversary crisis. For a 'Stage one alert' in NATO is a powerful and ambiguous signal to the Soviet Union.

To sum up, one might say that if the chief *function* of the adverse partnership is crisis management (moving, one hopes, eventually towards crisis avoidance), the main *instrumentality* by which this function is made possible is a system of signalling whose finer nuances should become increasingly well understood between the dominant powers. This clearly is a process far more advanced between the United States and the Soviet Union than between the United States and China. As between the Soviet Union and China it appears to have taken a giant leap backwards since 1963. Reckoning up the present obstacles to any co-opting of China to the adverse partnership, one would say that they are greater on the side of the Soviet Union than of the United States, and greatest of all on the side of China.

The degeneration of relations between the Soviet Union and China, over a mere ten-year period, 1958-68, from close alliance to near war, is a sobering analogy with which to begin consideration of the future of relations between the United States and the Soviet Union. Clearly the present ambivalence might be modified either by retrogression towards the more purely adversary relationship of the early Cold War years, or by further development of the elements of partnership, as yet fairly embryonic. If the latter proves to be the direction taken by events it might conceivably be possible at some future date to look back on the adverse partnership as a sort of way-station to an informal condominium of the two dominant powers. But that possibility is one which seems less probable now than it did in the early 1960s. Whereas then it seemed not unlikely that the two powers would become preoccupied with how much (jointly) they *might* do, now it seems rather more probable that they may become preoccupied with how little they *need* do. Both powers have learned recently how expensive it may be for them to preserve or cultivate vulnerable friends in the Third World. If one thinks of how much it has cost the United States to preserve a government friendly to the West in Saigon, or, on a lighter plane, how much the subsidy to Fidel Castro has cost the Soviet Union since 1963, it appears inevitable that enthusiasm for such expensive allies should wane, once the margin of power that their acquisition or retention formerly seemed to represent is no longer seen as important. Even in the ordinary field of foreign aid, the flow of funds has diminished with the settling-in of the détente. There is still an economic and humanitarian case for such transfers, but it is far less powerful than the old diplomatic case, based on the proposition 'if we do not make sure that they are for us, the other side may make sure that they are against us'.

Bearing in mind this essential uncertainty, one may still discern some factors which would nudge the relationship in the one direction or the other. The circumstance most likely to disrupt it altogether, and end the détente, would be some blatant disregard of the tacitly agreed rules as they have evolved to date, especially those concerning the vital power sphere of either. The second really fatal development would be a disregard or a wrong estimate of what degree of defeat either party would accept before moving from crisis manoeuvring to major hostilities. My view is that both parties will tend to accept very considerable local defeats at each other's hands (and perhaps ultimately at China's hands) rather than take new risks of over-commitment on the lines of Vietnam or Cuba. However, obviously neither will take an unlimited defeat; so that one of the main uses of the partnership is to keep a stream of messages flowing, to signal or agree the limits of defeat in any particular sphere. But there could obviously still be mistaken estimates of how serious and damaging a particular defeat could seem to a particular set of decision makers.

Assuming that total disruption of the relationship can be avoided, we have next to ask what are the other factors which will limit or blight its development (bearing in mind that blighting its development may be a desirable end, as with a healthily growing weed). The crucial case to be considered here is the question of whether the partnership is likely to be extended from relationships between the two powers themselves, and their immediate allies, to developments in the Third World. The limiting factor on this, I would suggest, is the experience of 'no imperial payoff' or, in gaming terms, 'negative payoff'. That is, there have proved nowadays to be more kicks than ha'pence in the imperial business. If you contrast the perceived rewards of being a member of the central balance partnership during the nineteenth century, with those in prospect in the late twentieth century, the game in the later period must seem hardly worth the candle. Some analysts have maintained that the only reason why the nineteenth-century system worked so well was the imperial payoff to the then dominant powers. If that were indeed the case future prospects would appear daunting. But we may optimistically hope that the dominant powers will feel enough incentive to take some action (because of the remaining risks of inaction) but that such action will not be so lavishly rewarded as to tempt them to seek an undue hegemony over the rest of the world.

Another factor which should conduce to this limitation is the tension generated between the dominant powers and their respective allies by the cultivation of relations with the adversary power. The instance of this usually cited is the impact on America's relations with its NATO allies of the cultivation of an understanding with the Soviet Union through, for instance, the SALT negotiations. But a better example of really disruptive influence on an alliance was the way in which the Sino-Soviet alliance was broken after 1959 by the Russian cultivation of relations with the United States.

It must be conceded that the existence of China as *tertius gaudens* is the factor which imparts the greatest unpredictability into the future of the American-Soviet relationship. If world politics in 1970 conformed to Maoist rhetoric about them, one would feel that the 'imperialists' and 'social imperialists' were left with not much option but to 'collude' against so formidable a power competitor. But the logical correlative of that Maoist view of the situation, a joint or tacitly agreed enterprise against China, is in fact never likely to recommend itself to the United States. For its upshot, if successful, would be to transmute the present triangle of forces back towards the old bilateral balance. And there is no prospect of American decision-makers thinking that would be to the advantage of the US. Whatever kind of China emerged after, perhaps, a pre-emptive strike by the Russians, it would not be likely to be one which could be a useful ally to the US. Presumably the Russians believe that it would be a Communist but not Maoist state, willing to revert to a subsidiary role within the Soviet sphere of power. Probably they are wrong, but the chances seem real enough to discourage any American impulse to believe that its own interests could be forwarded by helping the Soviet Union to pull chestnuts out of the Chinese fire. It should also rule out any callous assumption that hostilities in this quarter do not matter to the West. On the contrary, such hostilities would not only be abominable from a moral and humanitarian point of view, they would also be disastrous from a diplomatic and strategic point of view.

There is, however, another direction from which China's future status as a power competitor must be regarded as the great unknown in the future of relations between America and Russia. I said earlier that their present tendency might be less to reflect how much they *might* jointly do, than how little they *need* do. But this depends on their being able not only to take a relatively relaxed view of each other's roles in the Third World, but a similar view of China. And that in turn depends either on the co-opting of China to the adverse partnership, or on a conviction that it will not become over-formidable. Either assumption requires a good deal of optimism.

This essay appears, in expanded form, as ch. 3 of the author's *The Conventions of Crisis* (in press).

THE CENTRAL BALANCE:
ARMS RACE AND ARMS CONTROL

The decade of the 1960s saw the passing of the era of clear American numerical superiority in strategic missile launchers (ICBMs and SLBMs) over the Soviet Union, and the beginnings of a new era wherein the results of technological research and development in the 1960s—means of actively defending countries, cities, or single targets against ballistic missile attack, so-called ABM systems, and means of extending the destructive power of one missile launcher from one target to several, via the so-called MIRV —are likely to find their way into the strategic armouries of the super powers. And the passing of the 1960s is likely to see a translation of Chinese development work into some kind of strategic nuclear force which, at the least, will confront the United States with its first additional probable nuclear antagonist in twenty years and the Soviet Union with its third, and at the most could confront both with a rival nuclear super power.

One great influence at work shaping the strategic nuclear forces of the two major nuclear powers during the 1960s was the interpretation by each put upon the technical prowess and political intentions of the other, in other words the so-called action-reaction phenomenon whereby a military-technological advance by one side, whether real or imagined, exerts pressures on the other side for this advance to be countered by additions or alterations to its strategic armoury. Sometimes these pressures are modified, either accentuated or attenuated by other factors, technical, economic and political. And occasionally these modifying influences may be large enough to obscure or render insignificant the original action-reaction response, which is never, in any case, entirely free from these complicating factors (for example a statistical analysis of a graphical representation of the rise in numbers of the United States and Soviet ICBM forces between 1960 and 1969 certainly does not permit one to say very much about any relationship between the numerical size of the two forces beyond that they each have increased with time).

This chapter has benefited from comments by Geoffrey Jukes and Des Ball.

Without Soviet secrecy about its strategic nuclear forces there could scarcely have been a 'missile gap' crisis in 1960-1 but there is no major country on earth that is completely open about its military capabilities. Attitudes range over a spectrum stretching from China where information is least accessible, to the United States where military information is perhaps most easily available. But even the United States retains as secret much detail about its strategic nuclear forces, certainly to the extent that the Soviet Union finds it worth while to employ photographic reconnaissance satellite cover of the United States. And mutual secrecy has played an important part in determining the timing and nature of American and Soviet decisions regarding the composition of their strategic nuclear forces. It is uncertainty about what the other side has already deployed, or is about to deploy, as much as uncertainty about what it intends to acquire (which no amount of reconnaissance can determine), that has acted as a spur to new procurement decisions in many cases. The reaction side of the action-reaction phenomenon is often reaction to what is *supposed to be* the original action, which in the American case, and possibly to some extent the Soviet one too, means reaction not to what the Soviets (or vice versa the Americans) have done or intend to do but to what either country would itself have done or would have intended had the imperfect intelligence in its possession referred to itself.

The rapidity and scale of the American reaction to the missile gap was designed precisely to counter what the Soviets might have if they were to go about their business as the Americans go about theirs:[1] given the knowledge that the Soviets had a reliable large rocket booster technology, witnessed by their public success in space exploration during the late 1950s, production line techniques were estimated to be capable of giving the Soviets as much as a three to one superiority over the United States in ICBMs in the early 1960s if the United States did not react.[2] In fact by 1962 the Soviet ICBM force had increased from the forty of 1960 to eighty (in round numbers) whereas the American force by contrast had expanded from twenty to three hundred in the same period. The habit of assigning to an opponent one's own country's best capabilities clearly not only opens the possibility of wildly inaccurate estimates of the opponent's capabilities but also clearly reduces one almost to competing with one's self: a highly divergent, or self-feeding situation which without the intervention of other factors would quickly lead to the spending of a country's

[1] This is not meant to imply that the 1961 decision to increase the American ICBM and SLBM forces was taken in the firm belief at the time that the 'missile gap' existed. Yet, whatever importance other factors came to have in influencing the decision, it had its origins a year before in the previous Administration's inability to persuade the country and its political opponents that the missile gap did not exist.

[2] See Arthur M. Schlesinger, Jr, *A Thousand Days*. London: Mayflower Dell, 1967, p. 267.

entire resources on defence. It is nonetheless not a new habit, it has long been a tradition in professional military circles to exaggerate an opponent's abilities in peace-time, as in defeat.

Other examples of the action-reaction phenomenon during the 1960s are not quite so dramatic but one particularly baroque illustration, where the action-reaction process may have played an important part, was the Soviet construction of what is now believed to be an anti-aircraft defence network called the Tallin system, probably designed to counter the expected development of a new American strategic bomber but interpreted by some in the United States as an anti-missile system and used as one reason why the United States should develop new kinds of ICBMs and SLBMs which could penetrate anti-missile systems. The various Soviet anti-missile systems of the 1960s, one of which seems to have been installed around Leningrad as early as 1962, can be understood, in part, as a reaction to the American superiority in ICBMs over that period. And the most elementary example of action and reaction of all has been the imitation by the Soviets of some of what have proved to be the most successful aspects of the American strategic forces: solid and storable fuel ICBMs, hardened ICBM emplacements and sixteen-missile submarines. This following of example is, from the arms control viewpoint, perhaps the only desirable feature of the action-reaction process. From the pure arms control point of view qualitative and quantitative parity in armaments between two opposing nations is usually preferable to an imbalance favouring one side or the other.

One 'natural' brake to the unlimited operation of the action-reaction phenomenon, aside from the conscious efforts made by governments in the direction of limiting their armaments, which we will return to later, is that of cost. Both the United States and the Soviet Union have in the past allowed economic considerations to influence their strategic nuclear weapons procurement decisions. A Soviet desire for economising on central government expenditure in the early 1960s is sometimes thought to have been partly responsible at least for the slow rate of growth of the Soviet ICBM force during that period, and the American postponements of a decision to procure new strategic bombers or to deploy an ABM system over the same period were often defended on economic, as well as other, grounds. And the American decision in 1970 to limit the number of F-111 bombers to be assigned to a strategic role was defended by the government solely upon economic grounds.[3]

[3] It is important, however, as Albert Wohlstetter has already pointed out, that the economic impact of American spending on its strategic nuclear forces should not be overestimated. While at the beginning of the 1960s this spending was clearly considerable at between 20 and 25 per cent of the defence budget and only slightly less than total expenditure on conventional forces, by the end of the 1960s, while remaining roughly unchanged in money terms, it had shrunk to 10 per cent of the total.

FOOTNOTE CONTINUED OVERLEAF

E

It does not follow, however, that given internal economic situations—inflation, balance of payments difficulties, or recession, say—even in any one country have met or will always meet with the same governmental response with respect to its level of spending. This varies with the prevailing economic fashion and also, in the United States, sometimes with the political party that happens to be in power. The Democratic Administration's decision to procure large ICBM and SLBM forces in 1961 was taken at a time of industrial recession in the United States. It is not at all certain that had a Republican Administration been returned in the 1960 elections it would have authorised such a large increase in government spending at such a time; the previous Eisenhower Administrations had certainly no great reputation for Keynesian thinking and indeed had an inbuilt aversion to 'spending one's way out' of stagnation.

Equally, difficulties in the Soviet economy may not always be met in the same way; prevailing fashion in Soviet economic thinking has shifted during the 1960s away from indifference to the consumer towards paying more attention to his needs and, since the fall of Khrushchev, to a degree, back again in the direction of greater indifference, the middle period coinciding with a low level of central government spending on armaments.

Another 'natural' factor influencing the process of acquiring strategic nuclear arms in both countries is the advance of military technology. This provides governments with the choice often of a variety of new military products each usually offering some improved feature over the existing product and, by implication, over the products of the opponent's offensive or defensive technology. And while the advances are usually small and reasonably predictable they are occasionally large and relatively unexpected, as has on the whole been the case with MIRVs or the Soviet FOBS. Whereas economic factors are usually constraints upon the free growth of strategic armaments, advancing technology is more usually an accelerating factor, particularly when the products of the specific technological advance are merely added to, and not substituted for, the existing product, as the ICBM, for example, was by and large added to the strategic inter-continental bomber force in both countries, or when the specific technological advance leads to a search by the opponent for a counter to that advance, as ABM defence is an attempt to counter the ICBM, adding fuel to the action-reaction process.

Although the Vietnam War accounted for much of this increase in overall defence spending, expenditure on strategic nuclear forces as a percentage of the GNP has roughly halved from $1 \cdot 7$ per cent in 1963 to $0 \cdot 8$ per cent in 1969. In the case of the Soviet Union there are not the data available to make a similar analysis, but the manpower employed in Soviet conventional forces and the size of the Soviet strategic forces are sufficiently close to the American counterparts as to suggest that for the Soviets too the prospect of savings on expenditure on strategic nuclear forces may be far from decisive in conditioning their attitude to an arms limitation agreement.

Nevertheless technological advance occasionally exerts a braking influence on the arms race. The advent of the ICBM was accompanied by an almost total slowing down in the growth of strategic bomber forces and increasingly accurate techniques of ICBM guidance have, in both countries, tended to encourage the deployment of smaller thermonuclear warheads. Both developments tended to reduce, or slow down the rate of increase of, the total nuclear megatonnage likely to be exploded in the event of an all-out nuclear exchange and therefore have lessened, if only in terms of radio-active fallout, the destruction likely to be caused by such an exchange. Technological advance too has resulted in progressively more reliable and more efficient radar warning devices and surer command and control links and as such has probably acted to reduce the likelihood of some kinds of accidental war. Technological advances occasionally tend to cancel each other out as far as their effects on the stability of the strategic balance are concerned; advances in ICBM accuracy have, for example, prompted advances in techniques for protecting ICBMs against pre-emptive attack. Unfortunately while an advance and its counter-advance are often simultaneous within any one country they are sometimes far apart in time where two or more countries are concerned. The gap can often be quite long and dangerous; the Russians were for example slow to develop reliable means of hardening their ICBM force, partly because of an earlier decision to rely on large proven liquid-fuelled ICBM boosters, while the Americans were quick to do so.

This process of military technological advance is not of course a magical thing with its own life force; it is rather the result at any one time of what governments paid for when they purchased military equipment from the manufacturers some time previously. Armament manufacturers in the United States and their Soviet equivalents apportion out of their income, or are separately granted by their respective governments, funds for research and development which sometimes bear fruit some years afterwards as a new weapons system. This 'lead time', the period between the investment of funds for research and development and the emergence of a product ready for full-scale production, is another complicating factor to the understanding of the mechanism of the advance of military technology; research may, for example, be begun on an ICBM capable of penetrating not the ABM system the opponent currently possesses but the system he could possess in five years' time, which widens even further the scope for mistaking the opponent's capabilities. If the American MIRV warheads due for deployment in 1970 had been developed in response to the embryo Leningrad ABM system of 1962-3, and this could have played a part in the decision, the subsequent dismantling of the Leningrad system and the build-up of a new, less than one hundred anti-missile missile, ABM system around Moscow by 1970, makes the American decision seem a serious misjudgment.

And likewise the Soviet construction of the extensive Tallin anti-aircraft system, if connected with the American plans to build a new strategic bomber—and there could have been a connection—and with the severe cutback in F-111 procurement begins to look like gross over-reaction.

A final 'natural' factor with an almost wholly accelerating influence on the rate and scale of strategic weapons procurement in the United States is the pressure exerted directly, and via lobbyists, on Congressmen and officials by armaments companies and by the armed services, for, in the former case, new government contracts and in the latter for new weapons systems. This factor, more than any other, has drawn critical attention somewhat disproportionate to its actual influence on the rate of weapons acquisition. The pressures from industry have, however, become somewhat paradoxically progressively easier for Administrations to resist as military procurement contracts have become more valuable and weapons more complex, thus drastically reducing the number of companies physically and financially competent to handle them and in addition representing for those companies that can handle them such a large proportion of their income that governmental control over their activities has become both closer and harder to resist because of the risk of losing future contracts.

While industrial lobbying is still a factor in the American strategic nuclear procurement process it is hard to identify an example of its ever having been primarily responsible for a major decision. Lobbying by the military, on the other hand, while by no means always successful in overcoming civilian opposition, has been from time to time an important factor in shaping the American strategic nuclear forces, particularly in the early years. The original Polaris concept, for example, was more the product of the US Navy's desire to capture a nuclear strategic role for itself in challenge to the central part played by the US Air Force, which had responsibility for both bombers and the missile forces, than the product of a rational attempt by all responsible parties to invent a new strategic weapons system.

But the influence of the military is not always for change. Entrenched attachment by the Air Force to the concept of the manned bomber has probably been an important factor in the retention in being of such a large segment of the American nuclear bomber force even as large numbers of ICBMs became available. It has also been partly responsible, at least, for the retention by successive Administrations of a minimum of interest in the development of a new manned strategic aircraft. But the repeated rebuffs throughout the 1960s which met the US Army's persistent requests for funds to deploy an anti-missile system, more accurately reflects the decreasing effectiveness of military lobbying during the 1960s. The influence of the armed services on the procurement process overall was moreover progressively weakened throughout most of the decade by the presence of a strong Secretary of Defense, McNamara, whose seven years' incumbency saw the deliberate, gradual establishment of civilian ascendancy in the procurement sector, with the very substitution of more objective economic guides to military procurement decisions than had existed hitherto acting to put them further out of reach of modification by lay lobbyists, at least temporarily.

Indeed it may be said that in the decade following Eisenhower's famous warning on the 'military industrial complex' its actual success in securing new orders for major strategic nuclear items was demonstrably rather small, there having been no new order for strategic bombers, ICBMs or SLBMs placed between the first decisions of the Kennedy Administration and the decisions to deploy an ABM system of the Johnson and Nixon Administrations seven and eight years later (the MIRV procurement decisions, while of great strategic significance, were of a minor order economically and replaced existing ICBM re-entry vehicles).

The influence of industry and the military on the growth of the Soviet strategic nuclear forces, as far as can be judged, cannot have much in common with the American model. Private industry in the American sense does not exist, and rivalry between the services can only be presumed to exist with, until the comparatively recent launching of the Y-class Polaris-type submarines, the Navy playing a subsidiary role to the Strategic Rocket Forces and the Air Force.

None of these 'natural' factors of course operates in a vacuum, intervention in their operation by political leaders, in the interests of changing foreign and domestic policy requirements and in the light of a strategic doctrine or of arms control policy, has been and is likely to remain the overall moulding influence on the structure of the strategic nuclear forces of the super powers.

While the sophisticated thinking of American civilian strategists on deterrence in the nuclear age probably had some influence on the details of the thinking of American strategic planners even in the late 1950s (an example of which may have showed itself in the decision to place the Minuteman ICBMs in protected launch pads thereby protecting them from surprise attack), the guiding theoretical principle governing the size of the American strategic nuclear forces was that of superiority over the Soviet Union. While it was never made clear how the superiority was to be measured, it was an assumption fundamental to the thinking of military and civilian strategists and politicians alike, with few exceptions. That superiority certainly existed during most of the 1960s is undeniable, virtually irrespective of how it is measured, whether by total number of strategic nuclear delivery vehicles, number of ICBMs, number of SLBMs, or number of warheads. Only with the yardstick of total deliverable megatonnage was domestic doubt on the American superiority never wholly overcome. But by 1969 it became clear that US superiority in numbers of ICBMs was disappearing and with this knowledge the new Nixon Administration publicly rejected the principle of 'superiority' and substituted that of 'sufficiency'. Even so, at the end of the 1960s the respective numbers of deliverable strategic nuclear warheads were (including bombs): the United States, 4,200, the Soviet Union 1,880.[4]

While strategic superiority over its nearest rival or rivals was scarcely a novel goal for a great power, whether the superiority be measured in nuclear delivery vehicles or, as it might have been, fifty years ago, in capital ships, and receiving in general the same kinds of chauvinistic justification, a more precise and practicable doctrine and one more relevant to the nature of nuclear weaponry was developed beneath the heading of superiority. This was the doctrine of 'assured destruction plus damage limitation' whereby it became American policy that in order to deter the Soviet Union from nuclear attack upon the United States, or its vital interests, it (the United States) must possess a nuclear striking force large enough and refined enough to inflict damage upon the Soviet Union to the extent of destroying at any time between 20 and 30 per cent of the Soviet population and between 50 and 70 per cent of its industry even after absorbing a Soviet attack on the US strategic forces and penetrating Soviet active defences.

This definition is not so precise as it may seem. First, it was, as I have said, until 1969, subservient to the 'superiority' requirement. Secondly, the kind of American nuclear force that emerges from the recipe depends rather strongly upon how effective the Soviet first strike is expected to be and how effective the Soviet defence system is expected to be—each factor obviously capable of a fairly wide variation between reasonable estimates. The percentage destructions stipulated under the doctrine are moreover arbitrary in the sense that who is to say that they should not be a half or third of what they are; but they have some logical basis as *upper* limits. The demography and pattern of industrialisation of the Soviet Union is such that, in the case of population, the percentage killed (about 30 per cent) by a nuclear attack of 400 one megaton equivalent warheads targeted for maximum effect, is not much less than that (40 per cent) which would be killed by a nuclear attack of four or five times that size.[5] Similarly, with industrial capacity the percentage destroyed by a nuclear attack of 150 one megaton equivalent warheads (about 70 per cent) is only slightly less than that (75 per cent) that would be destroyed by a nuclear attack

[4] *Strategic Survey 1969*, ISS, London.

[5] The number of one megaton equivalents of any warhead is obtained by taking the 2/3 power of its yield in megatons. A 27 megaton warhead, for example, is 9 one megaton equivalents; the number of one megaton equivalents more realistically corresponding to the destruction caused by the explosion of the warhead in question.

ten times the size. In other words the 'assured destruction' percentages are set at a point beyond which further equal increases in destruction suddenly require increasingly large increments in the forces allocated.[6]

In fact by the end of the 1960s the total deliverable American megatonnage on the Soviet Union by ICBM and SLBM alone (less than 2,000 warheads out of a 4,200 total) even when multiplied by the least favourable (to the US) plausible reduction factors to allow for missile unavailability, unreadiness, unreliability, reduction after Soviet first strike and defensive action, still approached a total of 400 one megaton equivalents.[7] It would clearly therefore be wrong to suggest that the 'assured destruction' principle acts in practice as anything more than a general signpost to the minimum size of the US strategic nuclear forces.

I do not know whether the Soviets employ anything with the apparent precision of the 'assured destruction' principle but it seems reasonable to suggest they make some count of the number of targets they would wish to be able to destroy in the United States, and this would be a factor in determining the size of their forces. If the Soviets were to evolve an 'assured destruction' principle of their own the different distribution of targets in the United States would mean that the percentages of deaths and destroyed industrial capacity aimed at could be quite different from the American figures, if determined on the same basis, and could be used to 'justify' a much smaller force than 400 delivered one megaton equivalent warheads, given the higher American density of population and the different distribution of population and industry throughout the country.

While 'assured destruction' has provided a doctrinal justification for the minimum size of American strategic nuclear forces, however imprecisely, 'damage limitation' has provided the justification for anti-bomber defences and, more important, for increasing the accuracy of ICBMs and SLBMs beyond the point necessary for the destruction of industrial targets. It has been used as justification for increases in the accuracy of ICBMs to make them useful for destroying elements of the Soviet strategic forces before they could be used; and for keeping their numbers high enough to perform this task, to an unpublicised extent, in addition to the numbers required under the heading of 'assured destruction'.

While 'damage limitation' is always talked of by official spokesmen in the context of an American retaliatory strike after an initial Soviet attack, the

[6] Daniel J. Fink in 'Strategic Warfare', *Science and Technology*, October 1968, p. 60.

[7] Ibid., pp. 62, 63. These degradation factors are 20 per cent for missile unavailability, 20 per cent for unreadiness, 20 per cent for launch failure, 20 per cent for flight failure, 33 per cent destroyed by first strike, 33 per cent intercepted by ABM defences, leaving 18 per cent of the original force to reach Soviet targets (the overall factor is the same for SLBMs, their immunity from first strike being compensated by their lower availability).

kind of force it is used to justify can be used equally well, or almost equally well, to attack Soviet forces before any part had been launched, in other words to carry out a disarming first strike. 'Damage limitation' is then in a sense a euphemistic way of describing a part of American strategic policy—namely the option of being able at least partly to disarm the Soviet Union in a first strike. The extent to which the United States possessed a disarming capability during the 1960s is rather unclear, depending as it does upon largely classified information concerning the accuracy of American missiles in the period, the effectiveness of Soviet 'early-warning' radars, the alertness and reaction times of the Soviet bombers and ICBMs and submarine forces, and the degree of protection afforded to Soviet land-based forces by hardened silos or geographic dispersion. But while there may have been periods when the American disarming capacity could have been considerable, this could only have been in connection with the Soviet intercontinental nuclear delivery forces, i.e., those forces with the range to reach the United States; the Soviet capability to attack European targets even after absorbing an American first strike cannot have ever been in much doubt, in view of its numerical size.

Again, it cannot be said at this stage whether 'damage limitation' played any part during the 1960s in determining the size and technical characteristics of the Soviet offensive nuclear forces, whether in its first-strike or second-strike meaning. The Soviet inferiority in numbers of warheads deliverable on the United States and in ICBMs and submarine-borne missiles for most of the decade suggests not. Though the Soviets seem to have been aware from the beginning that the US forces have had a 'damage limiting' role, early Soviet ICBM sites were placed in southern Siberia some way from, at the time, the clearest US threat to them—bombers stationed in West Europe—and with Soviet anti-aircraft defences separating them, and, later, the Soviet ICBM sites were hardened against nuclear attack. Defense Secretary Laird has, however, referred to features of the Soviet SS-9 missile, in a MIRV configuration, displayed in test flights in 1969 and 1970, which have suggested to him that the SS-9 could be used to attack American ICBM silos. The SS-9 in this configuration could then be described as part of a Soviet 'damage limitation' force. And it is also possible that the Soviet SS-9 in its FOBS configuration, which was tested before an American decision to deploy ABM defences was taken, might be specifically designed for a 'damage limitation' role since its special characteristic, that of reducing the radar warning time of attack to a few minutes, is of no particular value against civilian targets without ABM defence. But it could be valuable against bomber formations which may be caught on the airfield with insufficient warning of attack to permit their take-off. On the other hand it is not expected to be a particularly accurate missile, nor to carry (by Soviet standards) a particularly large warhead in compensation.

But the other side of the 'damage limitation' coin, active defences, has played on the whole a more important part in Soviet strategic thinking than in American. Soviet ABM defence research began, as did the American, with research on offensive ballistic missiles, but in the Soviet case this was followed by an early decision to deploy. An ABM system appeared around Leningrad in 1962 and 1963, but was quickly dismantled, and then another was started around Moscow three or four years later. The Soviets have moreover taken anti-aircraft defence rather more seriously than the Americans; the Soviet Tallin system, almost certainly an air-defence network, is of more recent construction and presumably therefore more sophisticated than its American counterpart.

While the Soviet ICBM and SLBM (and other submarine-borne missiles) forces were considerably inferior to those of the United States, Soviet defensive 'damage limitation' measures could be unequivocally interpreted as just that, but as Soviet ICBM and SLBM forces have grown relative to the American so has it become feasible to associate Soviet 'damage limitation' measures with the possibility of a Soviet disarming strike on the United States, for it seems quite fundamental that ABM defences (and anti-aircraft defences) of the kind already deployed by the Soviets, and envisaged in the American Safeguard plan, are more effective against a small attack—such as that composed of forces which may have survived a disarming first strike—than against a larger one.

Whereas 'assured destruction' and 'damage limitation' can be said in varying degrees to represent political intervention in the 'natural' processes moulding the US-Soviet strategic nuclear forces, tending to encourage the growth and technical development of the forces both offensive and defensive, political intervention has also operated in the opposite sense, to limit the size of forces, to delay the introduction of new weapons and to lessen the chances of accidental war, to decrease the incentive to respond massively to a small attack, and to reduce the chances of all-out nuclear war breaking out.

It is extremely hard to identify any single decision with regard to their strategic nuclear forces of either the Soviet or the American government where such arms control considerations were uppermost, certainly no decision received its primary public justification as such. Yet arms control thinking has been influential in several American procurement decisions during the 1960s.

The most consistent actions of successive American Administrations during the 1960s, during the tenure of McNamara as Defense Secretary, which had an arms controlling effect were those designed to keep the numerical size of the American ICBM and SLBM force within the limits of the original procurement decisions of the Kennedy Administration, in the face of, at first, slowly growing Soviet capabilities, while at the same time satisfying the theoretical requirements of 'damage limitation' and 'assured destruction'. One inevitable and obvious result of this policy was the slow erosion of American superiority in numbers of ICBMs and SLBMs as Soviet strength in these missiles grew.

Its specific arms control effects were far reaching. The dispersal and flight alert of a portion of the strategic nuclear bombers force in times of crisis and the development of hardened sites for ICBMs decreased their vulnerability to a surprise attack and therefore provided an opportunity of maintaining US 'assured destruction' capacity as Soviet forces increased in number and in disarming capability without having to add to the US forces. Not only were these measures less likely to lead to a compensatory Soviet response than was an increase in the size of the US forces, but also, if properly understood by the Soviets, reduced the chances of a war being begun by them in the hope of reducing American retaliatory power. More than this, hardening reduced the American incentive to launch their forces *en masse* on receipt of a radar warning of attack, thus lowering the possibility of the Americans starting a nuclear war by accident, should the radar warning have proven incorrect, and offering in addition the opportunity to limit the scale and destructiveness of a nuclear war should the attack detected by the radar have proven to be a small one or one launched by accident.

And the eventual success of American publicity about these aspects of its strategic nuclear forces in persuading the Soviets to take similar steps with regard to their own forces (which was claimed by McNamara towards the end of his tenure to be the purpose of the publicity), hardening their ICBMs and deploying SLBMs (the latter resembling the American Polaris force even to the point of having exactly the same number—sixteen—missiles to a submarine), decreased the *American* disarming capacity below what it might otherwise have been.

Yet, ironically, the gradual acceptance of the notion, by Democrats and Republican Administration alike, that the American ICBM and SLBM forces should not be numerically increased, ultimately formalised with President Nixon's public rejection of 'superiority' as an aim of American strategic nuclear policy, was itself instrumental in encouraging the development in the United States of MIRVs. In the face of expected or actual Soviet ABM deployment and actual or expected increases in the Soviet disarming capability, and as the possibility of maintaining 'assured destruction' by increasing the number of ICBMs and SLBMs was ruled out, so multiple warheads were devised with the primary purpose of confusing, and thereby nullifying, the slow-reacting ABM defences which the Soviets had erected briefly around Leningrad. These were first produced with dummy additional warheads, and were incorporated into the US ICBM force

(Minuteman II), then later were made with small numbers of multiple but not separately guided warheads, and these were incorporated into the Polaris program (Polaris A-3). Towards the end of the decade the deployment of a faster-reacting Soviet ABM system and a rapid growth in the Soviet ICBM force, with the presumed increase in the Soviet disarming capability, possibly including the addition of MIRVs to the SS-9 missile, have been used to justify the development of even greater multiplicity of, and separate guidance for, warheads for the US ICBM and SLBM forces.

The restraint on offensive missile numbers exercised by the Americans in the 1960s found echoes in the postponement of a decision to deploy an American ABM system of any kind until 1968. The relative crudity of American ABM defence technology for much of the early part of the decade and its consequent inefficiency and doubtful viability as a defensive system, even when installed without regard to cost, made rejection by successive Administrations relatively easy on cost or cost/benefit grounds. More exactly it was relatively easy for McNamara to show that almost any American expenditure on an ABM system could be nullified by the Soviets, and much more cheaply, by adding to, or modifying, their ICBM forces.

At the same time this American self-denial of an additional 'damage limitation' capability with the implied refusal to take another step towards making the possibility of a disarming first strike by the United States on the Soviet Union a however slightly more attractive one, was not accompanied by a similar restraint upon the 'damage limitation' capability of the American ICBM and SLBM forces, which became progressively more accurate over the period, with this increase in accuracy being incorporated moreover into multiple warheads. And while a general reliance upon mutual deterrence with the Soviet Union and upon its indefinite continuance —a stable mutual deterrence in other words—was invoked by McNamara in defence of his refusal to procure an ABM system, the doctrines of 'assured destruction' and 'damage limitation' were not renounced, nor was the concept of an ABM system, if an efficient system could be found, for the defence of the United States ever rejected.

Soviet decisions on their strategic forces may have also been influenced by arms control thinking—it is certainly plain that they were aware of the kind of arguments that were being put forward by McNamara—and their decision to harden ICBM sites and develop Polaris-style submarines may have been accompanied by some understanding and appreciation of the 'stabilising' effects of these decisions, but nothing can be said for certain at this stage. The public Soviet attitude as to how their own ABM system should be interpreted does not betray any sympathy with McNamara's view and it is hard to know whether the Soviets are likely to hold different opinions in private. The traditional Soviet attitude to ABM systems has an

ideological content—that Soviet ABMs are purely defensive but that those
of other countries may not necessarily be—which is in some ways a mirror
image of the American ideological justification for its now discarded claim
to superiority in offensive missiles. But whether for arms control reasons
or not the Soviets have not built up their ABM system at all rapidly. For a
country which began to deploy a system in 1962 its size by 1970, some
seventy anti-missile missiles and associated radars round Moscow, does not
betoken rapid construction in comparison with the rise in their ICBM forces
over the same period.

It is too soon to say what kind of doctrines or rationalisations, if any,
are likely to emerge in support of a particular level of ABM defence in
either of the super powers, analogous to the 'assured destruction' condition
pertaining to the size of the American strategic offensive nuclear forces.
For one thing the entry of China, whose incipient ICBM forces were given
as the primary justification for the original American decision to procure
an ABM system, into the reckoning of strategic planners on both sides,
has to be allowed for; but on the American side at least there is wide agreement that for a given state of both offensive and defensive technology
there is always a level of ABM deployment beyond which one country can
nullify the procurement of additional ABM defences by the other by
improving its offensive forces (qualitatively or quantitatively) at less cost
to itself than the incremental ABM defence cost. This level of ABM defence is then said to be that at which the 'cost-exchange ratio' is unity.[8]
For current technologies this point would be reached by the United States
at a level of ABM deployment designed to reduce fatalities in an all out
Soviet attack to 30 per cent of the population or thereabouts. As with computing force levels to satisfy the 'assured destruction' requirement, the
'unity cost-exchange ratio' point cannot be determined with any great
precision. For example, Soviet cost structures and the state of technology
with regard to its offensive forces are difficult for the Americans to determine. But it is interesting to note that, if for want of better information the
Americans equated Soviet technology in offensive weapons with the best
of their own (and this is normal when computing 'assured destruction'
levels), the better in theory American offensive weapons became at penetrating Soviet defences the less easy it would be for the United States to justify
additional defensive weapons on the 'unity cost-exchange ratio' principle.

However, there is as yet no basis for assuming that 'cost-exchange ratio'
considerations will play an important part in dictating the size of a future
American ABM defence system nor that they even impinge upon the thinking of Soviet strategic planners. And it is too soon to be certain that

---

[8] The 'cost-exchange ratio' is the incremental cost the defence must spend to reduce
fatalities a certain amount divided by the cost to the offence to restore these fatalities.

mutually agreed constraints on ABM deployment will not supersede that of the 'cost-exchange ratio'.

The effect of the coming into service of MIRVs and ABM systems upon the stability of the strategic balance between the two super powers is likely to amount to a levelling off, or, depending upon the eventual scale of the deployment by both sides, a reversal, of the trend during the second half of the 1960s towards decreasing the relative advantage to be gained by either side in striking first.

It can be argued that the deployment of MIRVs, even if occurring simultaneously and at the same level in both super powers, eventually leads to a situation wherein each side can launch a surprise attack on the other with a high probability of disarming its opponent's land-based forces while using its ABM defences to intercept the depleted retaliatory strike, and therefore 'winning' the war. Thus each side is encouraged to use its forces first in a crisis. Or, alternatively, if one side or the other has a significant advantage in the number or accuracy of its MIRVs accompanied by a quantitative or qualitative advantage in its ABM defences, or believes that it has, then it may regard itself in a position to win a nuclear exchange and initiate a nuclear war to take advantage of what might be a temporary situation.

However, this presents an exaggerated picture. It ignores the property of MIRVs that they not only provide more warheads for a first strike attack but they also provide more warheads to retaliate with, although increases in accuracy and number of MIRVs per launcher will at some stage begin to favour the first striker. It ignores the property of MIRVs that they provide a means of evading ABM defences by their qualitative nature as well as through force of numbers. It ignores the likelihood that ABM defence of missile sites will be part of any large-scale ABM deployment, as well as the possibility that alternative means of protecting ICBMs such as making them land mobile are available; and it ignores the existence of the strategic bomber forces which to a degree are immune to MIRVs and ABM defences alike.

But while it may not always be clear how MIRVs and ABM systems will, if their deployment is unchecked, adversely affect the stability of the nuclear balance, it is very hard to see how they might enhance the stability of the balance, and therefore how they might contribute to making the situation of mutual deterrence more secure and permanent. There is of course no reason at bottom why stable mutual deterrence should always be the aim of either super power—its espousal during the 1960s by the United States might be called making a virtue out of necessity—and there is no reason to suppose that one or other side would necessarily hesitate to develop weapons systems which might give it an overwhelming military

advantage over the other, or that the suggestion sometimes made of a balance based upon defence rather than deterrence could not become a
reality. But the possibility that MIRVs and ABM systems, if deployed
without hindrance, will at worst lead to a situation wherein each side would
feel obliged to initiate a war in a time of crisis, or at best will recreate the
stable mutual deterrence of the 1960s with a new stable deterrence at much
higher costs to both parties, together with other factors regarding their
position with respect to each other and the rest of the world, particularly
China, has encouraged the two super powers to institute an arms limitation conference between themselves.

There are many reasons which suggest that the arms limitation conference begun in 1969 between the two super powers may in the end be productive of some kind of agreement. Both parties have tacitly or explicitly
made prior concessions. The United States has, explicitly, conceded its
requirement of strategic superiority and, tacitly, has lessened its emphasis
on intrusive methods for policing arms control agreements. The Soviet
Union has tacitly come round to an espousal of partial disarmament
methods and has risked exacerbating its ideological struggle with China by
its public willingness to meet with the United States on the question of
strategic arms. The success of the Non-Proliferation Treaty as a joint arms
control endeavour, although in the main an endeavour pursued for different reasons, and the coincidence in both countries of adverse economic
conditions which might be expected to be relieved by a reduction or postponement of armaments spending are reasons in common likely to encourage fruitful discussions.

The American interest in arms limitation talks has survived a change of
Administration and started as early as 1964 with the Johnson Administration's 'freeze' proposal for a cessation of further production and deployment
of nuclear delivery vehicles (but made at a time when the numerical dis-
parity between the ICBM forces of the two countries was greater than at
any time before or since—US 830 ICBMs; USSR 200 ICBMs). A regard
for Soviet susceptibilities was probably one reason for the American
description of its initial decision to procure an ABM system as anti-
Chinese. The Soviet conversion to the idea of arms limitation talks on
American terms, that is, where partial measures of limitation are discussed
as an end in themselves, has taken longer but has been encouraged both by
the growing hostility of China (and China's obvious intention to acquire
a strategic thermonuclear weapons force) and just as important by the real
growth of Soviet strategic nuclear power which has reduced the importance of bluster and purely propagandist proposals. And the process of
osmosis whereby American thinking on strategic nuclear matters in general
—the concepts of 'assured destruction' and 'damage limitation', the benefits

of hardening and submarine-borne missiles—has been transmitted to the Soviet Union has also, probably, been helpful in conveying to the Soviets some understanding of American arms control thinking too.

Yet it is difficult to see what sort of specific proposals are likely to meet the tests of equality of sacrifice, verifiability by non-intrusive methods (satellite and radar reconnaissance) and at the same time allow for accommodation of the different reactions of each super power to a future Chinese nuclear force (or that of some other nation or even group of nations), of their different alliance responsibilities, and of the advance of technology.

Any kind of policed control on the deployment of MIRVs seems ruled out on grounds of impossibility of verification alone: numbers of missile launchers and numbers of missile-carrying submarines can be counted at a distance but not the number of warheads carried on top of a missile launcher. Flight testing of MIRVs can be monitored by long distance radar in most instances and a ban on MIRV testing could be so policed. But the American MIRV program in 1970 was at the deployment stage and in advance of the Soviet equivalent and an immediate ban on further testing would be strongly disadvantageous to the Soviet Union and therefore, presumably, totally unacceptable to it.

The deployment of ABM defences can, it seems, be monitored quite effectively, although not perfectly, by non-intrusive means, although it would be difficult if not impossible to determine unequivocally whether a particular ABM defence system was designed for the defence of missile silos or civilian targets; this would be particularly true of the Soviet ABM system which relies on only one type of anti-missile missile.

What seems to be at least verifiable would be an agreed limit on the total number of offensive delivery vehicles, ICBMs and submarines, and a limit on the total number of anti-missile missiles. But the former would seem to be rather fragile in the face of the emergence of land mobile ICBMs, as a possible result of research into ways of counteracting the increased accuracy of MIRVs, and whose deployment rate and numerical size would be rather difficult to measure by non-intrusive means. While it is probably true that an arms control agreement limiting, say, the number of offensive missile launchers would help create an atmosphere less conducive to vigorous research into offensive missile systems in both countries, which could lead to less money being provided to finance such research, this research could not be stopped completely without causing the private or government owned armaments firms either to fall into decay or to divert their efforts to civilian enterprises. Neither government would seem anywhere near prepared for such a possibility and neither would willingly sacrifice the very remote but understandably attractive possibility that research might lead to a technological advance which would give one side or the other a decisive and reasonably permanent strategic advantage.[9]

But it is the question of how each side can to mutual satisfaction make adjustments to its strategic nuclear forces to take account of the emergence of a third major nuclear power, friendly to neither, that is likely to prove the least tractable. While this question is related to the more familiar one of how the nuclear forces of American European allies and the Soviet medium and intermediate range missiles targeted against European targets should be treated, it does not show signs of being amenable in the same way to solution through consultation with the third party (or parties) involved.

The central difficulty the emergence of China as a nuclear power hostile to both super powers is likely to pose to the calculations of each with regard to its strategic nuclear forces is a quantitative one. If both the United States and the Soviet Union were, apparently reasonably enough, to insist upon a force level sufficient to balance the combined levels of the other plus that of China—at its very simplest, say, if the United States wanted parity in ICBMs with the Soviet Union plus China, and, simultaneously, the Soviet Union wanted parity in ICBMs with the United States plus China—in the strictly quantitative sense there is no way at any one time in which such a three-power balance could be struck (other than that all forces were zero) and the search for such a balance would be bound to lead to advantages of one super power over the other with accompanying fluctuations in the stability of the balance between them.

Mercifully such rude quantitative arguments ignore considerable qualitative factors which have to be taken into account. The most important of these is the technology gap between the super powers on one hand and China on the other, and this is likely to persist throughout the 1970s. It means that while China may be able to deploy considerable numbers of ICBMs, say, the accuracy of these missiles, their capability of penetrating the ABM defences of the super powers and their security against destruction before launch are all respects in which they are likely to be inferior to the forces of the Soviet Union and the United States. To some extent therefore an adjustment to the Soviet or American offensive strategic armouries to compensate for any future incursion upon 'assured destruction' or 'damage limitation' strengths made by the Chinese forces may not seem sufficiently weighty to influence the central strategic balance one way or the other. But some qualitative factors operate in the other direction. It

[9] Remote in the sense that a striking feature of strategic weapons development since the early 1950s has been the tendency for both countries to develop qualitatively new strategic weapons within a year or less of each other; deployment of new weapons, on the other hand, has varied greatly in rate between the two.

is the same technological lead which has encouraged some in the United States (and conceivably in the Soviet Union too) in the belief that by deploying anti-missile defences the United States can postpone the day when it must take account of the Chinese nuclear force in its overall strategic calculations by denying China the capability of causing physical damage to the United States in a nuclear exchange. In order to do this a relatively large ABM defence effort is required, even on the assumption of a small Chinese ICBM force: in other words at a 'damage denying' level the cost-exchange ratio (see p. 54) heavily favours the offence. And a large ABM defence effort becomes, inevitably, a factor in the central strategic balance in the 'damage limitation' category. This is unlikely to remain a permanent feature; cost considerations alone may be decisive in putting a limit on how long the super powers may try to pursue a 'damage denial' policy in the face of a growing Chinese nuclear force.

The second important qualitative qualification that must be made to the quantitative analysis above is the simple one of geography. Both China and the Soviet Union can add to their offensive strategic nuclear forces in such a way as to increase their capacity for launching nuclear attacks upon each other without adding to their capacity for launching nuclear attack upon the United States proper by acquiring or re-deploying medium and intermediate range missiles or bombers. And there is some reason to suppose that both countries, even by the end of the 1960s, were already taking steps in this direction, partly, in the case of China, because shorter range delivery vehicles by the nature of things are more cheaply and easily manufactured than larger range types. Of course the United States may still have to adjust its strategic thinking as the Soviet Union and China deploy even limited range delivery vehicles targeted against each other. Limited range missiles manufactured by China for deployment with Soviet targets in mind can also be manufactured for targeting against Japan and other American Asian allies and, obversely, the Soviet force of medium and intermediate range missiles deployed against West European targets could be partly re-deployed to Soviet eastern frontiers with or without replacement in the west.

The emergence of a fourth or fifth nuclear challenge to the supremacy of the super powers in addition to that of China would further complicate and obscure the ways in which the two super powers could maintain a satisfactory stand-off between themselves while holding on to a clear and acknowledged level of nuclear superiority over the remainder of the world. How likely are such challenges and what will be the opportunities for preserving Soviet-American nuclear hegemony?

On the surface the evidence for the emergence of a *de facto* Soviet-American condominium based upon their military, economic, and technological

F

superiority over the rest of the world is quite impressive. By almost any yardstick the strategic nuclear force of each is overwhelmingly superior to the nuclear forces of the three smaller nuclear powers put together. This superiority has both quantitative and qualitative dimensions, the latter, as manifested in the development of MIRVs and ABMs, reinforcing and adding to the property of the former of going some way towards allowing the super powers to behave towards other nuclear powers as if the nuclear forces of the smaller powers were for most purposes negligible. In other words, large and effective MIRV and ABM deployments, while, possibly, not too large to endanger seriously the stability of the central balance, will nonetheless make it more difficult for other nuclear powers to acquire or preserve a second strike and even in some cases a first strike capability against either of the super powers.

And the coming together of the two nuclear super powers to discuss bilaterally ways in which the dangers their new strategic weapons may present to the central strategic balance may be averted and the reasonably successful conclusion of the nuclear Non-Proliferation Treaty jointly sponsored between them, with the aid of the United Kingdom, stand as examples of how significant differences need not present insurmountable obstacles to reaching common goals.

Yet for the space of the next ten years, even if we ignore the possibility that one or other super power should abrogate such common understandings as may exist for the sake of a political advantage, the joint military, economic, and technical advantages which raise the two countries above the rest of the world may not prove lasting.

The Vietnam conflict has outlined the extent of American conventional military power and its weakness in a particular military situation: it can be said that in Vietnam the combined North Vietnamese and Viet Cong forces—with considerable logistic support from the Soviet Union and China—have proved superior to the American expeditionary force in spite of the latter's even more bountiful and secure logistic support. This is not to say that another battlefield at another time will also find the US forces wanting, but it sets a benchmark against which future presumptions of American conventional military prowess should be measured.

The economic primacy of the two super powers is already beginning to be challenged by Japan and by the mid-1970s Japan will probably have by most tests overtaken the Soviet Union in economic strength. The primacy of the super powers in the field of military technology may itself not last out the 1970s; the Soviet Union is already in many respects the technological inferior of Japan and the leading West European countries. At some not far distant date Japan, or some consortium of West European nations, is going to be economically and technologically capable of mounting a challenge to the strategic nuclear superiority of the super powers on their own terms by matching MIRV with MIRV or ABM system with ABM system.

Although, as China has demonstrated, the challenge can be made much more cheaply by refusing to conform to some of the norms the super powers have laid down for respectable behaviour as a nuclear power, the Chinese challenge, like the still-born French challenge before it, has its own contradictions. For as long as China feels it necessary to make its challenge to the nuclear superiority of the super powers in their own military-technological terms, it is bound to fail for China does not possess the economic and technical resources of Japan or Western Europe, and is therefore quite likely to find matching the qualitative features of the super powers' strategic armouries, certainly for the next decade, beyond her. This does not, of course, mean that China will be totally unable to attain and maintain some kind of second strike capability on each super power but it does mean that this capability will be small and its very existence open to doubt and scepticism as the super powers' forces improve. A merely marginal second strike capability of this kind will place some limits upon a Chinese claim to super power status.

Not altogether surprisingly the smaller nuclear powers have so far chosen to imitate the two large nuclear powers in their choice of strategic nuclear weapons systems, just as the two larger powers have been each influenced by the other's choices. The bulk of American and Soviet strategic missiles are land-based ICBM types and it is towards land-based ICBMs that China (and, for a brief period France as well), has been working. The reasons for this fashion in certain weapons systems are somewhat beyond the scope of this chapter, but they probably include a definite political component in the form of a conspicuous demonstration that great power technology is being matched, qualitatively at least, with the side effect of helping defend the forces against charges of incredibility as well as, at another level, an economic component whereby following a proven design helps ensure a successful return on the investment of resources.

But it is essential to realise that this is a matter of fashion and that it is possible to imagine kinds of nuclear forces which are cheap and within the reach of a great many countries yet which would give these countries a second strike capability on the super powers. Just as the submarine in two World Wars demonstrated quite cheaply that a superior battleship fleet was not sufficient for mastery of the seas, so it is possible to imagine types of nuclear forces sufficiently different qualitatively from those of the super powers to be largely immune from the techniques developed by the super powers in the spirit of 'damage limitation'. For example, all existing systems designed to give advance warning of attack for active or passive defence measures to be implemented rely at some stage upon radar, yet a nuclear delivery vehicle which flies low in the air for the whole of its path can postpone its detection by radar almost indefinitely. To give another example, nearly all existing methods of delivering a disarming strike rely upon a precise advance knowledge of the position of the forces being attacked at the time of attack. Such advance knowledge is very difficult, if not impossible, to come by if the forces are mobile, on land or sea, particularly so if they are submersible and mobile as in the case of all submarine-borne missile launchers.

The sort of unorthodox nuclear forces imagined above will become increasingly within the means of small and relatively poor nations as their components become cheaper and technologically more commonplace. And while the two super powers with one hand have placed the Non-Proliferation Treaty in the way of a widespread acquisition of nuclear weapons, and it may prove to be a substantial obstacle, with the other they and other industrially advanced countries by way of normal trade practice continue to disseminate products of their modern technology, some of which have the highest military significance. Aside from the spread of nuclear power stations throughout the world with which the Non-Proliferation Treaty has been specifically linked, guidance electronic systems easily adaptable for use in guided missiles are becoming widely available for civil aviation; modern rocket technology is spreading as new countries, often abetted by the super powers, take up an interest in space exploration; and potential missile carriers such as submarines and surface ships of the most modern kind (with the exception of nuclear-propelled types) are available on the world markets.

Moreover, it is slowly becoming apparent, if the American and British experiences are any guide, that while the maintenance of conventional forces is becoming increasingly costly (socially as well as economically), nuclear forces are becoming relatively cheaper. The reasons for this are not hard to see; in general they are explicable on the basis that the products of a new technology nearly always become less costly (in real terms) with the passage of time and in particular because nuclear power stations and isotope separation plants, the two main sources of raw material for nuclear weapons, are becoming more cost-effective, and electronic equipment, the basis of missile guidance, submarine navigation, command and control, early warning, and missile defence radar, is becoming cheaper and more reliable.

It would be going too far to say that the super powers are kings with no clothes as far as their strategic nuclear forces are concerned, the technical limitations of the kind of nuclear forces that have evolved out of their competition with each other could presumably be partially at least overcome if the need to do so became apparent.

Yet if the present nuclear-military superiority of the United States and the Soviet Union over the rest of the world has largely come about as a result of their competing against each other, then an agreement to restrict this competition, such as may come about as a result of the Strategic Arms Limitation Talks, is likely to have the effect of slowing down or even reversing the trend of the 1960s towards increasing the gap, qualitative and quantitative, between their nuclear forces and those of their nearest competitors. And this movement is likely to be reinforced by the spread of technology and rising costs of conventional military forces referred to above.

In other words the features of the management problem facing the super powers over the next decade cannot be relied upon to preserve the pattern of the 1960s, during which time the only serious bid for an equal and distinctive voice in world affairs came from a country, China, poorly equipped to meet the current tests of economic and military strength and whose weaknesses therein have been, with reasonable success, exploited by the super powers to help keep a distance between themselves and their rival. In the future other countries may come to claim a management role with far better military, technological, and economic credentials than China and their claims, if unwelcome, may not be so resistable.

The managed themselves may become less manageable if the attractions of nuclear weaponry come to outweigh the barriers already erected. And this movement will be encouraged if the relevance of the armouries of the super powers to the deterrence of even small nuclear powers ever comes into question, in the ways foreshadowed above. With this, conceivably, may come an undermining of the kinds of military strength that it has been usual to believe carries political weight ever since nuclear weapons were invented.

THE NUCLEAR NON-PROLIFERATION TREATY AND SUPER POWER CONDOMINIUM

The Nuclear Non-Proliferation Treaty has now been signed by most states in the world, and ratified by less than half of them. Among the countries possessing nuclear weapons, China and France have not signed; among other countries with civil nuclear capacity on any scale, only India has not signed. The Treaty has been accepted by resolution of the United Nations General Assembly, and is the subject also of a resolution of the Security Council. Its declared objectives are unexceptionable—to limit the number of countries possessing nuclear weapons, and thus reduce the risk that one of them, accidentally or on purpose, may launch a nuclear war. Even one explosion would be a disaster; nuclear war would be a catastrophe for mankind.

Why then have not all governments signed and ratified the Treaty? There are many reasons, and reasons vary from country to country. One aspect of almost universal concern is the extent to which the Treaty represents a deliberate or implicit attempt at condominium by the two super powers, the United States and the Soviet Union. Not all who believe the Treaty to constitute such an attempt (or to have such an effect) will object to it on those grounds: they may well feel that it is far better to have two roughly balanced and reasonably rational powers managing nuclear weapons developments and their strategy, than to have three, four or more. Every new 'manager' or participant complicates the situation by geometric progression. Yet whether one supports the objection or not, the question remains as to whether the Treaty does constitute—and if so to what extent—a super power condominium over the system of world order.

The term 'condominium', in its liberal and governmental sense, denotes the sharing by two or more governments of legislative and executive authority over a particular territory. The most obvious condominium today is in the New Hebrides, where France and the United Kingdom have joint powers, dividing and sharing responsibility. In this sense, there is no super

For some of the points in this paper I am indebted to Elizabeth Young, *The Control of Proliferation: The 1968 Treaty in Hindsight and Forecast,* London: Institute for Strategic Studies Adelphi Paper No. 56, 1969.

power condominium in the nuclear weapons field. There are some shared responsibilities over the use of nuclear weapons within NATO; there are none between NATO and Warsaw Pact powers, or between the Russians and the Americans. What we are considering, therefore, are elements of condominium or of its corollary, a division of power. Any agreement to *divide* may also constitute, in effect, or can represent, a joint exercise of power at a higher level.

The two super powers are so far ahead of everyone else in nuclear weapons production that no one can at present challenge their superiority. They could, therefore, theoretically, separately or together, coerce all other states into abandoning their nuclear weapons or weapons potential. They have not done so, obviously, and for reasons most of which are obvious. But if not coercing others, they have themselves been uncoerceable. Thus while the Eighteen Nation Disarmament Committee, and numerous other bodies public and private, national and international, have sought to bring moral or intellectual influence to bear on the super powers, they have been almost totally unsuccessful. They have not slowed the growth of the super powers' weapons systems, and such checks or institutionalised arrangements that have been made have been essentially by agreement between the United States and the Soviet Union, on their initiatives, in their interest. They have been pushed and pulled by the rest of us, but they have moved at their own pace.

These arrangements have nevertheless been of some significance, even if largely in psychological terms. In 1959, the Antarctic was made an area in which all military activities were banned, being policed by a mutual inspection system. In 1963 the treaty banning nuclear tests in the atmosphere and under water gave some reassurance against nuclear fallout with its attendant physical effects. In 1967, nuclear weapons were banned from outer space. Latin America has become, in theory at least, a nuclear-free zone. But all these were *hors d'oeuvre*, and very insubstantial ones at that, for the main course: preventing the production of nuclear weapons by states at present not producing them, and arresting and reversing developments within states possessing nuclear weapons. Here again the world had to wait on, and to accept, the highest common factor or proportion of agreement between the super powers.

From the beginning—the early proposals about preventing proliferation (the 'nth power' problem)—the attitudes of the great powers and the super powers were a function of their desire to see the nuclear system limited to as few states as possible. The United States would have liked a total monopoly, hence the exclusion of Britain in 1945 from receiving nuclear information despite promises to the contrary and the substantial role she had played in developing the atomic bomb. The McMahon Act legislated for American monopoly to the extent of preventing others from legally acquiring relevant theoretical and technical expertise from American sources. When the Soviet Union demonstrated an independent nuclear capacity, the US did not then seek to extend Western capability by helping Britain and France to get nuclear weapons. On the contrary, American policy was designed to keep these states non-nuclear for as long as possible, and they were regarded with almost as much suspicion as the Soviet Union —perhaps *more*, because the Russians had made the bomb and nothing short of a pre-emptive war (which was never a serious possibility) could take it away from them.

The Baruch plan of June 1946 offered the first and perhaps only real opportunity to prevent nuclear proliferation. It proposed international inspection and control, the destruction of all nuclear weapons stocks, and a free hand for an International Atomic Development Authority. We cannot be sure what would have happened if the Soviet government had accepted this proposal: the United States may not have been so enthusiastic about implementing it. But it was spared this dilemma when the Russians rejected the idea outright. They were not prepared to deny themselves such weapons, nor to submit to international inspections (which could discover things other than nuclear capacity) or controls. This suspicion was partly a result of the way the Soviet dictatorship had developed. Yet combined with elements of paranoia were elements of reason. To undertake a full inspection of the United States would involve a whole army of skilled inspectors, and there was no such army available. Self-denying ordinances are possible if one's competitors are equally self-denying, but can you ever be entirely sure that they are? The effect of a mistake in judgment (so it was felt), or a wrong turn by the inspection team, could be annihilation or at least subjugation.

After Britain had made its own nuclear and then thermonuclear weapons, the American government saw this not as added Western capacity but as a threat to American interests. It did promote legislation allowing for nuclear information to be passed to Britain, but it also consistently played down Britain's independent capacity, and kept encouraging Britain to rid herself of this expensive and ineffectual encumbrance. As the British V-bombers became obsolescent, or at least inadequate, the Kennedy Administration had no hesitation in cancelling the Skybolt program which had promised to keep Britain with an independent deterrent capability. The replacements for Skybolt—Polaris submarines—had strong strings attached to them which Macmillan accepted at Nassau. They convinced General de Gaulle (so he said) that Britain was tied to American apron strings and was not a fit partner for the members of the European Economic Community. Equally, perhaps, the Polaris arrangement convinced de Gaulle that Britain would rather buy its deterrent from the United States and accept American restraints and hegemony than work with France towards a joint European deterrent. For Britain, the decision was entirely rational. Polaris was the next generation deterrent. It existed, whereas nothing remotely like it existed in Europe or would for many years. The restrictions were not on its use on behalf of Britain, but only on conveying the technology to others, or on using it outside of NATO while there was a NATO need for it. The United States had been a certain ally since December 1941; France was less certain in a range of respects, less stable politically, less capable militarily, less sure to share objectives and means in foreign policy, less easy to deal with. For the United States, the British Polaris deal was an impairment of nuclear hegemony, but a very small one. Only four submarines were involved. It gave Britain more a symbol than a reality, prestige without comparable power, a seat at the table without a substantive vote on decisions. It did not detract from America's leadership of the West. It made Britain more likely to go along with American proposals on nuclear proliferation or other foreign policy matters.

The public statements of the super powers suggested or implied that the Non-Proliferation Treaty would lead to a more peaceful world through a central balance of power. The bipolar system which had developed since World War II had its tensions and problems, but these were manageable. Each side needed a deterrent on the other, but it would best be an uncomplicated deterrent politically, preferably in a single intergrated force on each side, with a single finger on each trigger.

All these assumptions, and all the assumptions about the dangers of proliferation, can be questioned. Virtually unrestrained competition by the super powers has led and will continue to lead to bigger and more damaging explosions. Increasingly sophisticated weapons raise the possibility of one or other gaining an absolute lead, qualitatively and effectively, tempting it to trade upon that lead. Further, developments in nuclear technology have reduced the cost of less sophisticated weapons, thus expanding the range of countries economically and technically capable of producing them for themselves.

These are not arguments for proliferation. They are arguments for non-proliferation accompanied by a reduction in the weaponry of the super powers. The greatest objection to the treaty is on the grounds that there is no such accompaniment, and the continuing nuclear expansion of the super powers creates or continues client status among other nations demanding protection either against a super power or against a power considered hostile, by a super power ally, to its interests.

Let us consider those actual terms of the treaty which indicate the presence of a measure of Soviet-American condominium.

Article I states:

Each nuclear-weapon State Party to the Treaty undertakes not to transfer to any recipient whatsoever nuclear weapons or other nuclear explosive devices or control over such weapons or explosive devices directly, or indirectly; and not in any way to assist, encourage, or induce any non-nuclear-weapon State to manufacture or otherwise acquire nuclear weapons or other nuclear explosive devices, or control over such weapons or explosive devices.

This article thus puts restraints upon those states with a capacity to make nuclear weapons (provided they sign the treaty), preventing them from assisting in the proliferation process. In fact, for the twenty-three years between the first bomb and the treaty, there was extremely little transfer of information. The Sino-Soviet rift was in good measure a result of—or an expression of—the Soviet Union's reluctance to share nuclear weapons expertise with the Chinese. So far as we know, it has made no such expertise available to its East European partners. The Chinese have been equally secretive. The British worked with the Americans in the pre-Hiroshima research and development, but virtually on their own since then except for the Polaris submarine technology and missiles. Australians worked with the British and for a time with Americans, but have had no practical assistance from the United States since World War II. The French have been treated with the utmost caution by the United States and Britain. Accordingly Article I of the treaty, while it may become in due course a restraining factor on the spread of nuclear weapons technology or capacity, for the most part rationalises an existing situation.

Article II states:

Each non-nuclear-weapon State Party to the Treaty undertakes not to receive the transfer from any transferor whatsoever of nuclear weapons or other nuclear explosive devices or of control over such weapons or explosive devices directly, or indirectly; not to manufacture or otherwise acquire nuclear weapons or other nuclear explosive devices; and not to seek or receive any assistance in the manufacture of nuclear weapons or other nuclear explosive devices.

This is the necessary complement to Article I, but has a much more denying or self-denying effect. It is fairly easy to promise not to give away what you have; it is much harder to promise not to acquire what you want or feel you need. The non-nuclear-weapon states here acknowledge the monopoly—or oligopoly—of the nuclear-weapon states, and promise to help perpetuate it, *whether or not those states are signatories to the treaty*. As a further demonstration of humility, they accept in Article III the principle of inspection and safeguards by the International Atomic Energy Agency not only with respect to any nuclear weapons production but also (of necessity) to their use of nuclear energy for civilian and peaceful purposes. They accept these restraints while knowing that the states which do produce nuclear weapons will *not* accept the restraints.

The final key factor demonstrating the status of the nuclear-weapon powers is in Article VIII (2), which gives those states (providing they had exploded a nuclear device before 1 January 1967) a veto over any amendment to the treaty, even if every other government in the world wanted it. This veto lasts for twenty-five years, when a conference is to be convened (Article X (2)) to decide by majority vote whether the treaty shall continue in force indefinitely or be extended by an additional fixed period or periods. The idea of renegotiating the treaty is not mentioned, but obviously cannot be excluded.

The non-nuclear-weapon states signatory to the treaty thus accept the dominant military position of nuclear-weapon states whether signatories or not, and also rely on their good faith to make available at reasonable cost such fruits of nuclear weapons technology as are applicable to non-weapons productivity. As well as the two super powers, the nuclear-weapon states include Britain, France, and China, but only China constitutes a major strategic problem. Britain and France could foster low-level proliferation, but they are no threat to the peace or security of any non-nuclear-weapon state. They are not going to start a war against each other or anyone else, or threaten to use their nuclear weapons except in self-defence against a Soviet threat. Their weapons technology is not advanced, by super power standards. They are themselves client states, in nuclear terms, with a few modest dependencies but no satellites of their own.

The treaty was made acceptable to non-nuclear-weapon states only with (a) the addition to the Preamble of a pious statement about liquidating all nuclear stockpiles, and (b) a Security Council resolution (255 of 19 June 1968) to which the super powers added a declaration that they would provide or support immediate assistance, in accordance with the Charter, to any non-nuclear-weapon state party to the treaty that is a 'victim of an act or an object of a threat of aggression in which nuclear weapons are used'.[1] But Article 3 of the Resolution seems to let the cat out of this particular bag. It states that the Security Council

> Reaffirms in particular the inherent right, recognized under Article 51 of the Charter, of individual and collective self-defence if an armed attack occurs against a member of the United Nations, until the Security Council has taken measures necessary to maintain international peace and security.

Assistance to the victim of an attack in which nuclear weapons are used is no substitute for preventing their use. It would be most difficult to feel confident that any individual state, much less the Security Council, is going to threaten nuclear retaliation against any nuclear-weapon state negotiating with a non-nuclear weapon state. The only part of the arrangements that is at all credible—and it is not very much so—is Article 3 above,

[1] Cited in Article 2 of the Security Council resolution.

which clearly implies that any country which is in a treaty arrangement with a super power can be allowed to hope for support from its major ally before the Security Council has come to a decision. In other words, the best assurance against the fact or threat of nuclear attack is to have a security treaty with a super power. (This may not be true, but it is what the treaty and the Security Council resolution strongly imply.) The treaty therefore reinforces the client status of Soviet and American allies.

Yet, if it does so—and we will look at this further—most of them prefer it that way to having no assurance at all from anyone. Further, it implies not so much condominium as concert, agreed spheres of influence, joint agreement to separate hegemonies.

The Non-Proliferation Treaty is a concession to modern communications and education. The original method of preventing proliferation was by secrecy, by refusing to share information, and by improving barriers to the transfer of raw materials. This is no longer relevant. The raw materials are found in many countries. The processes whereby simple atomic explosions occur are known in every university physics department around the world, and the technology has been written up in a hundred magazines. More sophisticated techniques and products are less current, but are gradually coming on to the international market.

The treaty was thus designed to reduce the imperfections[2] of condominium by plugging the gaps, but it has many imperfections of its own. First of these is that China and France are not signatories and have said they will not be, although France has declared it will act as though it were a signatory. China has said that it will not be first to use nuclear weapons. Both have thus contributed (China much less certainly) to the spirit of the treaty, to the objectives *other than condominium* which the treaty seeks (as it were) to promote. Yet Gaullism displayed and expanded the doubts which more countries than France held about American capacity and will to engage in nuclear war on their behalf—unfairly so, in France's case, for American troops and families in Germany were (as they still are) hostages substantially assuring the implementation of promises made. And unfairly or fairly, such doubts prompt states to circumvent the condominium or blur the edges of the alliance, to take other actions to ensure their security. France herself sought an opening to the east, and in other directions as well.

While the great majority of states have now signed the treaty, a majority have not ratified it.[3] More than the minimum forty ratifications have now been deposited, and the treaty has come into effect, but no country is committed to the treaty until its own government has signed and ratified. With nearly seventy states not yet committed, the treaty is indeed imperfect. No

[2] Using the word in its economic sense.
[3] At the time of writing, 97 had signed and 61 had ratified.

less important than the number who have not ratified is the composition of that group. The treaty was designed in part to encourage pairs of countries in tense situations to sign together—Israel and Egypt, India and Pakistan—as well as other key states such as West Germany and Japan. Under strong American encouragement, West Germany and Japan have signed the treaty, but have not ratified. Egypt has signed but not ratified; Israel has not signed at all, and India has declared that it has no intention of doing so. A number of other states which could become nuclear powers fairly easily have signed—Sweden, Canada, Australia (reluctantly), and Switzerland; none of these is a country which, if it had not signed, would frighten its neighbours. Australia and Switzerland have not ratified.

States which do not sign and ratify the treaty, but which do not produce nuclear weapons or take steps towards such production, still remain, in a sense, within the condominium, especially in so far as they see themselves under actual or potential threat from either of the super powers, or from China.

This sense of ultimate dependence on the United States or the Soviet Union for protection does not necessarily prevent any independence of action. France, separated in some respects from NATO, is still dependent on the United States. In Eastern Europe, it is the presence of Soviet forces rather than a sense of Western threat which holds the Warsaw Pact together, and even countries which know very well where their nuclear bread is buttered are prepared to engage in occasional independent initiatives. Yet many states, perhaps almost all of them almost all of the time, find nuclear weapons irrelevant to foreign policy. For most African, Asian, and Latin American countries, nuclear weapons just do not enter their calculations. They would behave no differently if these engines of destruction had never been invented. They might behave differently if only one power possessed nuclear weapons, but even then the effect would be uncertain. No one kow-towed to Washington when it had, so briefly, a nuclear monopoly after World War II.

China's nuclear program presents the greatest imperfection to the condominium. Here is another major nuclear power—perhaps, eventually, a super power—able to threaten them, distort their tidy management of the system, providing its own independent pressures and opportunities. Both the super powers could have destroyed China's nuclear program by pre-emptive strike, but neither has done so nor is likely to do so. There are strong moral and political forces operating against such a move, and there is the near certainty that China would in due course resurrect its program and ultimately seek vengeance.

Yet if China destroys the duopoly, it also reinforces it in a degree. Some countries (Indonesia, perhaps) are more likely to fear Chinese nuclear weapons than Russian or American, and to seek help from a super power that it would not otherwise have sought. India has been offered reassurances, though in an uncertain form, by both the United States and Russia, only because of China's nuclear power. India may feel little confidence in these assurances, just as she sees little value in the treaty, but it is better to have them than not. Presumably Indian foreign policy, if it does not actively seek super power guarantees, is directed towards showing the Chinese that India has friends—especially the Soviet Union—which might react to Chinese nuclear threats. And even if India becomes a nuclear power, as seems increasingly possible, it will be extremely small, will be primarily for domestic political reasons, and will not reduce Indian dependence on Soviet or American protection.

Further, the existence of Chinese nuclear weapons has been a major factor in having the treaty in its present form, that is providing no restraints upon the nuclear armaments of the super powers. The vicious circle of competitive escalation which has produced the Soviet-American predominance has been reproduced as an argument between them and China. How can they disarm while China arms? How can they afford not to keep well ahead of Chinese technology? This consideration is not the main incentive to either state, and there are much more rational arguments for both slowing down against China than against each other. The United States, at least, has used the 'Chinese' argument to justify actions taken in fact on 'Soviet' grounds.

Within the treaty, there are stated and implied imperfections. Any signatory can withdraw (Article X), on three months' notice to the other parties and to the Security Council, 'if it decides that extraordinary events, related to the subject matter of [the] Treaty, have jeopardised the supreme interests of its country'. There is no *effective* time limit on negotiating inspection and other safeguards agreements with the IAEA—the treaty merely requires (Article III (4)) that negotiations shall *commence* within 180 days from the original entry into force of the treaty. A subsequent statement that agreements will enter into force within eighteen months of negotiations beginning can only be hortatory, not mandatory. The treaty does not limit research; indeed it specifically allows research 'for peaceful purposes'. Peaceful purposes could include nuclear propulsion of ships or perhaps eventually aircraft. Finally—a pin-prick point, perhaps—the treaty does nothing to prevent either a non-nuclear-weapon state party to the treaty, or a nuclear-weapon state not party to the treaty, from transferring information about the production of nuclear weapons to a non-nuclear-weapon state that is not a party to the treaty.

To sum up then, how is the condominium exercised—to the extent that it is—in the context of the treaty? By preventing non-nuclear-weapon states (under self-denying ordinances) from engaging in the manufacture,

acquisition, or use of nuclear weapons; by having unacceptable and overwhelming retaliatory power against any country displaying an urge to use
nuclear weapons, whether it is a signatory or not; by influencing states, who
fear retaliation by the other super power, to accept the existing hegemony.
Further, the treaty prevents peaceful nuclear explosions (e.g. for building
harbours or canals) by non-nuclear-weapon states. It reinforces super
power leadership in technology and seals the profits therefrom. It ensures
(if it is effective) that the super powers are so much more powerful than all
others that their nuclear predominance goes on indefinitely, with only a
growing China lurking around the stockpile. Yet China's nuclear weapons
without a broad national power base are not enough to give it either super
power or even great power status. Perhaps this applies also to Japan, with
a power base but without (as yet) nuclear weapons.

The Non-Proliferation Treaty is undoubtedly an *exercise* in condominium, or at least an attempt at joint control. It has not yet come off:
too few have signed and ratified and drawn up inspection agreements; too
few are reassured by the Security Council resolution; too many are worried
at the continuing pace of super power nuclear escalation; and enough are
affected by China. Yet if we resent the attempt being made, perhaps we
should also regret that it has not been effective, or that, not having been
effective, nothing else satisfactory has been thrown up in its place, by its
detractors, to slow down man's progress towards a capacity for total nuclear
annihilation.

CHINESE REACTIONS TO TENDENCIES TOWARDS CONDOMINIUM

The fact that it is possible to discuss Chinese reactions to the tendency to condominium at all is in itself rather surprising. Twenty years ago no one would have given a second thought to what China might, or might not, feel about any such development. China was a weak power racked by civil war, or just emerging from that disaster, which had come on the heels of a Japanese invasion and large-scale occupation of the national territory. Her economy was in ruin, her communications not functioning, rampant inflation had destroyed the value of money and wiped out investment. Such modern armed forces as she had acquired with American aid had been dissipated, routed, and dispersed. All that remained was a victorious guerrilla army and its untried political, social, and economic doctrines. These facts of recent history need to be remembered; modern China, armed *cap-à-pie*, did not drop from the skies, it was created by the Communist régime; whatever faults or evils that régime may be felt to have exhibited or promoted, it cannot be denied that it re-created the power of China as a modern state, and this was achieved with only Russian aid (for which full payment was exacted, and made). Thus China became a power to be recognised and feared, or respected, only since the Communist régime assumed power. The reactions of China to any present concern in international relations are therefore the outlook of her present rulers, and above all, of Mao Tse-tung himself.

Mao has never made any secret of his view of the world; he sees the recent past, as in China, a deplorable debacle of the old society; the outer world as divided between imperialists who are reaching the predestined term of their power on the eve of revolution, and Russia as a backslider which has lost the true faith and is slipping down to bourgeois ways of life —'taking the capitalist road'. In his view that road is a blind alley from which the only possible exit is revolution. Any tendency to condominium between such ill-assorted and, indeed, foredoomed partners, could be productive only of disaster for themselves, even if that also involved a world wide conflict. Russo-American condominium is a last attempt to bolster the forces of reaction by collusion between two powers whose fundamental

74

social bases are opposed and contradictory. There can be no long future before such an opportunist combination, whose main purpose is to delay, or if possible frustrate the development of the historically necessary and inevitable revolution, a movement which China is destined to lead and to guide.

In the short term such a condominium must operate to suppress or prevent wars of National Liberation, that is to say the immediate means by which the revolution is being promoted. China supports all such movements, not only because some of them are Communist led, but because all of them tend to the destruction of the existing order, are contrary therefore to American aims, and probably in reality to Russian objectives also, and are instruments which the true revolution can in time mould and shape to its own ends. The Arab resistance to Israel is not, or not yet, a Communist movement; but it is increasingly anti-American. Israel is the protected ally of the United States, so a foe. The fact that Russia is forced at present into uneasy support of Arab policies simply points up the basic weakness of a condominium, the contradictions which must exist between two great powers especially if their recent relations have been inimical. These contradictions can be exploited in favour of the revolution by showing up their insincerity, their inconsistency, and their inability to provide solutions acceptable to the revolutionary masses. Condominium may be outwardly designed, or justified, as a plan to maintain international order, but it is fundamentally a means to uphold US imperialism and Russian 'social imperialism'—two horses from the same stable.

It would be wholly inconsistent with the general line of Chinese propaganda, especially since the Cultural Revolution, to modify this stance. The picture of the Chinese people, purged of its own backsliders, dedicated to the furtherance of the true revolution, and the creation of a China strong enough to bear the main burden and leadership of such a vast upheaval, could not be reconciled with any evidence of collusion, secret dealing, or the old game of Chinese foreign policy 'playing off one barbarian against another'. It can be argued that one day China, and her revolutionary sympathisers in other parts of the world, will be strong enough to confront the super powers and assert her claim to lead the underdeveloped world; then will be the time, from a position of strength, to enter into some negotiation, but only when it is quite clear that China is in such a position and not in any way yielding to the traditional pressure from alien powers. In fact the Chinese leaders are not wholly their own masters in this matter. The national resentment against the bullying of a weak China in the nineteenth and early twentieth centuries is a very real sentiment, not by any means solely a product of Communist propaganda. Nothing was more awkward for the Chinese Communists than the Nationalist Chinese claim that they were subservient to Russia. The quarrel with the Soviet has produced one

G

consequence wholly agreeable to the Chinese Communists: no one now believes that they are pandering to Russia.

The official Chinese line must therefore continue to be unyielding opposition to any tendency to Russo-American condominium and unsparing condemnation of its motives. It is possible that the Chinese believe that this attitude may weaken the tendency, by arousing revolutionary opinion in other countries and by spreading doubt and alarm among devoted Communists in Russia itself. If such results are to be hoped for, they are at best marginal aims. The main target of Chinese propaganda is the Chinese people; again and again it has ignored the approach which might seem intelligible, or conciliatory to foreign ears, and preferred to concentrate on phobias which are attuned to Chinese prejudices. The Chinese people as a whole know very little of foreign countries and peoples; rarely do many millions of them so much as see a foreigner, still more rarely have any contact with the occasional traveller or foreign expert passing through their region. They also are more than indifferent to such foreigners as they might encounter, quite often they are rather hostile to them. What foreigners want to hear about China, or think would be appropriate for Chinese leaders to say or to do, is certainly no recommendation to the ordinary Chinese; his reaction would be to mistrust any leader who appeared to have these considerations in mind.

These are facts which the foreign resident in China, and the 'Old China Hand', were most unwilling to admit; yet it is the real foundation for very much of Chinese internal policy, a great part of the official propaganda, and no small part of China's standpoint in foreign affairs. The sense of being surrounded by hostile peoples, the age old fear of the northern nomad incursions, the strong tradition that China is the centre of world civilisation, beyond which all is inferior and mainly barbarous, these attitudes are normal and easily picked up. The Russians stand for the old northern enemies; the alien, Western peoples, who claimed to have a better and higher civilisation, are still taking the same line, denouncing the Chinese version of Communism, which to many millions has meant the difference between starvation and survival. To counteract these ideas, or even to modify them to a marked degree will be—or would be—the work of long years of education and deliberate effort. The Chinese leadership has no incentive to make such an effort. Chinese prejudices, and the facts which support them, are easily used to create the sense of national unity and dedication to the revolution which the party—or the Cultural Revolutionary leaders—see as the real foundation for their authority. It is highly improbable that they will put the arguments for or against a condominium of super powers squarely before the Chinese people.

What must be said in public, and can therefore be known to all the world, is one thing. What might be thought in private, or in confidential conversation and discussion is quite another. The question arises; how far do the Chinese leaders believe their own propaganda? Are they, as some observers think, actually self-deceived to the point of having created for themselves a world of their own imagining quite out of touch with reality? Or are they deliberately, for internal political reasons mainly, sustaining an attitude which they know very well to be far more extreme than can be expected to endure or provide a realistic hope of achieving their professed aims? There is no convincing evidence that Mao Tse-tung or his colleagues suffer from any form of mental disorder; there is much evidence to show that they have assessed the possibilities open to them, both at home and abroad, with great shrewdness. Few people would have predicted four years ago that China could indulge itself in the Cultural Revolution and escape with consequences which must today seem relatively trivial. Mao has overthrown his opposition which held the highest offices of state and party, he has overturned the structure of the Communist Party, his own creation, and if he has perhaps not yet remoulded it nearer to his heart's desire, he is certainly taking active steps to achieve that solution.

Shrewd political calculation based on the realities of Chinese popular sentiment and prejudices has paid off at home with what is unquestionably a great political victory; abroad, in spite of resounding denunciations and bellicose utterances, there has been in practice, after the first ebullience of the Cultural Revolution was brought under control, caution and restraint. The Chinese have always used violent language to supplement, or even to substitute for actual violence. A street quarrel was judged by the spectators on the merits of the rare and wounding nature of the abuse exchanged. But if ever it looked like blows, the bystanders at once intervened. On the personal level this is no doubt an outmoded 'bourgeois' mannerism; but on the higher level of politics it still holds good. The offending Liu Shao-ch'i was denounced in terms of the utmost opprobrium by the million strong demonstration which filed past his official residence for a whole day; but two policemen at the gate were all that was required to see that these infuriated citizens did not carry out their threats and haul the Chief of State out for a mob lynching.

America and the Soviet Union are constantly abused and their policies derided; but it is well known that the Chinese armed forces in the south have never, in spite of what might have been thought to be some provocation, retaliated against the airfields or ships from which intruding aircraft have come. As evidence slowly seeps out it is also more and more probable that provocations on the Russian frontier were of Russian instigation rather than Chinese. In the older Chinese world the enemy was always denounced in unmeasured terms, for both sides must claim that morality and Heaven itself were on their side; rebels were depraved wretches unwilling to abide by the elementary laws of decent human conduct; the imperial forces were ruthless oppressors, cruel fiends, merciless exterminators. But if it became necessary to pardon the rebels and enlist them on the imperial side against some more formidable enemy, or make a deal with the Emperor by which you could enter his service and save a cause which had no ultimate hope of complete victory, the depraved wretches became loyal and brave warriors, the ruthless oppressors became wise and benevolent rulers.

A nation does not shed its ancient mental habits overnight, even if there has been a revolution; much of what the Chinese say can be discounted, what they really think cannot be so easily apprehended, but may perhaps be deduced. It would seem most unlikely that the Chinese leaders really believe in an active, formal and operative agreement between Russia and the United States made to ensure their co-operation in ordering the affairs of the world. There is Vietnam, and there is the Middle East. In both areas the Russians give support to those forces which oppose US policy, to the revolutionary cause in Vietnam and to the Arab states and unofficial opponents of Israel in the Middle East. China happens to agree with both these movements, and if Russia is to be denounced it must be for half-hearted measures rather than for collusion with the United States. Yet if Russia and the United States cannot agree on the terms of settlement in Vietnam, nor find a means of pacifying the conflict between Israel and the Arabs, collusion between the super powers clearly has not made much progress. The American acceptance of Russian action in Czechoslovakia was not collusion, it was caution; no form of intervention was possible which did not involve a direct challenge to the Soviet on what the Russians would consider to be their home ground. Russian withdrawal in Cuba was equally not collusion, but caution, and for the same reasons. The Chinese charge of collusion is an anticipation of a danger which might evolve, not a denunciation of a fact which now exists.

On the other hand the Chinese, and not only the Chinese, are aware that the relations between Russia and the United States are not as bad as they used to be, that both sides fear and seek to avoid direct conflict while manoeuvring to gain local advantages. There has been, no doubt, a reasonable fear in China that such activities could amount to a tendency to team up against China, especially where purely Chinese interests are at stake (as in Taiwan) and where tacit acceptance of the attitude of one super power does not impinge upon the interests of the other. The Chinese are also right in thinking that in Russia revolutionary zeal has diminished, and in the United States the crusading spirit of anti-Communism—the Dulles outlook—has dwindled into insignificance. The first development is the basis for the charge that Russia is now a revisionist state taking the capitalist road back to bourgeois ways, and is both deplorable from the ideological point of view, but perhaps also not so unwelcome from the political point of view; if Russia has given up the great cause, all the more is China fitted to take over the leadership. There can be little doubt that the Chinese do believe that ultimately the revolutionary aims will be achieved, reshaped and guided on new and better lines by the thought and leadership of Mao Tse-tung. On the other hand the fact that America is disengaging from Asia, even if the full extent of that policy is still unsure, has given the Chinese new cause for confidence: interpreted, no doubt, as the reluctant acceptance by the American leadership of a popular protest with which they do not really agree, it is still the most important development for China for many years past. It is unlikely that the Chinese are seriously worried by the possibility that 'Vietnamisation' of the war will reverse a process which the large-scale intervention of the US armed forces could not arrest.

The decline of Russian revolutionary zeal gives China the opportunity to take over the spiritual leadership of the world revolutionary forces; the American withdrawal in Asia goes far towards removing the main danger of which Chinese leaders have had to take account since the Communists came to power, open war with the United States. But these changes are both negative; Russia is less zealous, America less 'imperialist'; neither of the super powers moves towards a policy which might satisfy some Chinese aspirations. Both seem to seek means of maintaining a *status quo*. But any such solution would, as the Chinese may well fear, be at their expense. If Russia agreed to reduce her interest in Vietnam in exchange for more positive American efforts to bring about Israeli withdrawal from occupied Arab lands, China would not benefit. Israel is far away, Vietnam is a neighbour state. China might be faced with the expense of fighting a long 'proxy war' in Vietnam, helping her side to fill a gap which Russia had left, while America poured arms, but not men, into a 'Vietnamised' war. The satisfaction of the hopes of Egypt or Jordan would not be of great comfort to China. Therefore a condominium, or any tendency towards such a situation based on mutual Russian and American agreement to uphold the *status quo* is contrary to the interests of China as they are formulated by the present leadership.

No matter what may be said in public, the Chinese leaders do not necessarily think that tendencies to collusion between the super powers are consciously and always directed against themselves. They can be partly a reaction to the dangers of a drift towards confrontation, which lead to support for existing alignments of power, and thus to policies which are inimical to Chinese interests even if that was not their original aim. Mao Tse-tung himself would see this as a natural consequence of the nature of powers which are anti-revolutionary or revisionist. The problem is how these natural consequences can be prevented from developing slowly into a firm and recognised anti-Chinese policy shared by both super powers.

One way is to use propaganda to alarm and dismay the Communists of other countries in the hope that their pressure and influence will act as a brake on the Russian leaders, perhaps even secure their replacement by others more in line with Chinese wishes. A secondary effect is produced in the non-Communist world by alarming and disturbing the extreme right, which still views Russia as the most dangerous revolutionary power. If these people can be made to believe that their leaders are really in collusion with 'international Communism' their influence and their electoral support will be cast against any tendency to collusion, or condominium. The American Right and the Australian Democratic Labor Party already show that this effect is being created. It is easier to judge what movement of opinion may occur in countries with a free press than to assess the effect, if any, of Chinese propaganda on Communists in the East European states, or in the Soviet Union itself.

A second method of seeking to impede collusion is to negotiate with one or other of the super powers themselves, and thus arouse the distrust of the other. The Chinese have, after a long delay, resorted to this method by renewing the Warsaw conversations with the US government. These discussions are always kept entirely confidential, but are admitted to cover a wide range of topics. A year ago the Chinese broke off the series, just at the time of the serious border clashes with the Soviet Union on the Amur and Ussuri rivers. That was perhaps why; it would not do to appear to be seeking American help in a crisis with the Soviet Union. Since talks with the Soviet Union itself have been started (although no results have emerged) this argument does not hold. China shows herself willing to state her case; she is not such an intransigent power as the capitalist press would have the world believe. But the talks with Russia concern the frontier, not an American interest. Those with the United States concern the world knows not what, and the Russians are left uneasily guessing. The United States has recently relaxed some of the restrictions upon trade and travel which were part of the Dulles apparatus for 'containing China'. So far the Chinese have made little acknowledgment of these changes in public, and what there was hardly sounded encouraging. But such matters can be raised in the private ambassadorial conversations, their nature explained, their intention clarified and possible reciprocal actions by the Chinese considered without the press on the one hand, or the propaganda machine on the other, being given any opportunity to sound warning cries or renew ritual denunciations of perfidy and greed.

How far, then, could the Chinese go, even if they appeared to be gaining the advantage of sowing mistrust in the minds of the Russian leaders—as some recent statements suggest may be true. America is seeking disengagement in Asia; but she is bound by treaties to the Nationalists in Taiwan, to the South Korean republic, and to Saigon. The Chinese have for many years made it plain that Taiwan is the issue with which they are most concerned. It shelters a régime which they defeated on the mainland, but cannot destroy so long as the US Seventh Fleet protects the island against invasion. It is not probable that the Chinese Communists are afraid of Chiang Kai-shek or entertain any doubts about his lack of support in the country at large. But the island of Taiwan is part of China; to accept a hostile government, a former opponent of so many years, established in a part of the national territory and protected there by American power is deeply repugnant. A 'Two China' situation, if accepted, would mean in Chinese eyes that their new and powerful régime was still unable to prevent the foreigner from interfering in China, detaching parts of the country from true allegiance, and sustaining régimes of their own choice contrary to the normal and proper form of international relations. The United States, Britain, or France, would never tolerate such intervention in their affairs; they have shown in Africa that they are not very willing to tolerate such separatist movements in other countries either. Why should China accept a lower status than the Congo or Nigeria? The US Taiwan commitment appears in Chinese eyes as a relic of nineteenth-century imperialism in its least attractive form. There can be little doubt that in this matter the Chinese government has the support of the nation as a whole and that even if it were willing to compromise it would be politically very dangerous to do so.

United States' support for South Korea is primarily a matter for North Korean concern, and China has not had entirely warm relations with her neighbour. The Koreans, of any colour, can be difficult people to handle. If China were certain that no new invasion of North Korea was possible, even if North Korea gives provocation, then American military support for South Korea is tolerable, as it has been tolerated for seventeen years; but North Korea is a vital shield to China's most developed industrial area, South Manchuria, or Liaoning Province. History has shown too many precedents for powers in control of all Korea invading Manchuria for any Chinese government to acquiesce in such a possibility. A tacit agreement to support neither Korean side in any war for reunion might pave the way for an improved relationship with the United States. Vietnam is another matter: the Vietnam War, so far from 'containing China', has been of great benefit to the policies of the Chinese Communists. It has strikingly demonstrated the limitations of massive and unchallenged air power; it has also shown that guerrilla war carried on with determination and steadfastness can frustrate the operations of very large conventional forces and undermine the support of the official government. Mao Tse-tung can well believe that his theories have proved once again correct, and that US involvement in the morass of Vietnam has been the real reason why the threat of US intervention against China has never materialised and is now insignificant. The lessons of the failure in Vietnam, and the revulsion of opinion which this has caused in American public opinion, are even more applicable to any war with China. If America now wishes to get clear of Vietnam under the cover of 'Vietnamisation' of the war, China has every reason to rest content.

From the short-term point of view some easing of strain in Sino-American relations is thus possible, and China may cautiously approach such a policy. In the long term America remains the citadel of the opposing ideology, the ultimate enemy. Russia, 'revisionist' and under its present leadership, is a short-term enemy; the Chinese may hope for a change in leaders, or they may expect a strong opposition to the policy of détente with the United States to develop within the Soviet Union; in either case there need to be no drastic breach with Russia, no war between Communist powers, if Russia can be induced to drop a policy of *rapprochement* with the United States. The Chinese, for all their propaganda, geared to arouse national feeling and solidarity, need not seriously fear war with the Soviet Union. A conventional invasion would expose Russia to the frustrations and inevitable failure which have attended the invaders of China in the past, dangers which American policy has wisely avoided. A nuclear attack, devastating as it would be, opens up such limitless possibilities of world wide involvement as to be daunting to cautious and realistic politicians, even if tempting to adventurous military minds. The one Chinese proposal at the conference with Russia which has been disclosed was that both sides should withdraw their frontier forces some scores of kilometres from the disputed border. This proposal puts the Russians in an awkward position; to agree means an admission that the Chinese are not being provocative, which runs counter to their propaganda; to refuse puts Russia in a bad light. To postpone the issue, as seems to have been done on the ground that other matters must first be settled, is also not a very forthcoming attitude and suggests unwillingness to cool off the conflict. The thought that the Chinese may well have confirmed this proposal in their conversations at Warsaw must be annoying. Mao Tse-tung has stated publicly that China will make no attack on any power, but if herself attacked, will retaliate with all her power. This is not a bellicose statement; it is the normal attitude of any national leader who believes that he is not entirely at the mercy of stronger powers.

If it is accepted that whatever the Chinese may say for public consumption, primarily for home consumption they think along some such lines as have been suggested, what circumstances could induce them to look with less hostility upon tendencies to a condominium, either of the two existing super powers, or at a later stage, one in which they would themselves participate. It would seem that some major changes in policy in the super powers themselves would be needed to create such a situation. If Russia proved willing to negotiate a settlement in the border disputes, preferably one which acknowledged in some form the fact that the Tzarist empire acquired its Far Eastern possession, by acts of imperialist pressure and aggression in no way different from those committed by the Western 'colonialists', and furthermore returned to a policy of support for Chinese interests—such as the settlement of the Taiwan problem—China's attitude to Russia could greatly change. Equally if the United States showed clearly that an anti-China front organised by the Soviet Union had no attractions for the Administration and further gave evidence, in relaxing the trade embargo and other hostile measures, of a real desire to effect a reconciliation with China, it is probable that there would be a cautious Chinese response. Taiwan would still be a stumbling block, but China might be content to wait upon events.

These possibilities may seem remote, or at best only likely to be fulfilled to a very limited degree. More certain, indeed progressively quite certain, is that China will acquire the nuclear armament which will compel the other super powers to re-assess their policies. It is always possible that such a change could mean increased hostility, and even a nuclear 'preventive attack'. But preventive wars, on the record of the past, have never prevented deeper involvement and ultimate disaster. The idea remains one more easily entertained by strategic analysts than by practical statesmen. It is more likely that the two present super powers would have to recognise the advent of a third, which at least would give greater scope for manoeuvre and act as a restraint on the stark confrontation of the United States and the Soviet Union. When this situation comes about China might be much less hostile to the idea of a condominium in which she would either be a member herself, or an outside critic strong enough to influence the policies of the two major powers.

If China found, within a few years, that Russia had changed her leaders for men either weaker in their political support, or more amenable to Chinese opinions, then even before she herself could claim membership in a super power trio, she could feel confidence that her views would be listened to in Moscow with respect and her wishes consulted. A condominium in which China had an indirect but powerful influence with one member might suit her well; whether it would be so attractive to the United States is another question. In practice these alternatives amount to a situation in which a condominium of the two present super powers could not work with China's acceptance, but only if the two members received China as a third partner, or at least as an influence constantly to be consulted and sometimes deferred to. This is not what is usually meant by a Russo-American condominium.

The terms on which China would freely and willingly join any such combination are at present well beyond the terms of reference which either Russia or the United States would consider admissible, or even worthy of consideration. China might claim, or rather certainly would claim, the role of predominant power in South-east Asia at the very least. History could be alleged to justify such a claim, and actual power might make it realistic, but at present the policy of the United States and her ally Australia is designed specifically to obstruct that objective. There seems no reason to think that Russia would now regard Chinese aims in South-east Asia with much favour either. On the other hand the Chinese are very unlikely to accept a secondary role in this region once they have the power to challenge those who would keep China out. Apart from being the natural field for Chinese emigration, the smaller and mostly much weaker South-east Asian states lie clearly within the zone where Chinese power could be effectively employed, just as the small republics of Central America are assuredly within the field of US dominance, and the East European states lie in the Russian sphere. The Chinese, if they are to be considered as a great power, would refuse to deny themselves the same standing in the area which concerns them to an equal degree.

The Chinese are likely to make an even more difficult condition; that in the areas of the world where China is directly interested the development of revolutionary movements should not be frustrated or impeded by the armed intervention of either of the other super powers. They would argue that just as Russia was allowed a free hand to suppress Czech deviation, and the US assumed the right to intervene in more than one Caribbean republic, so China must be recognised as having the same sort of authority in those parts of Asia which are closely related to her own territory. The Chinese might, perhaps would, claim a wider right on behalf of revolutionary movements in more distant countries, but such claims could be resisted on the grounds that China could not effectively intervene either in Africa or in South America. These claims mean that no condominium to which China would consent, even if she were acknowledged as a third member, could function to preserve the *status quo* as now established. It is conceivable that a condominium of the three great powers could operate on other policies, but it is hardly to be believed that such a change is within the present range of possibilities.

If a condominium were formed which did not function to maintain the present distribution of major power, it would in fact be committed to the acceptance of revolutionary changes in most parts of the world. Even if room was made for China, by acknowledging her predominant interest in South-east Asia, there could be no certainty that this would be the limit of her interests or ambitions. Half a continent is still much less than one-third of the whole world. A condominium which admitted the right of one of its members to support revolution wherever it seemed possible that such a movement could succeed would involve the virtual abdication of the

United States from her present position of world wide influence amid a very severe curtailment of Russian initiative. Russia, as a Communist state, could not oppose revolution; but if she was not herself an active supporter the leadership would fall to China. Thus a condominium on these Chinese terms would lead to the predominance of China in the Communist world, and the decline of US power.

It is of course possible that when such a situation arises as to make China's participation in condominium a real and urgent question the leadership in China will be in other hands, and the demands framed in less sweeping ideological terms. It might be that future Chinese leaders, while certainly expecting predominance in South-east Asia, would be content that the other partners, and the rest of the world should agree to accept the Chinese form of Communism as no less capable of acceptance, and normal inter-state relations, than is now accorded to the Russian-led Communist countries and to the USSR itself. Russia would be recognised, as now, as the dominant power in the eastern part of Europe; America would continue to be the ally of Western Europe and the effective overlord of South America, while China would not be challenged in South-east Asia. This arrangement would still leave Africa and the Middle East, and India also, outside the system, and in many parts of these regions revolutionary movements are more than possible, and causes for conflict and disagreement among the three super powers highly probable. This may be the shape of things to come, but it is again not what condominium is intended to achieve nor is it a very desirable future for mankind to expect.

It would seem probable that China would also expect that no fourth member should be permitted to join the super power group. Neither Western Europe, seen as the ally of the United States, when at some future date these countries are truly united, nor India, which is too close to China and potentially too influential in South-east Asia, nor, above all, Japan, the most likely candidate. For if there is anywhere a local possible check to Chinese power in eastern Asia it can only be a rearmed and powerful Japan. That country is part of eastern Asia, its destiny is intertwined with that of China. America may abandon Asia, and no great harm would come to her by doing so. Russia can find in Europe and the Middle East a compensation for accepting Chinese power in the Far East, but Japan must either live, in those circumstances, in the shadow of China, or compete for power and equal status. Japan is already an industrial giant and therefore a potential military power of the first order also; her economy is more developed than that of China can become in fifty years. The Chinese must certainly take account of Japan, not only now as the ally of the United States even if that relationship has obvious limitations, but still more of what Japan will be at the end of the century. It does not seem at all probable that Japan will then be a Communist state. On the other hand it may not be within the power of Russia or of America to keep Japan from taking her place as a major power. Japan is not a bargaining counter which the two present super powers can trade for their own advantage. The possibility of a complete American withdrawal from Asia is a stimulus to Japan to assert her position while there is yet time, and it would not seem likely that on the model of the Vietnam War, Japan would be willing to co-operate in the 'Japanisation' of the policy of containing China. Japan as a potential super power would not be amenable to direction from any other country, and it is not now possible to foresee what her future leaders would regard as the essential Japanese interests which could not be served either by alliance with the United States or by alignment with one or other of the Communist super powers. If China could come to contemplate a condominium of three super powers with a degree of acceptance, it is very possible that such a solution is not in fact viable, and that Japan would be the agent which would make it impossible to realise.

These reflections are based on the view that the leaders of China, including Mao Tse-tung, are not in fact as committed to ideological frenzy as their public statements would suggest. If this is a wrong assumption, the reactions of China to any tendency to condominium become all the more negative and unpredictable. *China contra mundum* may be an appealing cry to 'Great Han chauvinists' (not a group who receive public commendation in China) and sound good in the ears of ordinary Chinese living in the interior of the country, men with little or no personal knowledge of the wider world beyond their country. It would not seem really probable that it is entertained as a rational policy by the leaders. But the belief in a forthcoming revolution, that the capitalist powers are reaching the term of their natural existence, and that Russian revisionism is a false road which will lead those who follow it to disaster, is certainly held by men in power, and can distort their judgment. They may believe that their intransigent attitude is appropriate in a time when change is imminent, and that the present alignment of power is being undermined by forces which the capitalist and revisionist Communist countries cannot control. Over-emphasis is given to racial conflict in the United States, to student unrest in all parts of the world, and to the alleged debilitating effects of the return to bourgeois ways of life in the Soviet Union. Any adjustment of these beliefs to what most other people would regard as realities may be very difficult.

To accept the possibility that the capitalist system, changing constantly and far from static, is not going to collapse, but may find new forms of growth which are acceptable to the working classes, is to deny the fundamental assumptions of Marxism, which Mao Tse-tung has fully endorsed. To discover that revisionist Communism, even in the Russian form (let alone that of Mr Dubcek) can still offer a way of life which many millions find better than constant revolutionary activity is to deny the central doctrine of Mao Tse-tung's Thought. To assume that conflicts of race and generations in the Western world are unquestionable symptoms of decay and collapse in the countries where these problems are now acute is to ignore the infinite flexibility of human institutions, which have constantly met such challenges in the past and found workable solutions. The Cultural Revolution gave great impetus to the ideological aspects of Chinese life, and for a time submerged the practical intelligence for which the Chinese people have been renowned. It may be that this impetus has now spent its main force, and that cooler calculations will be made, even if their aims are not given any publicity. Ideals are not abandoned: their realisation has to be postponed, sometimes for ever.

If it will be difficult for the Chinese leaders to modify their ideological standpoint sufficiently to permit of hopeful negotiations with the Americans or the Russians, it will be almost more difficult for those two nations to give a favourable reception to the kind of terms which China would offer for tolerating, or participating in, a condominium. It is not, indeed, at all apparent that any such possibility has even been considered. Such hints of relaxation of hostility towards China which have come from the United States are concerned only with very marginal matters; there has been no suggestion that any major Chinese claim would even be discussed. On Taiwan, on the exclusion, if possible, of China from influence in South-east Asia, on the acceptance of Peking's delegation at the UN or on diplomatic recognition, there has been no public indication of any change, and on some of these issues the old attitude has been reaffirmed. This is rigidity, ideological or not, which is a fair match for the Chinese themselves. The Russians hardly show any flexibility at all. If America has relaxed some restrictions and welcomed a renewal of the Warsaw talks, Russia has maintained military presence on the Chinese frontier, is now thought to be responsible for at least the later series of border incidents, and if she was willing to open negotiations in Peking, has, it would seem, insisted that these shall have only a narrow scope. Moscow rivals Peking with mutual abuse, and plants anti-Chinese stories in the Western press with more success than the Chinese have so far been able to show. There is no sign that either America or Russia would give way to Chinese claims at any point.

This being the case there is no present prospect that China will be, now or soon, accepted as a partner in a condominium. If she is excluded, her reaction to any tendency to form one will be uniformly and continuously hostile. Present opposition will be confirmed as justified and inevitable, ideological intrasigence will be strengthened, and expectations fixed upon assumed forthcoming upheavals in the super powers themselves rather than upon negotiations with them on controversial issues. Under these conditions a condominium would assume the character of an anti-Chinese alliance, since China will be the only major power to oppose such an

arrangement openly. This prospect is not welcome to many other nations
who do not desire to be drawn into a quarrel on this scale, and have reser-
vations about both US and Russian policy towards China. A condominium
which does not have an anti-Chinese bias, but which is none the less unacceptable to the Chinese, could not long endure. It must be founded on a
common interest, which is the *status quo*. The Chinese do not accept the
status quo, therefore a condominium designed to uphold it will be opposed
by China, and must itself acquire an anti-Chinese character.

If China must be expected to oppose any condominium of the super
powers, what means has she to implement her hostility, and is it possible
for her to frustrate the formation of this combination? It must first be
observed that China is not the only country which views such a development with some concern. Governments may conceal their fears or mistrust,
but opposition political parties, the press and public opinion in many parts
of the world show openly their dislike of the prospect of super power
domination, especially if this condominium is obviously directed towards
maintaining a *status quo* which suits the interests of the two major powers,
but does not necessarily conform to the aspirations of other peoples. Arab
nationalists, African freedom fighters, South American socialists and often
liberals too, have no content in the present distribution of power within the
areas of their own concern. That the present situation might be guaranteed
and upheld by nations so different from each other and ideologically so
estranged as Russia and America strikes many observers as a cynical and
opportunist arrangement without any real prospect of endurance, and without any flexibility to meet impending change. China is thus not without
some sympathy in her stand, and if her present extreme ideological attitude
tends to discourage possible supporters, this condition could alter if China
maintains her opposition with more diplomatic skill.

There is among the younger generation in most of the countries of the
world a growing and strong resentment against the way the dominant
generation and their instruments, the governments of great nations, conduct affairs. Particularly the inflexibility of policies, whether Communist
or capitalist, is condemned. The critics will before long become the majority
of voters in democratic countries, and a strong force in the authoritarian
states. They will enforce some of their views, probably in a more coherent
form than they now express them. The Chinese are right, in this sense, to
expect changes within the super powers themselves, and among such
changes a more ready acceptance of China's own aspirations can be
expected. If the next generation of Western and of Russian leaders take
more account of the future and are less intent on upholding outworn doctrines and failed policies, some of China's claims will be reconsidered, and
her growing power will compel attention. The Chinese, despite strong
words, have shown caution in deeds, especially when military confrontation

might be the consequence of rashness. There is little probability that China would seek redress from what she deems to be her grievances by resorting to war against one, or both, of the super powers. There is no real prospect that the potential partners in a condominium could agree to or win the consent of their peoples, to waging a vast 'preventive' war against a China which offers no more than verbal provocations.

The idea, or the tendency towards a condominium of Russia and America is one born of the fear of change, shared by the ruling groups in both countries. It is not shared by millions of people in other parts of the world, or indeed, by very many within these countries themselves, and it is entirely repugnant to China both ideologically and as an unsatisfied power of growing strength. Even if China becomes less extremist and puts off ideological goals to a distant future, her claims and dissatisfactions as a nation and a power will remain, and will perhaps win more support if they seem more moderately presented. Thus the opposition of China to a condominium, although probably ineffective in preventing the formation of such a system by the present rulers of Russia and America, will constantly undermine the operation of the system, and ultimately frustrate it.

SUPER POWERS AND SECONDARY POWERS: WESTERN EUROPE AND JAPAN

In the discussions of bipolarity and polycentrism which took place in the climate of international politics brought about by the Soviet-American détente and the challenge by de Gaulle's France and Mao's China to the alleged hegemonial ambitions of the two super powers, little attention was paid to the role of secondary powers in the emerging international order. Indeed the concept of the secondary power, while scarcely a novelty, is not in general usage, nor is there any accepted list of secondary powers. The category of 'former great power' is more familiar, but its relevance to emerging relationships is open to question, even though any proposed list of secondary powers is likely to coincide closely with that of former great powers. There has recently been some interest in the contemporary role of 'middle powers', but these are usually taken to include states such as Canada, that is to say, states which ranked next after the traditional great powers.

For present purposes, secondary powers may be defined as those which play a major role in the affairs of one of the two principal regions of tension in world politics, Europe and Asia. These are clearly distinguished from lesser regions in terms of the magnitude of the stakes: the secondary powers have a place in the global balance which marks them off from the states in sub-regions such as the Middle East. In terms of this definition there are at least four secondary powers, Britain, France, West Germany, and Japan. The question whether China might more appropriately be regarded as a secondary power than as the third, still embryonic super power will arise in the course of the discussion.

Do any other states qualify as secondary powers? India does not at the present time: though it is the principal power in the sub-region of South Asia, it lacks sufficient weight in the Asian balance as a whole to be considered a player in the same category as the super powers, China and Japan. Conceivably a nuclear and more power-oriented India may assume such a role in the future, but this would be more than a matter of acquiring

This chapter has benefited from comments by Johannes Voigt and J. A. A. Stockwin.

nuclear weapons (which might make for a 'fortress India'): it would require a fundamental change of values in favour of projecting power, and a
change of régime that would make this possible for a country whose
resources are so tightly stretched as India's. The trend would appear to be
in the opposite direction, towards even greater preoccupation with internal
problems.

In Europe, Italy, despite its remarkable economic development, has not
played a role as a power in European and Atlantic affairs: the major
questions before the Common Market await the decisions of France and
West Germany, and North Atlantic diplomacy revolves around the relations
of these two with Britain and the United States. Italy, the former great
power whose status was never quite assured, has not recovered even the
status of a secondary power; France, despite its even greater debacle as a
power in World War II has, thanks to de Gaulle, increased its standing in
relation to its European rivals.[1] A European union, the prospects for which
will be discussed below, would be a potential super power, not just a
secondary power, if the union was sufficiently cohesive.

The question to be explored here is the role that the secondary powers
have been and are playing in world politics, and more especially the role
that they might be expected to play in a world order which has moved
towards a condominium or a concert. Are they capable of exerting decisive
pressure in favour of a concert rather than a condominium? Are they
likely to show solidarity or cohesiveness as secondary powers, or will their
influence be exerted in other ways?

The lack of cohesion among the secondary powers in the past is all too
obvious, as is the special position of Japan, which stands apart from the
intense interaction of the other three. In every challenge to the super
powers by one of the secondary powers, one or more of the others was to be
found supporting the super power.

The issue of super power hegemony has been pressed seriously only by
France: though Gaullism found its echo throughout Europe, the remaining

[1] This classification may be contrasted with that of a German study sponsored by
the Deutsche Gesellschaft für Auswärtige Politik, which distinguished between world
powers (super powers), great powers (which exercise influence in some part of the
world beyond their own region), and regional powers (which play a role in their own
region). Present great powers included only China, Britain, and France; one aim of
the study was to inquire which others might be expected to move into this category.
Middle powers, defined in relation to all regions, were: Sweden, Italy, Poland, Yugo-
slavia, Israel, United Arab Republic, South Africa, India, Pakistan, Indonesia, Australia, Japan, Canada, Mexico, Brazil. West Germany was also assumed to be a
middle power. Japan and West Germany seem out of place in this list, even granted
that the list is correct in terms of the defining characteristic (the exercise of influence
beyond one's region). See *Mittlere Mächte in der Weltpolitik*, Aktuelle Aussenpolitik,
Schriftenreihe des Forschungsinstituts der Deutschen Gesellschaft für Auswärtige
Politik. Opladen: C. W. Leske Verlag, 1969, p. 8.

H

governments saw their interests compelling them to side with Washington rather than Paris when de Gaulle thrust this choice upon them, as in the case of France's withdrawal from the NATO organisation in 1966. It remains unclear how far de Gaulle aspired to press his campaign against American influence in Europe, and whether he seriously over-estimated France's potential or merely exploited images of French power and independence in order to maximise the limited degree of independence that remained within France's scope. His successor President Pompidou, while not returning to the NATO fold and in fact maintaining many of the independent Gaullist policies (witness the Middle East) has reversed the style: the friendly banker has replaced the abrasive olympian.

West Germany had its own nightmare of the two hegemonial powers arriving at a 'deal' at its expense, which coloured German reactions to the Berlin crisis of 1958-62, the test ban, non-proliferation and détente diplomacy as a whole. However, setting aside the opportunism of de Gaulle's policy, a basic divergence between Gaullist France and Christian-Democrat Germany was that, while the former resisted American preponderance but sought by the mid-1960s to take the lead in détente diplomacy, Germany, having no objection in principle to American diplomatic leadership, dreaded the consequences of détente for its own diplomatic position until the belated initiation of a new *Ostpolitik*, hesitantly by the Great Coalition government, but with conviction under Willy Brandt.

Britain, which under Harold Macmillan in the late 1950s had been willing to antagonise the continental powers in its attempt to promote a Soviet-American détente, welcomed the achievement of such a détente under Kennedy and Khrushchev but found itself lacking a role in East-West relations. De Gaulle, at this point, reversing his earlier opposition to détente, succeeded in becoming its chief spokesman in the European context, but this was a uniquely Gaullist brand of détente, an attempt to take the substance of the East-West *rapprochement* out of the hands of the super powers, to promote a pattern of bilateral agreements among increasingly independent nations in both halves of Europe.

In the case of the Non-Proliferation Treaty, Britain was throughout a strong supporter of the attempt to negotiate a treaty, and played its part in the gradual erosion of support for the multilateral force, a major obstacle to Soviet acceptance of a treaty. Germany's legitimate grounds for hesitation toward the treaty found some understanding but little support in Britain, or for that matter in France, which opposed the treaty as an expression of the hegemonial tendencies of the super powers but was content to see Germany subject to further nuclear restrictions. Japan's reasons for reluctance to sign the Non-Proliferation Treaty (it finally did so in February 1970), were much less complex than Germany's and were largely a matter of economic concern and the demand for equal treatment with other advanced industrial states. Germany shared these reasons, but there was also on the part of the Christian Democrats a strong reluctance to give nuclear pledges to the Soviet Union and to accept any form of Soviet control over German nuclear developments, as well as overtones of the French rejection of a super power monopoly.

On European and Atlantic issues there is seldom unity among the three European powers *vis-à-vis* the United States, and when there is, it is typically more a matter of common interest and aspiration than of common policy—witness the technology gap. Typically the European powers have been divided among themselves: it is sufficient to mention the issues of European supranationalism, Britain's membership of the Common Market, NATO strategy and indeed whether NATO continues to be necessary. On all of these issues it is not so much a matter of clearly distinct national viewpoints, but of different attitudes throughout Western Europe, held in differing proportions in the different states.

Economic relations fall somewhat outside the present frame of reference, since the question of condominium does not arise: the world remains divided between two principal economic systems, even though the overlap is increasing. Within the Western economic system, de Gaulle found little support in his efforts to use gold as a weapon to undermine the dominant position of the dollar; and the uncharacteristically aggressive D-mark diplomacy carried out briefly by West Germany at the instigation of Franz Josef Strauss in 1968-9, far from being a concerted European move, had the effect of putting pressure on the then weakest currencies, the French and the British.

Japan's low-posture diplomacy has rendered it a spectator of most of these developments, welcoming the détente, taking a stand when its interests are directly affected, preoccupied above all with economic development and trade and, in the security field, its relations with the United States. The Security Treaty has been a major issue in Japanese politics, but more as a rallying cry for the Left than a mass grievance which could be used against the government. The resolution of the Okinawa issue has removed the main threat that the American alliance might arouse nationalist grievances at a time when a mood of cautious national self-assertion appears to be forming. Japan's relations with Russia and China remain secondary: little has come of the rumours of massive Japanese co-operation in the development of Siberia, and trade with Taiwan remains greater than that with China. The greatest tension in the relationship with the United States is now in the field of trade, but the economic relationship rests on a solid foundation of mutual interest and is far less vulnerable to national emotion than an issue such as the control of Okinawa. Japan has maintained a more normal though low-key relationship with China than any of the other powers: France's sympathy for Mao's challenge to the super powers has not led to an intimate relationship, any more than Britain's long-standing recognition and general desire to bring China into the international community. Notions of exploiting the Sino-Soviet conflict for national ends are among the fantasies of the German far Right.

Any pattern in these diverse responses of the secondary powers to the events of the 1960s is to be found not in any concerting of the policies of these powers, but in the diverse interests of each power as perceived by its leaders; the most notable change of orientation which has taken place is that in West Germany, gradually at first since 1966 but more sharply with the election of a Social Democrat-led government in 1969.

Perhaps a more realistic conception of the role of the secondary powers would focus on their individual attempts to limit the predominance of the super powers. In practice, due to Japan's low posture, this is mainly a question of the European powers, and the record is very uneven.

The role of Britain and France beyond Europe, far from increasing in the decade of polycentrism, has contracted along with their withdrawal from empire. One may contrast their central role in the Suez crisis of 1956 with their peripheral part in the Six Day War of 1967. French diplomatic support for the Arabs and Britain's efforts in favour of a compromise resolution at the United Nations had some limited significance in the post-war diplomacy, but the only external powers which counted seriously— potentially during the war, actually in the subsequent diplomacy and the rearming of the contestants—were the two super powers, a situation which became even clearer in the diplomacy over the cease-fire in 1970.

The same holds true for Indo-China. Britain and France were principals in the Geneva Conference of 1954, France as the embattled colonial power, Britain both because of American unwillingness to become involved unless it could win broad-based allied support, but also because Britain was still regarded as a world power. In the Vietnam conflict they were merely to be found among the legions of intermediaries and the chorus of critics.

Within Europe, the predominant trend has been the decline in American political pre-eminence, which was unchallenged at the time of the Marshall Plan and the foundation of NATO, remained a powerful force behind the expansion of the NATO armies and also European integration in the 1950s, but was clearly faltering with the failure of Kennedy's Grand Design for North Atlantic partnership, and is no longer sought by the Nixon Administration, which renounces American designs. Even here, however, there have been important cross-currents. John Foster Dulles failed in his attempt to pressure France to accept the European Defence Community in 1953-4, even though Germany was brought into NATO and the European movement recovered its momentum a little later. In a German perspective, the West German government exercised less influence in Washington under Johnson than ten years earlier under Eisenhower and Dulles: in particular, whereas Dulles had accorded Adenauer virtually a veto on issues of central concern to Germany, Johnson overrode German interests on nuclear sharing and the Non-Proliferation Treaty—at least, as these interests were perceived by most of the governing Christian Democrats. On balance, however, American influence has become much less pervasive. Western détente diplomacy has been characterised by increasing independence on the part of all the Western protagonists. And the United States could no longer claim a major part in deciding such essentially European issues as Britain's joining the European Economic Community. Even Kennedy's attempt to do so proved counter-productive. This does not, of course, preclude the silent use of pressure, such as economic leverage or the question of troop withdrawals, though such pressure would have to be exercised with delicacy.

In general, one may accept Henry Kissinger's assertion that conflicting tendencies are at work: politically, the world is becoming increasingly multi-polar, but the movement of arms technology, discussed elsewhere in this volume, is reinforcing the bipolar aspects of the strategic balance as MIRVs and ABMs are incorporated into the nuclear forces of the super powers. However, it must be asked whether such a divorce between political and military relationships can persist: will not strategic bipolarity undermine the movement towards greater political independence, unless political independence is consolidated by the development of secondary power nuclear forces at a comparable technological level to those of the super powers?

Kissinger attempts to meet this problem by suggesting that there is a decline in the political significance of military power, especially nuclear power, the use of which becomes less and less credible as its enormity increases.[2] However, this is by no means the only possible projection. One reason for doubting its long-term validity is the prospect of a large-scale withdrawal of the American forces which have been stationed in Europe since 1950. The Nixon Administration has undertaken not to withdraw any American units before mid-1971, but it is reasonable to expect substantial withdrawals after that date. But for the invasion of Czechoslovakia, pressure from the Senate would probably have brought about withdrawals already, and such pressure is likely to regain strength, the more so since the present Republican Administration does not share the commitment of its predecessor, especially former Defense Secretary Robert McNamara, to the 'conventional strategy', i.e. the policy of planning for extended non-nuclear fighting, preserving the option to withhold or introduce tactical nuclear weapons, instead of being compelled to introduce them early for

[2] Henry A. Kissinger, *American Foreign Policy: Three Essays*. New York: Norton, 1969, pp. 53-64. Kissinger's view is summed up in the statement: 'The age of the superpowers is now drawing to an end. Military bipolarity has not only failed to prevent, it has actually encouraged political multipolarity'.

want of alternatives. The probability of American troop withdrawals is perhaps the major factor which could precipitate a restructuring of European attitudes and policies in the coming period, as regards nuclear weapons, political integration or a search for political accommodation with the Soviet Union.

The present position may be summed up as follows: there is greater regional autonomy in Western Europe and greater flexibility towards the East; Japan shows signs of working towards a similar autonomy, and pursuing a more flexible diplomacy. However, despite de Gaulle's challenge, NATO has not been replaced or transformed, and the major disturbing factor is the prospective reduction in the American contribution. To the extent that a system of international order dominated by the collaboration of the super powers is emerging, the attitudes of the secondary powers range from support through acquiescence to a now muted and uncertain resistance on the part of France. The challenge to the United States is strikingly less serious than China's challenge to Soviet supremacy in the Communist world. This may be seen as a measure of the difference between France as a secondary power and China as a potential super power, but it may rather reflect the greater overlap in the interests of the Western secondary powers with those of the United States, in contrast to the near-total rivalry of China and Russia at all levels, not offset by comparable shared interests.

There is nothing in past experience which would point to an alignment of secondary powers, collectively confronting the super powers. It may be supposed that a condominium would have to operate in a blatantly oppressive manner to provoke this sort of alignment. On the other hand, the reaction to the Non-Proliferation Treaty may point toward the possibility of successful resistance by most or even all the secondary powers to super power initiatives, not necessarily in a common front but with at least tacit co-ordination.

There is even less indication of pressure by the secondary powers in favour of a concert in matters of global diplomacy, as against condominium. France provides no more than the venue for the Paris peace talks, Britain even under the Conservatives is to retain only a modest presence in Malaysia-Singapore: the national mood as reflected in the 1970 election campaign appeared to be inward-looking, even the Common Market issue being played down. Great power diplomacy in the Middle East is essentially Soviet-American diplomacy. Japan shows little interest in affairs beyond Asia; except in the economic field there seems no basis for its becoming involved in European issues. The prevailing tendencies, then, point in the direction of regionalism, European and Asian, with an enhanced role for the secondary powers solely within this context. There is a greater basis in past and present experience for informed speculation in the case of Europe than of Japan, but the diversity of past European tendencies points to the need to be conscious of exceptions to the pattern, diversions from what appears to be the mainstream of events.

The interdependence of the European powers is so great that it is more fruitful to examine the issues which seem bound to remain at the top of the diplomatic agenda rather than the policies of each country in turn, which inevitably lead to the discussion of the wider European issues. First, there is the future political structure of Western Europe, as well as the membership of the EEC, which raises the question whether the secondary powers will remain independent powers or attempt a political merger. Second, and closely related, is the question of European security: the level of American participation, the roles of the European powers and the possibility of a security agreement between East and West. Third is the question of relations with Eastern Europe and the Soviet Union more broadly: is there a prospect of anything more than incremental change? Clearly, all three issues are interrelated: for example, any further measure of integration in Western Europe, especially in the military field, would have major repercussions on relations with the East. Another possible issue, especially if there is increasing European autonomy, is the balance of power in Western Europe itself, not in terms of certain national aspirations to 'leadership' as in the past, but in terms of inner and outer groupings, and in particular the possibility of the emergence of a dominant pair among the three powers.

Despite some recent expressions of faith in European union and clarion calls to begin the process of constructing a federal Europe, it is difficult to discern much political momentum behind the 'European idea' at the present time.[3] The technology gap has not provided the necessary stimulus. The present governments of France, Germany, and Britain appear highly competent, capable of meeting immediate national pressures with considerable flexibility, but they do not project a long-term vision. A contemporary Jean Monnet would find no such receptive national leaders as Schumann, de Gasperi, and Adenauer.

A number of more general factors appear to be working against European union in the period immediately ahead. Some of the most obvious problems of the moment, such as educational reform, must necessarily be solved within the national framework. To the extent that present discontents reflect a reaction against the increasing power of impersonal bureaucracy, proposals that conjure up the vision of a sprawling supra-national super-bureaucracy lack appeal. Whatever the economic advantages of size, the political disadvantages have become more salient, not only in the case of

---

[3] For two recent European manifestoes, see John Pinder and Roy Price, *Europe After de Gaulle*. Harmondsworth: Penguin, 1969 and Norman Macrae, *The Phoenix is Short-Sighted*, supplement to *The Economist*, 16 May 1970.

the United States but world wide: and even in economic terms the greatest progress among the underdeveloped countries is to be found in some of the smaller states, not the giants.

In the short run, whether it succeeds or fails, Britain's bid to join the EEC will impose serious strains on the Common Market as it is now constituted. It still seems likely that Britain's entry would further weaken the forces making for supranationalism, but if these are as weak as suggested, the stresses may be of a more mundane kind, the need to make extensive specific adjustments to allow for new members, the change to a less homogeneous membership and a much less manageable number of members. On the other hand, Britain's entry seems more and more a prerequisite for any future move towards European unity. A united Europe based on a Franco-German axis seems less and less likely as the circumstances which forged the Adenauer-de Gaulle relationship (the Berlin crisis, the peculiar tensions in Franco-American and German-American relations, de Gaulle's unique ability to project an image of France as a great power) recede into the past.

For every European persuaded by Franz Josef Strauss that Europe must become a power, several are scared or alienated, not only because of Strauss's image in Germany and abroad, but also because this vision of the future clashes directly with the concept of détente as the gradual normalising of relations between the states of Western and Eastern Europe.[4] The emergence of a nuclear power in Western Europe, whatever its specific political form, seems bound to make for more rigid Soviet control over Eastern Europe, and even though the invasion of Czechoslovakia has dimmed the prospect for détente it has not entirely destroyed the hopes placed in it. For the present, the new *Ostpolitik* rules out any consideration of the Strauss approach.

However, many of the factors referred to may change or lose their salience in the longer run. What emerges most clearly from a recent study by the Institute for Strategic Studies of 'Models of Western Europe in the 1970s' is that all the models are likely to involve a great deal of tension and to promote resistance to the emerging 'structure', whichever it is.[5] This holds true for the case of drifting along with 'evolutionary Europe' as much as for the attempts at more radical change. However, the study can find little evidence of pressures great enough to impel Europe towards one of the more radical solutions, but opts cautiously for a future marked by more intensive and diverse functional co-operation.

In the eighteen months since the Institute's study was completed, one

[4] For Strauss's views, see Franz Josef Strauss, *Challenge and Response*. London: Weidenfeld and Nicolson, 1969.

[5] Alastair Buchan (ed.), *Europe's Futures, Europe's Choices*. London: Chatto and Windus, 1969. The six models examined are: Evolutionary Europe; Atlanticized Europe; Europe des Etats; Fragmented Europe; Partnership Europe; and Independent Federal Europe.

factor has emerged which could prove more of a force for change than the mainly economic and technological factors then prominent, or the waning spirit of Gaullism in Western Europe. This is the foreshadowed American troop reduction. It is possible that this may be implemented in a manner which minimises its wider repercussions, though this would require not merely a circumspect American policy but also agreement among NATO's European members on an appropriate response and a reasonably co-operative Soviet policy. The consequences would be minimised if American troop reductions formed part of an East-West agreement on force levels and were perceived by West Europeans as a limited response to the détente, not affecting the credibility of American nuclear protection. On the other hand, it is possible to imagine circumstances in which the reductions could undermine American credibility in European eyes: if they were carried through in the face of an unco-operative Soviet attitude to overall arms reductions, for example, and if they appeared to be a response to domestic pressures beyond the control of the Administration. In such circumstances the certainties which have underpinned European politics for two decades could be eroded and the question of Europe's political unity reopened. Needless to say, it is the aim of the Nixon Administration to avoid any such development. Like its predecessors, it seeks 'a partnership', and it asserts further that 'we can no more disengage from Europe than from Alaska'.[6]

The prospects for an orderly development towards burden-sharing and partnership are not better than in the past. The gloomy paradox remains that so long as the West Europeans are confident of American protection they lack the incentive to make the drastic adjustments that would be needed if they were to make a contribution to their security more commensurate with their economic strength. Only a loss of confidence in American protection seems likely to bring about the shock that could bring Europe to reorganise itself to assume the responsibility for its own defence, but this would not be as a junior partner of the United States but in a desperate attempt to provide deterrent forces to replace those in which it had lost confidence. Short of a near-cataclysmic shock (it will be recalled that the very considerable loss of confidence in the United States during the 1961-2 Berlin crisis provoked no such movement in European defence) the factors working against European union in the nuclear field seem likely to prevail. In brief, in addition to the effect of the détente these include the difficulty of making the British and French deterrents, or a joint Anglo-French deterrent, into a technically plausible or politically credible nuclear umbrella. If a technically adequate force required wider collaboration, as seems likely, the problem of control would arise in an acute form. On the one hand, Britain and France would doubtless prefer a merely symbolic form of

6 Richard Nixon, *A New Strategy for Peace*, Report to the Congress, 18 February 1970, p. 31.

shared control, or consultation along the lines of the 'McNamara Committee' in NATO; there would still be especially strong misgivings against a German finger on the trigger. On the other hand, the Germans and perhaps others would expect something more than mere consultation in return for their contributions to a deterrent whose capability would inevitably be less impressive than the American.

The transformation considered here—the most radical that appears even faintly in prospect for European security or for Europe as a political entity —is not envisaged as a consequence of condominium.[7] It would represent a radical unilateral redefinition by the United States of its role as a super power. The discussion bears out the view that bipolarity survives in matters of fundamental military relationships: the secondary powers are little more than middle powers in this context. The relative military weight of Europe's secondary powers is declining, not increasing. Only a crisis with an impact greater than, say, the Korean War, seems likely to precipitate the fusion of the secondary powers which would mean, if the international order could stand the shock, the rapid appearance of virtually another super power. The discussion has explored some of the outer limits of the theme: we may return to the more marginal issues usually raised in connection with European security in the present context.

The more likely developments are a general scaling down of the NATO forces and the initiation of protracted negotiations on European security. A conference on European security, should it be held, will not change the basic security structure. It is perhaps tempting to suppose that, contrary to all recent expectation, Europe might be approaching a real watershed: that *Ostpolitik* and especially a Berlin settlement—now conceivable for the first time—might symbolise the final passing of the military confrontation in Europe, just as the Berlin blockade symbolised its onset and Khrushchev's 1958-62 Berlin crisis brought on its tensest moments. But this would be to overlook not only the geopolitical pressures for the retention of a substantial American presence in Western Europe (in the last analysis this could change if there were a sufficient change in the psychological climate) but more important, the irreducible Soviet requirement to station large forces in Eastern Europe in order to maintain the Soviet position there beyond challenge.

If a European security conference is not to degenerate into a futile exchange of unreal blueprints, or merely to offer Moscow a vantage point

---

[7] A US-Soviet agreement to impose a new system of European security over the heads of the protesting Europeans is a logical possibility, but so unreal in practice as to merit no more than cursory mention. Agreed troop reductions would not fall into this category, since most Europeans wish to see them. A revival of the 1950s proposals for disengagement or a nuclear-free zone could drastically affect European, especially German, attitudes to the US, but there is little chance of this under the present Republican Administration.

for attempts to detach some of the more marginal members of NATO, it may be necessary to supplement the rather unpromising proposals for agreed force reductions by disinterring some of the long-forgotten arms control proposals, selecting those that minimise intrusiveness and political anxiety, but at the same time offer some modest benefit to general security, as has been done at the global level.

One of the most notable developments in recent years has been the common approach of Britain and West Germany to NATO affairs. Both would like to see negotiated force reductions, but neither is under pressure for major unilateral reductions: both favour the maintenance of substantially the present levels until agreements can be negotiated. So long, then, as the American Administration does not lose control over American policy, in the manner of Vietnam, changes are likely to be incremental, with Britain and Germany, in particular, playing a major role in any negotiations. An American troop reduction, however, is unlikely to lead to increased contributions from the European members, but rather to European demands for greater emphasis on tactical nuclear weapons in NATO's strategy, and the indications are that the Nixon Administration may not resist these demands as previous Democrat Administrations would have done. So long as the danger of war in Europe continues to recede, there is little to counter the deceptive attraction of a tactical nuclear strategy, but it is a choice which the NATO governments may come to regret if a war crisis should again arise.

The situation as regards European security is not one of condominium but remains one of confrontation between rival blocs. The confrontation may be made safer by agreed restraints, the tension may be reduced, but so long as the United States remains a world power, so long as it remains interested in world order, it cannot collaborate with Russia in the dismantling of NATO. This would not be condominium, but abdication—the unilateral renunciation of the role of super power. There is no general community of interests to sustain collaboration between the two super powers in Europe, which remains divided into two systems by the choice of the Soviet Union.

Nonetheless, relations with East Europe are likely to count for more than, say, at the time of the build-up of NATO when a more rigid Soviet system in Eastern Europe was taken to be an acceptable price for Western security. There will be reluctance, especially perhaps in Germany, to foreclose avenues that could open up more normal relations. In contrast to de Gaulle, who at one time seemed to be calling for a loosening of the alliance systems in both halves of Europe, present governments, and notably West Germany, recognise that it will be self-defeating to try to attract East European states out of the Soviet orbit, and consequently they conduct a parallel diplomacy with Moscow as well as the states of East Europe. The

West Europeans, including the secondary powers, are more concerned about East European contacts than the United States, but there is no major divergence of interests such as was suggested by de Gaulle's playing on the memory of Yalta to suggest continuing super power collusion to maintain the two blocs intact. The real problem remains Soviet reluctance to tolerate greater flexibility in Eastern Europe, internally or externally: the questions of condominium versus concert scarcely arise, since the region has been accepted *de facto* as falling within the Soviet system of influence since 1945.

It seems likely that international conflict in the next decade will continue to be centred on Asia rather than Europe. A degree of Soviet-American collaboration in Asia is possible after Vietnam, though whether this can amount to condominium will depend on China and on the role of Japan. Japan's starting-point is a preference for a continuation of the emphasis on economic development which has served it so well since 1945, continued low defence spending, which thanks to rapid economic growth enables a steady expansion of armaments to take place, and continued avoidance of contentious foreign involvements. One major uncertainty is whether the international economy will continue to afford Japan the opportunity for this sort of growth, and if not, whether economic difficulties would lead to a more active foreign policy. Political contingencies which could induce Japan to realise its power potential include a decline in the credibility of the American alliance (of which there is at present little indication) or a conflict with China.

It is questionable whether Japan is rightly to be regarded as a secondary power if China is classified as a potential super power. Of course, either might experience economic or political setbacks which would place it firmly in the secondary category. If present trends continue, the power resources, though remarkably different in kind, suggest that they may potentially be powers of much the same order. Japan is more advanced industrially and educationally, has a higher growth rate and much higher *per capita* income, and thus potentially greater resources, in terms of finance and technology, available for military purposes. China has been influenced by a tenacious nationalism and power drive, springing partly from ideology but more from the humiliations of the past century, it claims a world role as leader of the true revolutionary forces, and has a nuclear force in which it is investing heavily.

But China is militarily far from being a super power. It may soon achieve a limited 'assured destruction' capability against the United States, but this is not yet certain, in view of the development of missile defences. If even a small nuclear force perceptibly increases China's bargaining power, this may furnish an incentive to further proliferation in Asia, which in turn would limit China's scope. While China is a military giant around its own frontiers it lacks the capacity to deploy its forces outside its own neighbourhood. China has little to offer remote revolutionary movements beyond moral support: its claim to be the third world power is mainly symbolic. Even if the situation in many developing countries comes to favour Maoist revolutions, this will be a success for Chinese ideas and example rather than its power.

In South-east Asia, which is sometimes regarded as China's natural sphere of influence, China lacks economic strength and attractiveness: if any state is moving towards economic dominance in the region it is Japan. China could gain a dominant position only through violence, either outright invasion or the support of insurgencies, which is likely to antagonise Japan as well as the super powers. Whether, when, and how any of them would intervene militarily raises too many unknowns to be a fruitful topic for speculation.[8] One can envisage one possible situation in which both China and Japan cultivate their peculiar forms of power, avoiding a direct clash, Japan winning the substance of regional influence, China being left with the symbols of super powerhood. The possibilities range all the way from a direct clash between the two Asian powers to Japan's taking the lead in a *rapprochement* with China. What seems unlikely is that either will be able to intimidate or dominate the other.

Should there be an easing of Sino-American relations, it is unlikely that Japan would be content to follow in the wake of US policy: it would surely seek to anticipate, if not influence, America's China policy. The issue of China's UN seat will surely reveal a more flexible diplomacy. It is likely that Japan will demand a say in any major Asian negotiations. While there is still relatively little pressure for nuclear weapons or for an activist diplomacy, there is by now a strong demand that Japan's interests be respected.[9] There would, clearly, be a danger that any attempt by the super powers to establish a condominium in Asia, or to treat Asia as a three-power world including China, would provoke a vigorous Japanese reaction. However, in view of the American attempt in recent years to induce Japan to play a more active role in Asia, this particular danger is unlikely to arise. Perhaps a more serious threat to American-Japanese relations is that the Americans may postulate too great an identity of interests, hence may be unprepared for a Gaullist style of foreign policy if Japan should in future seek to demonstrate its independence.

[8] Some observers cannot conceive of Japan's becoming involved militarily in South-east Asia. Some Japanese participants at a conference in Canberra in 1967 did not reject the idea out of hand, even though they judged it unlikely; one suggestion was that if Japan's trade was adversely affected, the constitution's restrictions on armed force might be amended. See J. D. B. Miller (ed.), *India, Japan, Australia: Partners in Asia?* Canberra: Australian National University Press, 1968, p. 21.

[9] See, e.g., K. Wakaizumi, 'Japan Beyond 1970', *Foreign Affairs*, vol. 47, 1969, pp. 509-20. The government is fostering a more positive attitude towards defence and plans for Japan to assume full responsibility for its own non-nuclear defence, the US providing only the 'nuclear umbrella'.

The assumption underlying this discussion is that the prospects for
condominium depend on its being limited to what might be termed the
backstop of international order, and that it be unobtrusive. The nuclear
arsenals of the super powers would be held in reserve as a deterrent against
reckless or over-ambitious policies on the part of lesser powers. This is a
difficult role: each super power will be primarily concerned with its own
interests, and will be discouraged from giving high priority to joint action
with the rival super power just because they are rivals on most issues for
most of the time—also because it would damage relations with friends and
allies.

The super powers cannot 'manage' international politics. Not even small
powers, so long as they are independent, will accept super power management of their relations. The secondary powers will certainly resist two-
power management of world politics: they are by definition the powers
which have been playing a major role in Asian or European affairs or which
now expect to play such a role. It is likely that the super powers will concede this claim: the United States at best will be a reluctant crisis manager
for some time after Vietnam. Should the claims of the secondary powers be
persistently neglected, however, they possess a remedy which amounts
to a deterrent against super power arrogance: they have the potential to
become virtual super powers, Japan individually, the European powers
collectively. It would be very costly, and also perhaps very provocative
and dangerous to translate this potential into reality: hence there is a reasonable prospect that a certain asymmetrical mutual deterrence will bring
about stability in the relationship between the secondary powers and the
super powers. The potential of the former will impose a degree of restraint
on the latter, but the massive power of the latter will ensure that the super
power potential of the secondary powers remains merely potential unless
their grievances are commensurate with the shock and possible turmoil that
would result from the emergence of another super power.

GREAT POWER RELATIONS AND THE THIRD WORLD

It is an important question whether the categorisation of a large number of new states spread over three continents as the Third World is at all relevant for any meaningful analysis of the problems of international politics. As area specialists often point out, each of these countries is unique in many ways and there are inherent risks of grave distortion of realities in any attempt to treat them as an undifferentiated mass of nations. Yet, to those who are concerned with the broad underlying dimensions of world politics it appears as a convenient device to group the poor, weak, and problem-ridden states of Asia, Africa, and Latin America as a distinct and different element in international affairs.

Notwithstanding the many dissimilarities among them, these states share certain qualities which are of considerable significance for the analysis of the nature of the international society or of the problems of creating and sustaining a viable international order. The main attempt in this essay is to discuss the impact of the changes in great power relations on the position of the Third World states in the international system and to analyse how the interests of these countries could be affected by future developments in the relationship among the great powers.

It may be worth while to begin this discussion by trying to identify the attributes which these countries share as states and which qualify them to belong to the Third World and to discuss the extent to which these are of relevance in shaping their attitudes and behaviour as members of the inter-national society. It is apparent that while they have some important ele-ments of commonness they are very different from one another for many purposes: the relative strength of the pulls exerted by their similarities and dissimilarities determines their ability and inclination to evolve a set of common attitudes to questions of international order in general and to problems of great power relations in particular.

The most obvious of the common problems of the Third World states is that they are poor and that the gap between them and the richer coun-tries is widening. It is true that there are great differences among them in terms of *per capita* income or of the level of industrial progress. But they are all technologically backward and relatively unindustrialised. What is more, the consciousness of difference in levels of development among them is much less relevant as a political factor than the consciousness of their collective inferiority in relation to the developed world. Frequent references to the less developed countries as the great problem areas of the world in the speeches and writings of leaders of both the developed and the under-developed world have deepened this consciousness, just as the creation of bodies like the UNCTAD has institutionalised it. The economic division of the world between its North and its South has by now become as much a perceived division of the world as the political division between the East and the West has been ever since the last World War.

The second attribute of the Third World states is that virtually all of them are going through the first phases of modernisation of their societies and are engaged in adapting their political institutions and values to the needs of social change and economic growth. Hence, most of them, in varying degrees, are showing signs of political instability of one kind or another. It is a controversial question whether the social tensions generated by the process of transformation of a pre-industrial to an industrial society are any greater than those created by the transition from an industrial to a post-industrial society: what is undoubtedly true is that the political values and institutions created in both the Western and the Communist societies seem less vulnerable to such tensions than those in the developing countries.

The importance of this phenomenon as a factor in foreign policy making is difficult to measure, nor is it easy to suggest how and in what direction it might influence the views and attitudes of these countries. There is on the one hand the facile argument that the ruling élites of these countries, conscious of their insecurity in their domestic environments, tend to evolve flamboyant foreign policies and press them into service in order to stabilise their position in internal politics. But it can be argued with equal plausibility that these internal tasks make them basically inward looking. What is less controversial and more important is that the social and political instability of the Third World states influence the views and attitudes of the rest of the world towards them: it is to most of the developed countries the chaotic and disorderly part of the world.

A third common characteristic of the Third World countries is that an overwhelming majority of them have, till recently, been under the direct colonial rule of Western nations. Even those states which formally retained their independence were brought under an overtly unequal relationship with one or more of the West European or North American powers. The most widely shared political experience of the Third World is the experience of Western domination, and the most commonly shared feeling in the Third World is that they are new as independent nations, though not necessarily as peoples or civilisations.

A fourth quality, which is to some extent a corollary of the third, is that there is in varying degrees in all these countries a consciousness of being non-Western and non-white. Though the racial differences between one Third World state and another can sometimes become a source of greater friction than this broad division between the white and the coloured peoples of the world (particularly when racial differences are invoked to bolster up conflicting territorial claims), what lends extra meaning to it is that the issue is inextricably mixed up with the broader issue of the relationship between the advanced Western and the backward non-Western peoples. To many Third World states, racial discrimination and colonial domination are but two facets of the same problem—the white rule in Rhodesia or South Africa is regarded as only a variant of colonialism—and the North-South division has as much a racial as an economic and a political connotation.

Lastly, with perhaps a few exceptions, all the Third World states are relatively powerless and weak. Many of them are just not big enough to acquire military strength of any consequence; others are not technologically well-equipped to build up their forces on the basis of self-reliance. Most of those Third World states which have set out to build up strong national defence forces have done so with the help of one or more of the nations of the East or the West. Once again, the difference between the weakest and the strongest of the Third World states may be much greater than that between the strongest among them and the weaker among the powers of the developed world. But the consciousness of being underpowered is widely shared—a consciousness that is reinforced by and in its turn reinforces the general consciousness of being inferior and underprivileged.

In brief, it is the fact of their being poor, unstable, new, non-white, and weak that gives the Third World states their common identity and their distinctive character as a group of nations or as a group of members of the international society. What is more, the élites of the Third World states have often been brought up in those Western intellectual traditions which attached considerable importance to the problem of uplifting the weak and underprivileged sections of societies and which extrapolated the theory of the need for solidarity among the underprivileged within a society for collective struggles to improve their lot into a theory of international relations which thought of associations or leagues of 'Oppressed Peoples'. The Leninist theory of imperialism has had great impact on the minds of the peoples who formulated the world views of these countries, and without being Communists or Socialists in their attitudes to internal social problems, many of them regarded their anti-imperialist struggles as parts of a world-wide effort to improve the lots of the international 'have-nots' (as indeed Lenin and Stalin had anticipated). The consciousness of being the have-nots of

I

the world has influenced and will continue to influence the behaviour and attitudes of the Third World states.

Yet, it is easy to exaggerate the importance of these factors and overlook other realities regarding the individual and collective world views of these nations. Interestingly, both the revolutionaries and the conservatives of the world make the facile assumption that because they are underprivileged and have-not in some ways, the Third World states are like the proletariat of the international society: the former hope and the latter fear that the underprivileged nations of Asia, Africa, and Latin America will seek to bring about radical transformation of the institutions and arrangements which sustain the present international system. Neither the professions nor the practices of the leaders of the Third World states justify such a conclusion.

In the first place, not many of the Third World states are radical in their attitudes to internal institutions and problems. No doubt some of them genuinely intend to rebuild their societies on a new basis and virtually all of them are apparently committed to bringing about fundamental social changes: but in actual practice the élites of many of these countries are as much concerned with conserving the social structure as with achieving the maximum possible economic growth. Even those nations which have accepted socialism as the declared goal of their policies define it in a manner which stresses the importance of gradualism and they often take great care to differentiate their ideologies from those of the Communist countries. To bring about radical social transformation through revolutionary methods is for many Third World élites tantamount to passing a death sentence on themselves. This aversion to internal radicalism, or the unwillingness to conceive revolutionary transformations within one's society, tempers the zeal to act as international have-nots.

Secondly, the new have-not nations have more reasons to be afraid of international anarchy than the powerful 'have' states of the developed world. For one thing, a situation of international anarchy may aggravate their domestic problems of nation building; what ensures the unity and integrity of many Third World states is that the United Nations and the international political system that sustains it is virtually underwriting the political map of the various continents. In the absence of some commonly accepted international codes and some authority to enforce them, at least some of the new states would find it difficult to survive in their present form. It is possible that neither Congo nor Nigeria would have remained a united country if their unity was not legitimised and enforced by the United Nations and the great powers. It is also clear that in any situation where international might becomes international right the weak and powerless states of the Third World would have more to lose than others.

Thirdly, unlike the have-not Axis Powers of the pre-war world, only a few of the Third World states are territorially have-nots. There are, of course, a few countries in Asia, Africa, and Latin America who have national *irredenta* and a few others who aspire to change the political maps of their regions. But by and large the Third World states are content with their present boundaries. It is significant that the document adopted at the Cairo Conference of the Non-Aligned Nations in 1964 referred to the inviolability of the traditional frontiers of nations. Though there was some opposition to this principle at Cairo, there was overwhelming support in its favour, which is some indication of the fact that many of these countries do not regard themselves as territorial have-nots. This is not to deny that there are important boundary disputes among the new states and that a few of them have a compelling urge to change their regional maps. But the point is that most of the Third World is as anxious as anyone else to lend some permanence to the present international boundaries of states: their fear of international anarchy, as mentioned above, makes them *status quo* oriented, as far as questions of territorial changes are concerned.

What is even more important as a factor restraining their urge to achieve the solidarity of the have-not nations is that new nations, no less than the older ones, conduct their foreign policies to promote their national interests, as perceived by their ruling élites. While at one level they may see many great advantages in the solidarity of the Third World against the rest, the search for a more equitable international society can only be one of their many national goals. Some of them see the safeguarding of their security in the face of threats from neighbours (often fellow members of the Third World club) as the primary tasks of their foreign policies. Indeed, if the Third World consciousness was a primary motivating force, India and China, Pakistan and Afghanistan, Ethiopia and Somalia would have found it easier to resolve their disputes and problems in order to be able to present a united front before the rest of the world. Many of the Third World states have in fact sought to promote their national interests *vis-à-vis* their neighbours' with the help of the very nations who are most unquestionably the haves of today's world.

The foreign policy preoccupations of many of the Third World states are, and in all probability will continue to be, more varied than one of the seeking of structural changes in world politics.

Again, the Third World states are very different from each other in regard to one major motivation of international behaviour—their potentialities as powers. Some of these countries—India, Indonesia, Pakistan, United Arab Republic, Nigeria, Congo, and Brazil—may well be classified as middle powers. Others like Chad, Gabon, Singapore, Laos, Peru, and Ecuador are small powers and likely to remain so. It is extremely difficult to aggregate the interests of these countries on questions like the relative power and status of nations in the world. While all of them may be

equally happy to see themselves in a world of general and complete disarmament, in the absence of such a Utopia their interests and hence their
attitudes are likely to be very divergent indeed. It is not accidental that on
an issue like the Non-Proliferation Treaty, the small powers readily perceived an identity of interests between them and the super powers in preventing the spread of nuclear weapons among the world's middle powers,
some of whom belong to the Third World itself.

The picture that emerges is therefore much more complex than one of a
few haves, who are guardians of the international order, struggling against a
large group of Third World have-nots who have no stakes in preserving the
existing international order. On the one hand, there are some bases for the
Third World to see itself as the underprivileged section of the international
society and this perception must inevitably lead the new states to reject any
idea or concept of international order that equates it with stagnation or
seeks to preserve and freeze the existing pattern of distribution of economic
and military power in the world. On the other hand, they not only want to
promote their individual and collective interests through manipulation of
the existing international forces but also to avoid any contingency in which
international anarchy or disorderliness hinder their efforts to build their
nations and consolidate their independence. Gradual improvement of their
position within the international system, through orderly change rather
than the collapse of whatever order exists, is therefore the rational goal
for most nations of the Third World.

Although only a few of the leaders of the Third World states have tried to
articulate the collective interests of their countries and ever talked of a
calculated attempt to bring about changes in the world political system, the
contradictory pulls of the various considerations mentioned above can be
well illustrated from the course that the foreign policies formulated by
them have taken in the past. The two questions on which these states have
shown the greatest degree of unity of purpose and on which they have tried
their utmost to reform the international system are those of colonialism and
racialism. The undoing of the world system which rested on the integration
of large areas of the world into empires has been the most explicitly stated
and the most consistently pursued goal of the Third World states. The
anti-*status quo* aspects of their international role has been equally evident
in their opposition to racial discrimination and domination in various parts
of the world.

Another form in which the reformist aspirations of the Third World
found expression over the last two decades is non-alignment. There are
many bases of non-alignment: the natural urge to remain uninvolved in
other people's quarrels, the urgent need to diversify the international contacts of these countries without ending the historical ties with the metropoli-

tan countries of Europe, the desire to reconstruct their societies through a non-capitalist and a non-Communist approach, the intention to prevent the polarisation of political forces within their countries and the apprehension that the Cold War would relegate other international issues which are more relevant for their future in the world to a position of relative insignificance, were all factors leading to the evolution of the policy of non-alignment. What made non-alignment a reformist effort, however, was that it was a method of preventing the West from promoting a post-imperial international system under which the Western powers would organise the entire non-Communist world as a single political area, integrated through military pacts and alliances and through other forms of regional associations.

The degree of unity of outlook among the countries of the Third World in various stages of the growth of their foreign policies depended on what they were seeking to achieve in relation to the West, or, to put it differently, on the degree of change they were seeking to bring about in the world system. On questions like colonialism and racialism, which were issues of great emotional and practical relevance for all of them, there was a large measure of agreement, at least as to the goal. There was lesser unity among them on issues like alignment and a few of the Third World states saw it to be in their national interests to belong to Western sponsored alliances.

The similarity of outlook was even less pronounced when it came to a question of deciding what the attitude of the non-aligned to the West should be. Some of the non-aligned nations like Tunisia and Malaysia believed in maintaining cordial relations with the Western powers; others like Ghana and Indonesia perceived a continued relevance of an anti-Western posture in view of what they regarded as the neo-colonialist threat to their independence.

The issues that these countries faced in determining their attitudes to the international system in various phases of its evolution were many and are worth enumerating. In the first place, could the Western and Communist worlds be equated and a policy of equal irrelevance of both be accepted? Both the Communist and the Western powers were trying to prove to the Third World that it was in their interests to make a difference between them. The Communist powers appealed to the anti-*status quo* part of the Third World's consciousness and asked them to carry forward their struggle against the West to a new phase of further limiting and if possible eliminating Western influences in their societies. The Western powers, on the other hand, appealed to the *status quo* part of their consciousness and pointed out the grave risks that these countries might take of changing their internal political systems as well as of disturbing the local and global power balance through a policy of collaboration with the Communists.

A contradiction was inherent in the positions of the Third World states: on the one hand, there was little doubt that the Communist world was the

great anti-*status quo* force in what was basically a Western dominated
world system and that it was ready to lend support and sustenance to
anything that the Third World might do to change it. On the other hand,
domestically most of the Third World states were engaged in a type of
nation building effort which could not permit the growth of Communist
revolutionary activities within their societies. Also, the West's capacity to
reward them with aid and assistance and further their developmental efforts
was far greater than that of the Communist world.

In the 1950s, the attitudes of the Third World states to the West and the
East (and hence to order and change) tended to be determined primarily
by the degree of insecurity that the élites in these societies felt in their
domestic and international environment. It appeared to many ruling élites
who were hard pressed at home that to enlist the West on their side would
give them the breathing space they needed to consolidate their positions
within their countries; others wanted Western support to withstand the
challenges from without that they faced. The West, in its turn, conscious
of its power and its capacity to influence events as well as of its interests in
building an integrated world under its auspices, was prepared to stand by
them. It prevented many political changes in areas where the situation was
ripe for such changes; equally it helped the smaller and the weaker states
to meet what they regarded as threats from their bigger and stronger neighbours. The Communist powers, motivated by ideology and conscious of
their relative weakness and incapacity to shape the course of events, tended
to side with the forces of change within certain societies and with the
stronger states in certain regions.

As a result of these trends in Western and Communist policies, the more
secure élites of the relatively larger states tended to be less pro-Western
and more pro-Communist than the insecure élites of the smaller states.
Thus, in South-east Asia, Indonesia looked more to the Communist countries than to the West and was up against a number of problems in its relationship with the West; Malaysia on the other hand looked more to the
West than to the Communists. Similarly, in South Asia, India was less pro-
Western than Pakistan, just as in West Asia post-revolution Egypt was less
pro-Western than the monarchical régimes of the smaller Arab countries.
It was a logical consequence of the dominant position of the West in the
world power structure that the reformist powers of the Third World should
find a degree of community of interests with the Communist countries.

A different source of conflict of attitudes among the non-aligned states
themselves which assumed increasing salience in later years, was the importance that their respective élites attached to internal as against external tasks
and the way they organised their societies to be able to carry them out. At
the Belgrade Conference of the non-aligned, Nehru urged the members to
build in their own countries 'societies of free men, where freedom was real';

at the Cairo Conference three years later Sukarno said: 'we must under-stand that it will not work just to turn our attention to economic develop-ment and social welfare and to ignore the diversion of our efforts to serve the interests of the old powers . . . we cannot develop economically nor socially nor culturally until we have removed these sources of domination'.[1]

The radicals among the non-aligned saw the need for a struggle against the established order while the moderates among them saw the need to maintain and promote order to be able to tackle their domestic problems. Both perceived the long-term importance of attaining economic, political, and military independence from the great powers but while some felt that the way to do so was to carry on with the struggle against those who wielded power and authority in the world others felt that the salvation for these countries lay in promoting international co-operation. The idea of orderly change and a gradual readjustment of relations between the developed and the developing world through a co-operative effort at diffusion of technology by the former and its absorption by the latter appealed to some; others were attracted by the concept that the restructuring of the world through industrial and technological progress in the developing countries could not be a purely economic exercise and that political confrontation was a basic precondition for the economic progress of these societies. The ideas of 'confrontation' as formulated by Sukarno and of 'international co-opera-tion' as formulated by Nehru constituted the two opposite ideological poles for the developing world. The implication of the two sets of belief for the world system and for questions of order and change in the world were very different.

The problems of unity of the Third World states were further exacer-bated in the 1960s by the trends within the Communist world. The gradual transformation of the Soviet Union from an anti-*status quo* to a *status quo* power and the growing evidence of the Soviet anxiety to participate in the efforts to preserve the new international system based on peaceful co-existence among the great powers had changed the entire background of international politics. It was easy for many of the newly independent states to agree to prevent the growth of a post-imperial Western oriented pattern of world order; it was difficult for them to evolve any agreed approach to basic international issues once the question was one of determining their attitude not to the Western, but to the Soviet-American world. The rise of Khrushchev in the Soviet Union was followed by a perceptible change in the Soviet attitude to the West as well as to the Third World. This brought to the fore the problem of the Third World's attitude to a new world system.

---

[1] For a discussion of the differences between the Indian and the Indonesian approaches to the problems of non-alignment, see Sisir Gupta, 'Asian Non-Align-ment', *Annals of the American Academy of Political and Social Science*, November 1965.

The moderates among the non-aligned found no reason to adopt a negative attitude to such a system and enthusiastically welcomed the opportunity it offered of peaceful change.

For the national bourgeois élites of these societies, significant progress had already been achieved in restructuring the world through the replacement of the 'Western' system of international order by a Soviet-American system: the task now was to make the best of the new scheme of things, bring about marginal changes in the world system to improve their position in it, preserve the basic structure of relationships among the great powers on which the prospect of peace and order rested, promote the idea of international co-operation under which the knowledge and resources at the disposal of the developed countries of the East and the West would be available to the less developed areas, and take advantage of the climate of global peace to create viable and secure regional systems to enhance their security. The alternative path of confrontation appeared to them as utterly counter-productive: apart from the risks of greater international anarchy that were inherent in it, there were some grave implications of such an international course for their internal progress and their internal systems.

The legitimacy of a Soviet-American system, however, was challenged by China, which is, in one sense, a leading Third World state, an entirely independent centre of power and a source of Communist theories. The Chinese accused the Soviet of colluding and collaborating with the United States, suspected that Moscow was now bent upon creating a joint Soviet-American system in the world, expressed their conviction that such a system could only stagnate the world and freeze the existing internal systems and external policies of the Third World states and detested those in the Third World like Nehru who seemed to welcome such developments. (This, in this writer's view, is the origin of the Sino-Indian conflict.) Soviet efforts to build a new order found expression in the many joint steps they took with the United States to preserve the dominant features of the existing structure of world politics (particularly the present pattern of distribution of power in the world) as well as attempts to strengthen the United Nations: the Chinese, in response to such Soviet policies, began to regard redistribution of power in the world and prevention of the growth of a legitimate international authority in the form of a stronger United Nations as their primary tasks. The Third World's response to such a situation was naturally confused and contradictory and although only a few among them showed any inclination to accept the Chinese view of these developments (only Indonesia withdrew from the United Nations), the differences among them became too wide to be bridged through international conferences and through new solidarity slogans. By 1965, the Chinese and their supporters, no less than the moderates among the Third World states, had come to the conclusion that it was fruitless and futile to try to bridge this gulf and organise the entire Third World into a Bandung type association of nations.

It appears in retrospect that 1965 was also the year in which the conflict between the radicals and the moderates in the Third World ended in a victory of the latter and isolation of the former. Earlier in the year the Chinese were eager to hold the Afro-Asian conference at Algiers and were prepared to make heavy diplomatic investments for its success; the indifference towards such a conference was then shown by India and other moderate countries. By October 1965, however, the Chinese were pleading for the postponement of the conference while India was eager to hold it. It is interesting to reflect on the causes of this basic change in the correlation of forces in Afro-Asia. Firstly, the fall of the Sukarno régime in Indonesia had dramatically underlined the futility of external militancy if internal problems remained untackled: the failure of Sukarnoism could not but impart some lessons to the militant states of the Third World. Secondly, Indonesia's action in withdrawing from the United Nations, which was blessed and encouraged by China, had alienated many Third World states, particularly those of Africa, which saw a big advantage in their membership of the United Nations. For a number of African states which are small and very new in the world, membership of the world organisation is not only the fulfilment of their aspiration to emerge as a recognised member of the family of nations but often the most potent available instrument to project themselves in an international role. Thirdly, the fear that a more militant Afro-Asianism would result in an increase of Chinese influence in their societies would have been present in the minds of many; Prime Minister Chou En-lai had earlier in the year created concern in many African states by saying that Africa appeared to be ripe for revolution. Fourthly, the Soviet Union had thrown its entire weight in the Third World behind the position adopted by the moderates, who had carefully raised the issue of Soviet participation in the Afro-Asian Conference in order to isolate the Chinese and their friends. Fifthly, local conflicts among some leading Afro-Asian nations (India and Pakistan, Malaysia and Indonesia) and unexpected government changes in some of them (Algeria and Indonesia) had brought to the surface the enormous problems of international relations within the area and of internal stability in some of these countries. Lastly, the onset of the Proletarian Cultural Revolution in China led to a temporary withdrawal of that country from diplomatic competition in many areas of this world.

Subsequent events in Asia and Africa underlined the need to avoid any attempt to confront or even opt out of the existing international system. Another pillar of Third World militancy against 'neo-colonialism' fell when Kwame Nkrumah was ousted from power in 1966; the breakdown of the Nigerian federation and the indispensability of great power support and co-operation for the restoration of unity in that country had its own lessons to impart; India and Pakistan—exhausted by a short war—found a friend and guide in the Soviet Union and both hoped to improve their positions *vis-à-vis* each other with great power support and sympathy; caught between China and Pakistan, India's military dependence on the super powers continued to grow, just as two successive droughts had created an impossible food situation within the country which aid from the West alone could have helped to overcome; some Arabs were increasingly looking to the Soviet Union for military aid and political support while others expected the West to sustain their local anachronistic political systems.

An explicit declaration was made by the developing countries in their meeting at Algiers in 1967 that there was no need for a confrontation between the developed and the developing countries for the creation of what was called a just economic order. In fact, the Algiers Charter, as drafted by the Group of 77 (of the developing countries) in their meeting at Algiers in October 1967, provides an example of the way in which the Third World states could still jointly formulate their demands on the world system in the changed circumstances of the late 1960s.

Pointing out that all indications showed a further worsening of their relative position in the world economy, the meeting called for the creation of a greater awareness of the need for concerted efforts for the economic development of the Third World countries. Among the demands of the developing countries was the following: each developed country should comply with the target of a minimum of one per cent of its gross national product for net financial outflows, in terms of actual disbursements, by the end of the development decade. The same kind of demands had been formulated by these states earlier in the United Nations.

The Third World's have-not awareness was now finding expression in a pattern of behaviour that is more akin to that of the legitimate trade unionists in a welfare state than that of the revolutionary proletariat in a highly exploitative society. It was basically an attempt on their part to function on the basis of such codes of conduct as were regarded as legitimate by the existing international system and to make use of the available international institutions like the United Nations to advance their common interests.

The issue on which the attitudes of the reformists and the revolutionaries within the Third World proved to be totally divergent was that of great power relations. To China and the few other new nations which accepted its interpretation of world events, the relaxation of tensions among the established great powers and the détente between the two contending super powers was not only irrelevant for the poorer and weaker countries of the world but positively harmful for their interests. The stability of Soviet-American relations ensured a degree of order in the world which made any significant structural change far more difficult to accomplish; the détente would deprive the Third World of one of the few available methods of first weakening and then radically transforming the international political system. To India and a large number of non-aligned states, on the other hand, the détente and the gradual improvement of Soviet-American relations appeared to be a pre-condition for the success of their efforts to reform the international system. The Chinese view is dealt with at length in another contribution to this symposium; it is worth while therefore to concentrate here on what leaders like Jawaharlal Nehru had perceived to be the advantages of the mitigation of the Cold War and the improvement of great power relations for the countries of the Third World.

In the first place, Soviet-American co-existence was necessary for world peace, which was imperative for the success of the developing countries in planning the reconstruction of their societies and in providing them with an international climate in which the basic task of transformation of their economies assumed greater importance than that of solving the problems of insecurity created by threats of an all-engulfing war. Secondly, there was an inverse relationship between the salience of East-West and North-South issues in world politics: the less the world's concern for the former, the greater would be its awareness of the latter. Thirdly, the mitigation of the Cold War would strengthen those elements in the Communist and the Western societies which believed in a new welfare oriented international order. Fourthly, any resources that the developed world could save out of its huge expenditure on defence, as a result of relaxation of international tensions, might well be diverted towards the uplifting of the backward regions of the world. Fifthly, the détente could also mark the beginning of a process of convergence of the two systems—the Western system accommodating the principles of social ownership of means of production and equality of incomes and opportunities and the Communist system accommodating the Western principles of political freedom and liberty. Such a situation could make the countries of the Third World which essentially believed in democratic and socialist goals the areas of agreement between the two power blocs. Sixthly, the co-existence of the United States and the Soviet Union was the first step towards a more meaningful co-operative relationship between them: the challenge that the underdevelopment and poverty of two-thirds of mankind presented could only be tackled through great power co-operation and the creation of international institutions. Lastly, accord and amity among the great powers in general and the Soviet Union and the United States in particular were necessary for the strengthening of the United Nations—the only international forum where the small, weak, and underdeveloped powers had any chance of making an impact on the course of world events.

In the model that Nehru advocated for the Third World, emphases were evenly distributed between the need for change and the need for order: what is more, transformation of the world system was to be brought about through the efforts to create a higher order in the international society out of the existing world political infrastructure rather than through the demolition of what was already existing. For example, while great power accord was basically viewed as a necessary condition for world order, it could also have appeared to some as the only available method of unfreezing the bipolar world structure. Soviet-American *rapprochement* would make it difficult for both the Soviets and the Americans to maintain the strict bloc discipline that they had enforced for years over a number of countries. Soviet-American co-existence and co-operation would mean less Soviet and American control over their respective spheres of influence and competition in the developing areas. Nehru said in the early 1960s:

> As more and more nations keep joining this peace club, as against the nuclear club and Cold War club, we expect this unaligned grouping to grow and absorb other nations, the Big European nations like France or Czechoslovakia, which today belong to NATO and the Warsaw military alliances. We want the whole world to become part of this area of peaceful co-operation, including ultimately, the United States and the Soviet Union.[2]

The expectations of Nehru, who stood out as the most consistent champion of this particular line of thinking, could be well illustrated from the following extracts out of the record of his conversation with an Indian journalist towards the end of his life:[3]

> The vital issue before us both in the national and international sphere is one of achieving social justice, economic equality and co-operation, national co-operation as well as international co-operation. We want to create a socialist co-operative commonwealth within our country, and, also, help the world move towards a similar international order—that is, a co-operative world order, by removing the dangerous economic division of humanity between the under-developed and the developed or over-developed regions of the world.
>
> If the United Nations wants to serve humanity it must divert the attention of the bigger powers from the cold war by getting them together to rehabilitate the backward regions of the world. At the moment we are considering a proposal that the United Nations should devote a whole year to international co-operation towards this objective.
>
> The issue of peace and disarmament is linked up with this most dangerous threat projected by a world divided between the overdeveloped and underdeveloped regions. I have mentioned this danger before and I would like to say again that we consider this to be a more real division with potential for trouble than the other artificial division of the world between capitalism,

[2] R. K. Karanjia, *The Philosophy of Mr Nehru*. London: Allen and Unwin, 1966, p. 47.

[3] All the extracts are from the book cited above, which is the record of a series of Mr Nehru's talks with the author.

communism and all that. It presses upon the Big Powers the absolute necessity of crying halt to the Cold War, calling off their crazy armament race,
and of co-operating with each other for the rehabilitation of more than half
the world of underprivileged, impoverished, hungry people. If we cannot
bring them round to tackle this problem, which is basically an economic
problem but lends itself to racial fanaticism, then it might blow up in a fatal
conflict between the underdeveloped, overpopulated and overdeveloped and
underpopulated races and peoples of the world.

Certainly, we cannot compel the more advanced countries to share their
abundance with the less developed world; but we can certainly tell them that
this division of humanity between wealth and poverty is about as bad and
dangerous a source of trouble as such imbalance in the economy of a single
country . . . today, fortunately, the Big Powers have come round to appreciate our point of view . . . *In fact, this area of peace of ours—that is of the
non-aligned countries, most of whom are underdeveloped—is becoming a
sort of workshop of peace for both sides in the cold war.* Today they are
helping us individually in a sort of competitive spirit. Tomorrow, or the
day after, we might get the Soviet Union and the United States as well as
others to co-operate in the building of a Bhilai or an Aswan project.

It should be noted that Nehru and other such leaders of the Third World
were not the only ones who fostered such dreams of a transformation of the
world political system: a great many liberals in the Western world had for
long been holding out the vision of a world in which the meaningless pattern
of relationship among nations based on simple calculations of power politics had yielded place to a more meaningful pattern of relationship that
ensured international efforts for the solution of the deeper problems of the
world. For Nehru, who had all along been sustained in his thoughts by a
particular strand of West European liberalism and attempted to add a
Third World dimension to it, it was natural to adopt this optimistic model
of orderly change in the world. His personal contacts with the great liberal-
isers in the Communist world—Khrushchev and Tito—would have further
encouraged him in his belief that it was not impossible to bring about a
world-wide awareness of the need for such a co-operative approach to the
solution of world problems.[4] The fact that any alternative model could
prove to be highly detrimental to the values and ideals he had learned to
cherish provided the negative reasons for his growing faith in such a
course.

It is worth while to view the changes that have occurred in the pattern
of great power relations in the 1960s from the viewpoint of these two contending schools of thought in the Third World.

The two outstanding trends in great power relations of the last decade
have been the transformation of Soviet-American relations from one of

[4] For a more recent expression of such sentiments within the Communist world
see: A. D. Sakharov, *Progress, Coexistence and Intellectual Freedom.* Harmondsworth: Penguin, 1968.

intense rivalry and hostility to one of restrained rivalry and limited co-operation and the loosening of the two alliances and the emergence of China as an entirely autonomous great power. The problem from the Third World's viewpoint is to assess the significance of these developments for its own position in the world and to separate the positive and negative aspects of these trends in order to be able to mitigate the latter while preserving and promoting the former.

The most serious difficulty that one faces in this exercise is that great power relations have not yet crystallised into an easily recognisable shape; the world political system is more fluid than ever before and even the great powers themselves do not know how the search for a new pattern of relations among them will end. But the countries of the Third World have an additional problem in viewing these developments because of their inability to participate in the affairs of the great powers. The two super powers have tended to deal directly with each other, not only on such bilateral problems as arms control, but on a number of other issues like the enforcement of non-proliferation of nuclear weapons and the resolution of local conflicts which involve many other nations as well. It is a matter of great significance that while they seemed unresponsive to the frantic appeals by the leading nations of the Third World for a renewal of contact between them after the abortive Paris Summit of 1960, they found it possible to adopt a series of measures to improve their relations following the Cuban missile crisis of 1962, when no such Third World initiative was forthcoming.

What has made the Third World's confusion worse confounded is that the major powers of the world have sought to describe these changes in their relationship in a manner that would help them retain their advantages in the outlying continents and among the smaller powers of the world. On the one hand, the propaganda machines of the two super powers have consistently minimised the significance of their *rapprochement* and the various agencies of their governments which were geared to conduct a vigorous Cold War have been at pains to prove that it continues unabated. China, on the other hand, has alleged that the two super powers have not only improved their relations but also brought about a new system under which they are collaborating with each other to build a duopolistic international order.

As the objects of their rivalry and competition, the Third World states have found it difficult to accept the simplistic Chinese view of collusion between the two super powers for a redivision of the world; they have found it equally difficult to ignore all the evidences of a qualitative change in the nature of great power relations and sustain the old 'two scorpions in a bottle' image of super power relations. The Non-Proliferation Treaty, the Test Ban Treaty, the meeting at Glassboro, the parallelism of Soviet and American policies in the Indian sub-continent, their identical assessments of the Chinese threat, their common anxiety to preserve the *status quo* in certain regions, the continued dialogue between them to arrive at such arms control arrangements as would suit their interests have all been indicative of a change which is too significant to be immaterial for world politics. The Third World has found it difficult, as a result of these factors, to enunciate a clear position regarding the changes in great power relations.[5]

It is apparent that there are some important positive aspects of these developments for the Third World: to the extent that the Soviet Union and the United States have attained a greater stability in their relations, the world has become more peaceful and the spectre of a nuclear confrontation between them has ceased to haunt the peoples of the world. The global balance of power appears more stable at the end of the 1960s than it did a decade ago; though there are still many anxieties as to how and where the Soviets and the Americans will find a stable level of mutual deterrence, their ability to resolve these problems has been demonstrated. The general improvement of relations among the great powers and the greater confidence in their capacity to avoid a world war may eventually help the evolution of peaceful solutions to many of the pressing problems in various parts of the world.

Secondly, the modification of the bipolar structure of world politics has, while complicating the task of management of great power relations, added to the room for manoeuvre of individual Third World states in their relationship with the great powers. The emergence of China has also been a reminder to the developed world of the risks of leaving the problems of the Third World untackled: the anti-*status quo* and revolutionary stance adopted by Peking helps to underline to the *status quo* powers of the world the importance of urgent steps to tranquillise the Third World.

In brief, the stability of Soviet-American relations and the independence of action acquired by other major powers as a consequence of this phenomenon can both be regarded as conducive to the kind of orderly change in the world that Nehru and others had thought of. India's own experience suggests that it is now possible for many states in the Third World simultaneously to invoke the support of both the Soviet Union and the United States to promote the security of these states and to stabilise the present political map of certain regions: it is also possible for them to secure assistance from both the super powers for their economic development.

Similarly, the evolution of distinctive foreign policies in some West European countries has helped the countries of the Third World to create a more diversified pattern of foreign relations. The Arab states, for example, have

[5] Mrs Indira Gandhi told an American correspondent in early 1969 that a 'strange situation' has been developing in Soviet-American relations: 'While there is a certain amount of cold war, they do sometimes get together also'. Interview with Selig Harrison, *International Herald Tribune*, 15-16 February 1969.

derived considerable benefits in recent months from the French desire to differentiate its West Asian policies from those of Britain and the United States. Finally, the old Cold War pressures on them to align themselves with one or the other of the blocs have become less.

Yet, if one applies the test of how far the dreams of leaders like Nehru have been fulfilled by the structural changes in world politics in the last decade the conclusion becomes inescapable that neither the improvement of Soviet-American relations nor the loosening of the blocs has yielded all the results that they had fondly anticipated. In fact, the new problems and anxieties that these developments have created in these states are of far greater significance in the short term than those that they have resolved. It is necessary to enumerate these problems to illustrate the inadequacy of the present international system from the Third World's viewpoint.

The first painful reality is that the period of the improvement of great power relations has also been the period of a sharp decline in the developed world's concern for the economic development of these countries and a general adverse movement in the economic relationship between the Third World and the rest of the world.

As the Algiers Charter pointed out:

[there has been] the increasing squeezing and isolation of developing countries in the world economy, evidenced by the fact that the share of developing countries in total world exports has steadily declined from 27 per cent in 1953 to only 19 per cent in 1966 . . . the developed countries are adding approximately $60 per annum to the average income of their people while the average growth in income in developing countries amounts barely to two dollars . . . In the mid-1960's the developing countries have been able to buy, for a given volume of their traditional exports, 1/10 less imports than at the beginning of this period . . . This has aggravated the problem of the increasing indebtedness of developing countries . . . Although modern technology offers developing countries great possibilities to accelerate their economic development, its benefits are largely bypassing them due to its capital and skill intensive nature, and is drawing away from them such limited skills as were developed . . . in spite of the final act of UNCTAD I, no new commodity agreement on primary products of interest to developing countries had been concluded . . . while flow of development financing to developing countries amounted to 0.87 per cent of GNP of developed countries (at the beginning of the development decade) it came down to 0.62 per cent in 1966 . . . the terms and conditions of development finance were becoming more and more onerous; the proportion of grants was declining; the interest rates were increasing; repayment periods were shortening; development loans were becoming increasingly tied. . . .[6]

The decline in the net outflow of assistance from the developing countries as a part of their GNP could be attributed to many factors: domestic

[6] *Charter of Algiers*: Adopted by the Ministerial Meeting of the Group of 77 on 24 October 1967. New Delhi: Government of India, 1967.

problems have assumed urgency in many affluent societies, aid has not produced all the results that were expected of it, and there is greater diffidence in the developed world about its capacity to help the underdeveloped. But to a large extent the growing indifference of the major powers of the world towards the Third World's problems could also be explained in terms of the new confidence they have developed in their mutual relations and the lesser need they now feel to enlist the support of these countries for their conflicting political goals in the world. There are some political and moral considerations that still cause them to offer aid and assistance to the less developed areas but the compulsions to do so are now fewer.

Nor has the improvement of Soviet-American relations led to any great progress towards disarmament or limitation of their arms, or any reduction in their defence spending. In fact nothing has proved the inadequacy of the new pattern of international relations more than what the great powers have done with disarmament. It was easy for the Soviet Union and the United States to agree to limit the scope for other nations to emerge as nuclear powers; the Test Ban Treaty of 1963 was obviously designed to prevent China's entry into the nuclear club. Once China demonstrated that it had the will and the capacity to defy them, their energies were inevitably turned towards the task of excluding other nations from the membership of their exclusive club. They saw in the possible proliferation of nuclear weapons a threat to the stability of their system and agreed that efforts should be made to see that new and uncertain elements were not introduced into the world power structure. Not even the Vietnam War could hinder their joint efforts to draft and push through the Non-Proliferation Treaty.

But they have found it impossible to make the treaty the beginning of a serious effort to limit and control their own arms race, although the preamble of the Non-Proliferation Treaty morally binds them to such a course. In fact, the conclusion of the treaty has been followed by a number of steps on the part of the super powers to augment their power and to add to their arsenals new and more expensive weapon systems. It is now evident that even the SALT talks which they have undertaken are designed mainly to determine an optimum level of their power—a level at which they would be able to retain a pronounced superiority over a third country that challenges their supremacy and yet maintain a degree of stability in their mutual relationship.

The growing nuclear might of China has no doubt made the problem of disarmament more complicated; so long as China does not agree to enter into an arms control dialogue with the other powers, the United States and the Soviet Union would find it necessary to try to maintain a clear superiority over her. The logic behind this is the assumed belligerence of China: it is the view of the two *status quo* powers that until such time as China shows signs of accepting the need for stability in the world it would

K

be dangerous to permit her to function as an equal of the two sober and restrained great powers of the world. It is difficult to be certain to what extent China provides the legitimacy for what the Soviet Union and the United States might in any case have done; if there was no Maoist China they might have had to invent one!

The point, however, is that by the end of the 1960s it became clear that the great powers had conceived their proposals for general and complete disarmament as mere propaganda devices and that, in the foreseeable future, their efforts towards arms limitation and control would be designed more for stabilising their present position of power superiority rather than to achieve a reduction of their arms. Disarmament as a method of reducing the existing inequalities of power distribution among the nations of the world remains a chimera.

Even as a method of achieving greater stability in great power relations, the current arms control dialogue between Russia and America has serious limitations. The very fact that the debate in the United States on these and related issues has not yet become conclusive is one indication of uncertainty. The other is the persistent reports in Western newspapers that the Russians have, in fact, been pursuing such a goal. It is true that there is greater confidence among all concerned that whatever the future pattern of weapons development the two super powers will not permit their mutual relations to be disturbed easily. But it is little consolation for those who regarded arms limitation and reduction as an important objective that any future arms race will be conducted with greater restraint.

A problem that did not appear in sharp relief to those who assumed that steps towards disarmament would lead to greater spending on the Third World is that there are formidable competing demands within the developed societies for any funds that may be saved through cuts in defence expenditure. The socialist countries have enormous problems of satisfying the pent-up demands of their peoples for a better life and all of them will find it necessary to balance carefully the external compulsions to offer more funds to the developing countries against the domestic compulsions to spend more on urgent internal needs. The Western countries have a much greater affluence but the nature of their political systems are such that even relatively unimportant domestic problems assume greater urgency there than in the Communist societies; the manner in which the problems of pockets of poverty amidst their general affluence have been thrown up in recent years leaves little hope that the problems of the Third World will receive any priority in their schemes of things. The Communist world's ability to curtail domestic demands and invest their surplus in the Third World is more but the surplus itself is small; the Western world's surplus is greater but so is the salience of domestic demands in their priorities. Apart from this, the advanced countries of the world have to pursue their technological competition, irrespective of the arms situation: the low level technological effort which is possible through and necessary for investments in the Third World cannot be a substitute for things like space research. The possibility indeed is that in a world where arms have been limited and controlled and where the sanctions behind the less developed countries' demands are more moral than political the technological race would assume even greater importance as the determinant of a country's status and prestige in the world, necessitating huge investments in these fields.

Leaving aside the hopes of disarmament and of greater emphasis on international development efforts, it is necessary to ask the question how far the trends in great power relations have contributed to stability and peace in the world as a whole and to the security of the countries of the Third World in particular. The outstanding feature of Soviet-American relations today is their duality: concord and conflict, amity and animosity exist side by side. The military revolution has made them aware of the need to avert wars and head-on collisions; the growing challenge to their supremacy in the world from certain quarters has made them conscious of the need to preserve a particular pattern of world politics and of the identity of their interests in some spheres; the discovery of the possible costs of conducting an unmitigated rivalry in all parts of the globe has made them perceive a few areas of agreement. As a consequence of these developments ideological considerations have lost much of their earlier relevance and both the super powers have begun to approach international problems from a more pragmatic angle. Equally, however, as the two leading powers of the world they still have a great need to limit each other's influence in many areas of the world and there is intense competition between them to improve their relative positions in the world, whenever and wherever this can be done without seriously jeopardising their basic agreement to avoid wars.

This affects the Third World adversely in two ways: in the first place, the very stability of the global power balance and the determination of the great powers to avoid a confrontation makes them prone to seek lower levels of conflict and less dangerous ways of conducting their rivalries, which in effect means a concerted attempt to confine their conflicts to problems that impinge on them less directly and to localise them in such areas as are far removed from the areas where their vital interests are involved. To fight out their battles in the Third World is one way of ensuring that their own worlds are not touched by their conflicts and that they retain a greater measure of option to escalate and de-escalate these conflicts according to the needs of their relationships.

Again, the nature of their competition in the Third World has undergone a change: they are no longer in need of the Third World's conciliatory efforts to help them avoid wars nor are they in need of enlisting the support of individual Third World countries behind their global postures. Formerly, the competition between Russia and America led them to make efforts to persuade the established governments of Africa and Asia to take up such foreign policy postures as would be of use to them; now, the broad foreign policy stance of these governments is accepted and the effort is not so much to make a difference to what they are doing as to ensure that future internal developments in these countries will be in accord with their respective long-term interests. This transformation of the character of great power competition in most of these countries has contradictory impli- cations in the short and the long term: in the short term it is helpful for these states to know that none of the super powers is greatly interested in pushing them one way or the other; in the long term, however, it exposes them to grave risks of being converted into less than independent states.

The second adverse effect of this pattern of Soviet-American relation- ship is that it increases the dangers of local clashes and conflicts among the states of the Third World. To the extent that the central power balance has become immune from the contagious effects of Third World conflicts, to the extent that the stability of great power relations can be maintained in spite of local and regional disturbances, such conflicts and such disturbances have become permissible. The two super powers have demonstrated their capacity in situations like the Indo-Pakistan War to disengage themselves from such conflicts; even in the Arab-Israeli situation, where their direct interests are involved, they have shown a remarkable ability to reassure each other that a clash among their clients need not disturb their mutual relationship.

Indeed, the 1967 agreement at Glassboro is of great relevance in this context, as indication of what the great powers can and cannot do. In pur- suing their competitive interests the two super powers had lined up on opposing sides in the Arab-Israeli conflict; this eroded their capacity to prevent a major conflict in the area in 1967. All that they could do in response to the situation was to disengage themselves quickly from the conflict and to decide not to escalate it into a wider clash. They also hurried to decide that the stability of their mutual relations would not be permitted to be disturbed by these events. Having done so, they relapsed into their old postures and began to buttress their competitive interests through aid and encouragement to the conflicting parties. Although they formally entered into negotiations among themselves to devise ways and means to restore peace in the area, the awareness that their own relationship was not under any immediate threat deprived the great power discussions on the Middle East of the kind of urgency that alone could have brought them together to conceive and implement a reasonable peace plan. It was only when Soviet arms supplies to the United Arab Republic had increased the possibility of a great power clash over the region that forces were set in motion to bring about a cease fire.

In brief, although the relations between the super powers have been stabilised, there has been a perceptible rise in the level of permissibility of chaos, conflict, and violence in those regions of the world which are peripheral for the purposes of the central power balance. The evident fact that conflicts and clashes among the states of these regions provide the great powers with a high degree of leverage on them and a great opportunity to increase their influence over the parties in such a conflict must be appearing to the United States and the Soviet Union as a matter of some advantage, though as *status quo* states they cannot but be interested in maintaining a minimum degree of stability even in the remote regions of the world.

The core of the problem, therefore, is that the changes in the Soviet-American relationship have not been carried forward to the extent where they could have become meaningful for the Third World and that the process of change seems to have been arrested long before it could begin to produce the expected results. The two super powers have arrived at a stage of their relationship when they perceive the need to safeguard the present structure of modified bipolarity in the world, limit the power and influence of other competitors in the field, defuse those explosive situations which might affect their ability to preserve the stability of their relations and maintain a degree of co-operation in the face of the multifarious threats and pressures to alter the present world political system to their common disadvantage. But the assumption of the Third World leaders that this limited accord will automatically expand into an awareness of the imperative need jointly to help the less developed nations of the world and to an effort to create a new pattern of world order which will promote the welfare and security of *all* nations has proved to be facile.

The decline of bloc solidarity and the rise of China as a third super power have also had some adverse effects on the Third World, though, as noted earlier, there are some important positive aspects of these developments.[7] It was the Third World's hope that as the Soviet-American Cold War became less intense the salience of North-South issues would increase;

[7] It is obvious that there is still a vast gap between the military power of China and that of the two established super powers and it is still an open question whether this gap will ever be bridged. The industrial-technological resource base of China is in no way comparable to that of Russia or America. What is evident, however, is that the determination to bridge this gap is shared by the entire ruling élite of China. The main reason why China is listed as a super power in this essay is that it has already achieved and demonstrated its capacity to sustain an entirely autonomous power role in a world of super powers. This cannot be said to be true of other great powers like Britain or France, which, according to some, should now be treated as middle rather than great powers. The present writer is inclined to accept this new classification of the major powers. Hence the terms great power and super power are often used interchangeably in this essay.

in practice, however, the détente had shifted the focus of the world's attention to the policies and postures of the major allies of the two super powers
and the 1960s appear in retrospect to have indeed been the decade of the
disgruntled partners. As China broke away from the Soviet Union and
France began to defy the United States, the nations of Asia and Africa
found themselves reduced to the position of the fifth or the sixth world
in terms of their importance in the world.

The loosening of the Western bloc and the disintegration of the Sino-
Soviet alliance have both signified the decline of ideology as a factor in
world politics and thereby enhanced the role and relevance of the traditional
factors such as national power and the diplomacy of alignment and realign-
ment to create new power balances. To the extent that the salience of the
Third World was a function of the ideological tussle among the great
powers, the decline of ideology has adversely affected them. Similarly, the
free play of power politics tends to expose their individual and collective
weaknesses: lacking power and the necessary diplomatic skills to play the
game of power politics, the Third World states have been gradually rele-
gated from the position of an active and effective group of participants in
the processes of world politics to the position of a passive and ineffectual
set of extras on the world stage.

The rise of China as a super power has created new anxieties for many
Third World states, particularly in Asia. The vision that India once had of
creating an area of agreement in Asia among the great powers has faded
away; though the Soviet Union and the United States were at one stage
prepared to live up to these expectations, China clearly refused to act as a
stabilising force in Asia and demonstrated her intentions to change the
political map of the continent before considering any complementary role
vis-à-vis the other super powers. A triangular agreement on Asia is indeed
a chimera till such time as there is a wide gap between China's image of its
own legitimate role as a power in Asia and those of its adversaries about it.
The alternative that the other two powers will co-operate to create and
enforce a new political system in Asia, in the face of China's expressed
opposition to it, has also become less and less possible as China has
acquired the power to back up her foreign policy objectives. For one thing,
the revolutionary movements in Asia cannot be wished away by the great
powers and the Soviet Union cannot afford to side overtly with the forces
of status quo in Asian societies, so long as it competes with China for the
loyalty of the revolutionary forces. For another, the creation of a stable
triangular power balance and the eventual accommodation of China into a
new super power system (steps which must precede any effort to create a
triangular system) are more important items on the great powers' agenda
than the creation of a Soviet-American area of agreement in Asia. The
advantage that a super power may derive against its adversary by enlisting

China on its side (for at least certain purposes), and the disadvantage of pulling it too far towards the other, are also considerations that inhibit any attempt in this direction.

At the beginning of the 1970s, the major question that creates concern in the world is whether the transition from a two to a three power world would be easy and what rules of the game would have to be evolved to sustain a triangular power balance. The anxieties of the Third World are many: will a triangular balance be as stable as the Soviet-American balance or will it mean that the world will again be obsessed with the threat of a catastrophic nuclear conflict among the great powers? Will the rise of China tend to exacerbate the internal tensions within developing societies? Will China, as the weakest of the three super powers, continue to try to augment its power by posing as the champion of the cause of revolution in Asia, Africa, and Latin America? Will China's emergence as a super power mean the acquisition by her of a sphere of influence in Asia? Will it be a corollary of a triangular balance that the influence of the three powers would have to be demarcated on ground through recourse to the orthodox method of defining and delimiting spheres of influence? Will it mean a further erosion of the role of the United Nations or, alternatively, a greater role for the Security Council as against the General Assembly? Will the increase in the number of the major actors on the world stage further reduce the import- ance of the mass of small and weak states of the world?

It is not easy to anticipate the shape into which the present fluid inter- national system will eventually solidify. At one end of the spectrum of the practical, as against the theoretical, possibilities is the emergence of a three or four great power system,[8] in which the roles of each of them have been more clearly defined in geographical terms and under which the smaller and weaker powers of the world are mainly preoccupied with determining the pattern of their relations with the dominant great power of the region, in much the same way as the smaller nations of Eastern Europe and Latin America are today preoccupied. It can be argued that this indeed is the inevitable ultimate consequence of the coming into being of a situation in which there are more than two or three independent centres of power, as in the pre-war world, but in which, unlike in other periods of history, each is constrained by the logic of the military revolution not to resort to large- scale wars to press its claims against another great power. Since it is danger- ous for any new incumbent to challenge the predominance of the older great powers in regions where their supremacy has been recognised for years, the only available course for it to satisfy its urge to acquire a great

[8] The emergence of a fourth great power in the world would depend on the manner in which Western Europe tackles its problems of unity in the coming years.

power status and for others to confer it is to try to have some of the grey areas of the world allocated to it.

At the other end of the spectrum of possibilities is a pattern of great power relations in which they fail to evolve any agreed approach to the problem of creating a new global system and confine their area of agreement to the bare minimum of the need to avoid a nuclear war or a direct confrontation among them. A pre-condition for the success of the working of such a model of great power relations would be their common and conscious design to relegate the problems of other powers and regions of the world to a position of such insignificance and marginality as to reduce their capacity to affect the stability of great power relations. A minimal world order, which would essentially rest on the principle of separation of the problems of great power relations from those of the peripheral regions would appear to be the logical goal of the great powers if they are unwilling or unable to attempt the creation of a global order.

If one is asked to hazard a guess on the basis of the current trends in world politics one would be inclined to take the view that it is in fact one of the variants of such a model of minimal order that the great powers can in the foreseeable future seek to create. In the first place, the outstanding feature of the politics of the last decade has been the steady decline of the relative power and influence of the West—or of those Western powers which have been historically concerned with the problem of maintaining a pattern of world order and guarding the *status quo*. The disengagement of the Western European powers from their involvements in various parts of the world, which were bequeathed to them by their empires, is nearly complete. The inescapable reality that the United States is not able, even if it is willing, to act as the world's gendarme has already created neo-isolationist tendencies in that country. It is likely that the United States will in the future give up its ambition to reorganise the world according to its own preferences and adopt a more modest goal for its foreign policies.

The great but unanswerable question is whether the Soviet Union, conscious of its strength and power in the 1970s, will try to step into the shoes of the West and perform certain order enforcing roles that the West had been performing in various parts of the world. There are certainly a few indications that the Soviet Union does not like the idea of an anarchic world: it has been regarded by many analysts for some time as the world's second most important *status quo* power and the ideas of European and Asian security that are occasionally thrown up from Moscow can be cited as instances of the Soviet search for order. In regard to China, in particular, the Soviet Union has a greater compulsion even than the Western powers to try to limit its influence through the creation of orderly regions around that country. As against this, however, account must be taken of the fact that the Soviet Union is still committed to an ideology that attaches greater importance to change than to order, that it will find it difficult to burn its boats with the revolutionary forces in the developing countries of the world, that its *status quo* role may not find full expression till the West's rejection of a predominant role for itself it total and complete, that it may have derived some lessons from the West's discomfiture in enforcing order around the world and that its relative power and influence as one of the world's three super powers may never be comparable to that of the West in the 1950s and early 1960s. A more viable Soviet line would be to work in co-operation with the West to preserve and promote a minimum degree of order and stability, while pursuing its competition with it in selected areas.

As for China, it is extremely unlikely that in the next decade or so it will develop such an overwhelming stake in world order as to share the burden of maintaining it with other great powers, thereby denying to itself the advantages that are now accruing to it as the world's most identifiable anti-*status quo* force. The road to parity with other super powers will be long and arduous; its internal needs will point towards a revolutionary stance in the world; there will be no world war to legitimise its expansion into certain areas; it has a number of significant middle powers like India, Japan, and Indonesia to contend with; and finally, what partially makes up the gap between its physical capabilities and those of the other super powers is its anti-*status quo* stance. As a revolutionary and anti-*status quo* force it requires a lesser foreign policy input to produce a given amount of foreign policy output in a region where the situation is revolutionary and ripe for change; the resources required to preserve a *status quo* in a region like Asia are much greater than those required to upset it. The most that can be expected of China therefore is that it will formally agree to enter into a dialogue with other powers on issues like arms control and agree to adopt a public posture which is conducive to the creation of stable great power relations; the minimum that can be expected is that it will, without entering into such dialogues, abide by certain rules of the international game, as indeed it may have been doing all along.

A triangular balance will mean the lowest possible level of order in the world; any agreement of the great powers to regulate their own relations will for some time to come have to be upheld by a simultaneous agreement to permit the free play of forces in other areas of international relations. A slightly neater variant of this model, which would aspire to create a higher level of order, is the one that would treat China as an outsider, at least temporarily, and emphasise the relationship among the developed countries as the key to peace and stability of the world. This has been cogently advocated by some Western theoreticians and public men and it is necessary to discuss this in some detail.

The core of this idea is that the old concept of one world is either too unwieldy or too difficult to implement: it is overambitious for the central powers of the world to think that they will be able to erect a global system; for they are not individually capable of doing so and a collective effort on their part must in the foreseeable future remain beyond the realm of possibility. Hence the need for a new concept of what may be called an 'inner' and an 'outer' world—a concept that would apply the Lin Piao theory in reverse.

The assumption is that the relations among the world's central powers, or its cities, are the key to global peace and stability and North America, Western Europe, the Soviet Union, and Japan must act as the four pillars of a world system of the future. The hope is that if the relations among these countries can be maintained at a satisfactory level, the inner world or the world of the central powers can be insulated from the pressures and problems generated in the outer world or the world of the rural slums of the Third World. Should these powers be able to evolve a very satisfactory relationship among themselves, it might be possible for them eventually to integrate the Third World into their system; but so long as their own relations are less than co-operative, the major effort must continue to be one of ensuring that these are not disturbed by extraneous elements.

The primary need from the viewpoint of this school of thought is therefore to give up the old style globalism, to separate the problems of stability in the inner world from those of the outer, and to prevent the latter from casting its shadows over the former. If the relative power at the disposal of the central powers remains as high as it is today and if the relationship among them is one of mutual co-operation, the authority that will emanate from the inner world will probably be adequate to manage the world's villages. If it is not, the cities of the world would still be able to live with a high degree of instability and turbulence in the outer world.

George Ball has suggested as 'a first principle of American foreign policy', that 'we should make a crucial conceptual distinction in our foreign policy between the problems of the Northern Zone on the one hand and the peripheral Southern areas on the other'. To him a hard but quite obvious reality is 'the fact that the loud and insistent problems of the Third World are in a real sense a hostage to what we accomplish in the industrialized nations —to how we Americans and Europeans and Russians and Japanese order and structure our own relations'. He also believes that 'while shifts in the industrialized world can deeply affect the power balance that preserves a fragile armed peace short of general, nuclear havoc, political changes in the less-developed areas are likely to have only a marginal influence'.[9]

The same idea of a community of developed nations has been advocated by Brzezinski,[10] though in more universalised terms, just as this scheme of

[9] George Ball, *The Discipline of Power*. London: Bodley Head, 1968, pp. 233, 346.
[10] Z. Brzezinski, 'Peace and Power'. *Survival*, December 1968.

things has been anticipated in a slightly different manner by the British Committee on reforms in the Foreign Office.[11]

The less tidy model, in which China assumes a larger role than that allotted to it above, attempts no such system building but concentrates mainly on the regulation of the relationship among the three super powers and leaves a large area of international politics to the free interplay of the multifarious forces of global and regional power politics. It is a natural concomitant of the attempt to create a minimum area of agreement among the super powers whose interests, motivations, and goals are still largely incompatible that a great deal of chaos and conflict over a wide range of subjects and areas should be regarded as inevitable.

But there is no indication as yet, notwithstanding the Cultural Revolution and other internal excesses in China, that Peking will play the role of the catalytic agent to bring about such a world system. In fact, it has already shown a remarkable agility in varying its attitudes to its two major adversaries in order to prevent any such possibility. It would of course be wrong for China to believe that it can disturb Soviet-American relations to a point where it can make either of them pull its chestnuts out of the fire. But it seems to have already succeeded in burying many of the ideas that were being toyed with by Western and Soviet system builders in the late 1950s and early 1960s.

It is apparent that such a minimal world order would by itself be of little help to the Third World. It may be reassuring for them to know that no such neat great power dominated world system in which their room for manoeuvre would be further curtailed is in the offing. But the progressive reduction of the influence of great powers over the world is not an end in itself; it is a means to achieve a more equitable world order and of greater participation by the Third World states in the international political processes. A system of world politics in which the Third World is quarantined or left to stew in its own juice, while the great powers and their partners enjoy the relatively healthier climate of an immunised and insulated world of the central powers, can be no more a desirable goal than the one of a world dominated by a few great powers.

The basic interests of the Third World states in the changed environment of the 1970s remain what they were when they began to emerge as independent nation states: the maintenance of stable great power relations so as to ensure world peace, the strengthening of international organisations and institutions, the improvement of their position as a factor in global politics, the projection of issues of North-South relations into world political debates, the creation of a climate in which their tasks of internal progress

[11] *Report of the Review Committee on Overseas Representation*, 1968-69. London: HMSO, 1969, pp. 12-13.

become easier to achieve and the promotion of their security through the gradual elimination of the lines that now separate their affairs from those of the central powers. The implications of the pursuit of these goals are, however, very different now from what they were two decades ago.

While non-alignment itself was a policy of being equally friendly (or aloof) from the two blocs, its implications in a triangular situation have not been spelt out. The fact that many of the Asian countries are either directly or indirectly involved in political conflicts with China makes it unlikely that all the Third World states would be able to opt for non-alignment in a triangular contest with as much ease as they refrained from joining the Soviet-American tussle. Yet, the improvement of Soviet-Chinese and American-Chinese relations are the pre-conditions for the kind of stabilisation of great power relations in which they are interested.

It is not impossible that once the Chinese begin to pursue the same set of objectives in their diplomacy in the Third World as the other great powers are doing, it will become easy for these countries to fall back on their traditional policies of non-alignment and to try to be friendly with all the three great powers. But the Chinese may not choose to pursue such a course. For one thing, they may show a greater inclination than others to join the internal political battles in the Third World countries, thus pushing the ruling élites of these societies away from their path of non-alignment and equidistance. For another, the Chinese expectations from the Third World countries may be higher: China may regard itself as the vanguard of the Third World's struggle against the established order and seek to enlist the positive support (and not mere neutrality) of many of these countries behind its policies and programs. As said before, the crucial thing about the triangular balance of power is that a power of self-admitted inferiority is trying to emerge as the equal of two other powers who are on all available indications far superior to it. Till such time as an effective parity of power between China and the other super powers is established, it would be natural for it to seek to offset their advantages by other means. Ideology, encouragement to revolutionary forces, pressures on the non-aligned to align, attempts to get the other great powers caught in the quagmire of the Third World's conflicts are all methods which are open to China to make good the power gap between it and its adversaries. The Third World's ability to play any role in the affairs of the great powers would largely depend on how it responds to the various kinds of challenges and opportunities that the rise of China as a super power would mean for them.

China is even more important for the Third World when it thinks of its goal of strengthening international institutions. The exclusion of China from the United Nations has already crippled the world organisation; if it continues to remain outside the United Nations the tendency to shift the responsibility for making the fundamental decisions of world politics to other agencies, where China is represented, would become stronger. Already the United States is busy devising institutions like the Warsaw talks to maintain lines of communications with China: it would not be surprising if the current border negotiations between Russia and China were to expand into a wider dialogue on relations between these two super powers. These trends could easily find more concrete expression in the creation of tripartite institutions, for such purposes as arms control. The exclusion of China from the United Nations has thus become a matter of even greater significance now than it was in the decade after the Communist Revolution in China.

The problem of strengthening the United Nations is, however, greater than one of seating China; basically, it is a problem of underlining to all the great powers that it would be safer and easier for them to throw the onus of finding solutions to international problems (and of enforcing agreed solutions) on the world organisation, rather than to carry it themselves. It is only to the extent that the inefficacy of the great power mechanism in solving the world's problems are demonstrated that there will be any need for them to turn to the world body. So far, the United Nations has been largely engaged in playing the role of the legitimiser of such agreements as the great powers have been able to evolve; to emerge as a more important factor in world politics it will have to take upon itself the role of peace-making and peacekeeping on a greater scale.

The identification of its goals and objectives is the less important part of the task that the Third World faces: the more important task is to determine the extent of its leverage over the policies and postures of the great powers and to find out the options it can avail of to make itself a more important actor on the world stage. While it is true that in the last decade the Third World's influence has declined and that great power relations have assumed a degree of autonomy that they did not have earlier, there are still many reasons for it to feel confident that any idea or scheme that relegates it to a position of insignificance will be very hard to implement.

In the first place, notwithstanding the decline of ideology as a factor in foreign policy-making, both the Western and the Communist societies still contain many elements which are concerned with long-term world problems and which think of global solutions to many of the emergent problems of their countries. For example, some of the problems of environment, which are assuming increasing importance, can only be tackled through international co-operation. Likewise, many of the technological pursuits of the developed countries (the exploration of the sea beds or the conquest of outer space) require world-wide consent and support. These specific questions apart, there are idealistic men in all societies who still regard it to be not only immoral but unwise to ignore the problems of the welfare of the impoverished sections of humanity; a degree of moral and political pressure on the developed countries to help the underdeveloped is therefore likely to continue. It is true that many of the protesters in today's America or Europe have shown a singular lack of interest in wider international issues. But it is reasonable to hope that the present ferment in affluent societies of the West will result in the evolution of a more meaningful international-ism than the globalism of the imperialists and the Cold War enthusiasts meant. Similarly, the trends towards liberalism within the Communist world will hopefully lend further emphasis on the humanitarian aspects of Marxist ideology, both nationally and internationally. The Third World countries do not have the resources needed to join the issues within the developed countries in the same way that the great powers have been try-ing to join the issues within their societies. They can, however, make their preferences clear and do whatever little is possible to strengthen those elements in the affluent societies which are internationally oriented.

Secondly, the countries of the Third World still possess considerable capacity to exacerbate the conflicts among the great powers by varying their attitudes to them. For example, Israel and the Arab countries have already succeeded in converting their region from a region of low level great power tension to a region of high level great power tension. In the same way, the Sino-Soviet competition offers to some Asian (if not African) countries new opportunities to assert what may be called their nuisance value: it would not be difficult for an Asian country to pursue a set of policies which are so clearly advantageous to one great power that they are bound to create anxieties among the rest. Admittedly, there are grave risks for any smaller power in trying to follow such policies; the whole exercise may end in its being named as a part of the sphere of influence of the great power that it begins to favour. Yet, pressed to the walls and driven to desperation, some of them may well think of so modifying their policies of non-alignment as to be able to tempt one or more of the great powers to become involved in its affairs. In other words, many of the Third World states still have the capacity to disturb any agreement among the great powers over their future, though this will require a great deal of re-evalua-tion of the basic tenets of their foreign policies and expose them to grave risks.

Thirdly, they may hope to re-emerge as an important factor in world politics through a renewed bid to achieve a degree of solidarity among themselves. While there has been no attempt since 1965 to hold another Afro-Asian conference, the Third World states have found it possible to keep alive the idea of consultation and co-operation among the non-aligned. The fact that Afro-Asianism has declined at a faster pace than non-align-ment is partly a reflection of the reality that great power rivalries (particu-larly those among the two Communist powers) tend to be a more important divisive force in the former than in the latter; moreover, there is less problem of acceptability and legitimacy for an association of the smaller and weaker states of the world than there is of an association of the small and large underprivileged nations of a given region of the world. Though the significance of any conference of the non-aligned has considerably diminished in the last few years, it may still provide the Third World states with some kind of a forum for articulating their common demands.

A more obvious area where common action is necessary and possible is the one covered by the Group of 77 within the UNCTAD. Behind the political militancy of the Third World states has been an acute awareness of their social and economic needs: once the politicians of the Third World have had their say in well-publicised international conferences, the technocrats and officials of these countries have found it easy to sit down quietly and evolve a number of concrete economic proposals which are of practical relevance for all of them. Whatever might happen to political co-operation among the poor nations of the world, it is only likely that they will continue to perceive the need for and succeed in presenting a solid front in international conferences dealing with such issues as trade and development.

A degree of co-ordination of the policies and attitudes of the Third World states is also possible at the United Nations. Of particular relevance to the Third World are issues on which the interests of the smaller and the larger powers are divergent and conflicting. For example, it is extremely important for the smaller countries of the world to have the principle of internationalisation of the control over and use of sea beds and outer space accepted, just as the great powers are naturally interested in extending their own control over such matters. Similarly, the question of reforms in the structure and organisation of the United Nations are of vital significance for the Third World, whereas the great powers find the existing arrangements, concluded in a phase of history when their predominance over the world was more marked, quite satisfactory.

One of the ways in which some Third World leaders have been hoping to augment their political leverage is regional co-operation. In fact many of them had grand visions of regional solidarity before and immediately after the achievement of their independence.

Their early enthusiasm for regional co-operation was, however, soon marred by their discovery that it could turn out to be the most potent available instrument in the hands of the West to organise the entire world of new nations into various pro-Western regional blocs. Also relevant as inhibiting factors were their awareness that the mutual fears and rivalries among them were often acute, that their historical ties with the metropolitan countries of Europe were stronger than those with their neighbours and that their own assessments of their security problems could be very divergent. However, the growing power gap between them and the great powers, the fear that individually they would be unable to withstand the various challenges to their integrity and sovereignty and the hope that through regionalism they would be able to project themselves as significant quantities in world politics have all combined once again to insert regionalism as one of the items on the agenda of the foreign policies of many Third World states.

The most important question that the Third World states are faced with is whether they can ever re-introduce themselves as active participants in international politics without acquiring a relatively higher degree of power than that which they now possess. This indeed is the question that China has forcefully posed. The problem, however, is relevant for only a few of the Third World countries which have the potential to emerge as regional powers of some consequence and thus to enter the select band of countries which will be regarded as the pillars of a world system of the future. Indeed, the pursuit of power by the middle powers of Asia, Africa, and Latin America can bring about a greater differentiation within the Third World and adversely affect the other goal of its solidarity. Nevertheless, as Kahn and Weiner have said, if a community of developed nations should come into being 'the Third World might indeed need countervailing power either to protect itself or to stimulate the possibly apathetic and indifferent community to take an interest'.[12]

Such conscious designs apart, it is quite possible that internal political trends within the Third World countries will tend to rectify some of their present internal weaknesses and to increase the level of interest of the great powers in their affairs. The revolution of rising expectations, the increasing politicisation of the masses, the growth of revolutionary movements, the urgency to absorb Western technology and the rapid improvement of communications among nations are all contributing to the creation of radical politics within the societies of most Third World states. There are still a few countries which have all the social, economic, and political infra-structure for stagnation, but in many Third World countries the low level political equilibrium has been disturbed beyond redemption. Though this could well mean a prolonged period of political gestation before more productive systems are evolved, it appears reasonable to hope that a stagnated Third World has already become a contradiction in terms. The capacity of the Third World to project itself in any important international role will ultimately be a function at the pace at which internal changes and internal progress are achieved in their societies.

The possibilities mentioned above make it obvious that though the Third World may not be able to achieve all its aspirations in the foreseeable future, it is by no means entirely without options when it begins to consider its problems in the changing world environment. Much will depend on whether the developed nations, led by the great powers, will regard them-

[12] Herman Kahn and A. J. Weiner, *The Year 2000*. New York: Macmillan, 1967, p. 379.

selves as the secure power élite in a welfare oriented international society or as a highly insecure privileged group in an international society which is still in the state of nature. In case they get over their present feeling of insecurity individually in relation to each other and collectively in relation to future claimants, it should be possible for the developing countries to behave like the legitimate trade unionists in a welfare state. In case they do not, the Third World may have to tread the much longer and the much more arduous road to power and prosperity through self-reliance before they can break the vicious circle of political insignificance, social stagnation, and economic underdevelopment.

L

WORLD ORDER AND THE SUPER POWERS

Sometimes when we speak of world order (or of *the* world order) what we have in mind is the totality of relationships among states, the international political system as a whole. But this is not what we mean when we ask the question with which this concluding chapter is concerned: what is the contribution of the super powers to world order? For here we are thinking of order as a quality which may or may not obtain in international politics at any one place or time, or which may be present to a greater or lesser degree: order as opposed to disorder. And this raises the question of what world order in this sense is.

To say of a number of things that together they display order is, in the simplest and most general sense, to say that they are related according to some pattern, that their relationship is not purely haphazard but contains some discernible principle. A row of books on a bookshelf displays order, while a heap of books on the floor does not.

But when in international politics (or in politics or social life generally) we speak of order as a goal to be striven after, an objective to be pursued, we have in mind not any pattern, but a pattern of a particular sort. For a pattern may be evident in the relations of two states confronting each other 'in the state and posture of gladiators', or in the relations of desperadoes locked in a struggle to the death, yet these are situations which, viewed in relation to order as a goal or objective, we should characterise as disorderly.

The order which we take to be desirable in social life is not any pattern or regularity in social phenomena, but a pattern drawn so as to produce a particular result, an arrangement of social life such that it fulfils a certain goal. In this purposive sense a number of books display order when they are not merely placed in a row, but arranged according to their author or subject so as to facilitate the purpose of selection. It was this purposive conception of order that Augustine had in mind when he defined it as 'a good disposition of discrepant parts, each in its fittest place'.

This is a definition which at once raises the question: 'good' or 'fittest' for what? Order in this purposive sense is necessarily a relative concept: an arrangement (say, of books) that is orderly in relation to one purpose

140

(finding a book by a particular author) may be disorderly in relation to another (finding a book on a particular subject). It is for this reason that disagreement may legitimately obtain as to whether or not a particular set of social arrangements embodies order, or that political systems that are opposed to one another may both embody order: the political orders of the *ancien régime* and of Revolutionary France, of Imperial Russia and of the Bolsheviks, the international order of Napoleon and of the Quadruple Alliance, of the Soviet Union and the United States, have each been orchestrated so as to fulfil different goals or promote different values.

But while order in this purposive sense exists only in relation to given goals, certain of these goals stand out as elementary or primary, inasmuch as their fulfilment in some measure is a condition not merely of this or that sort of social life, but of social life as such. Whatever other goals they pursue, all societies recognise these goals and embody arrangements structured so as to promote them. These are the expectations that life will be in some measure secure against violence resulting in death or bodily harm; that promises will be kept or agreements honoured; and that possession will remain stable to some degree, and will not be subject to challenges that are constant and without limit.

The order which is taken to be desirable in social life is a pattern of activity drawn so as to promote these elementary, primary, or universal goals of social life: characteristically, it is a pattern drawn by rules requiring that the taking of life be limited, that agreements be kept and that property be respected. This, at all events, is a close approximation to what is commonly meant by the everyday notion of order as a desirable feature of social life.

International order is a pattern of activity drawn so as to fulfil the equivalent elementary or primary goals of the society of sovereign states, goals which are secured by the rules (expressed in international law, but prior to international law itself) requiring immunity for envoys, the keeping of agreements, and mutual respect for sovereign jurisdiction. These and related basic rules express the requirements not of this or that sort of international society, but of any attempt to found the political organisation of mankind upon the conception of a society of states.

World order is a pattern of activity drawn so as to promote the primary or elementary goals of social life in human society as a whole. It is as a society of sovereign states (rather than, for example, as a universal empire or as a single cosmopolitan society) that mankind as a whole is now politically organised, but international order is in the last analysis only a means of sustaining world order.

At all events if our moral starting-point is the proposition that the justification of political institutions must ultimately relate to the interests and the rights of individual human beings rather than of states or nations, and these interests and rights belong to all individuals equally, irrespective of the special groups or associations to which they belong, then we are committed to the view that order among sovereign states is valuable only to the extent that it promotes order in the great society of all mankind.

If this is what we mean by world order then in thinking about it there are certain pitfalls of which we should be aware. We should avoid the temptation to identify world order with a patterning or structuring of international life towards the preferred goals of some particular power or group of powers, to confuse world order with, for example, an American-preferred, a Soviet-preferred or a super power-preferred world order. When in the Western world today terms such as 'order' or 'stability' are used, it is an ordering of international relationships that subserves such American-preferred or Western-preferred goals that is often meant. What is meant here, by contrast, is a quality of order that may be abstracted from particular 'preferred' international orders, that comprises a structuring of international life in relation to elementary or primary goals.

Furthermore, we should avoid making the assumption that order is the sole or the overriding goal of international society, the only or the chief test in relation to which the worth of international institutions and practices is to be assessed. World order as we have described it implies norms or rules, and we single it out for attention partly at least because we ourselves assent to these rules, treat them as having 'value'. But it is important to recognise that order in world politics is only one of a number of contending values, that its claims have to be weighed alongside those of change, justice, prosperity, and perhaps peace, and that to show that some course of action is a requirement of world order is not to have established that it should be undertaken.

The term 'super powers' may be traced back at least as far as 1944, when Professor W. T. R. Fox applied it to Britain as well as the United States and the Soviet Union.[1] It is erroneous to define the super powers in terms of military nuclear capacity: although (as Professor Burns points out above) nuclear capacity is a necessary condition of super powerhood, it is not a sufficient condition; moreover, the super powers were recognisable as such before their strategic nuclear armaments were fully developed (and, in the case of Russia, before they existed at all). What the term super power essentially recognises is the appearance since the end of World War II of a new class of power, superior to the traditional European great powers, and alone capable of undertaking the central, managerial role in international politics they have traditionally played. The emergence of the United States and the Soviet Union in 1945 so dwarfed Britain, France, and

[1] See W. T. R. Fox, *The Super Powers: The United States, Britain and the Soviet Union—Their Responsibility for Peace.* New York: Harcourt Brace, 1944.

Germany that it has ever since seemed inappropriate to use the term 'great power' to describe a status which all of these countries have in common. It has seemed necessary either to reserve the term great power for the United States and the Soviet Union, and to treat the major European powers as having an inferior status (for example, to treat them as secondary powers, as Mr Richardson does above, or as middle powers), or to speak of the United States and the Soviet Union as super powers, possessing a status higher than that of merely great powers. The former practice is to be preferred; only the super powers are today in the full sense great powers, and the role they play in world politics is one they have inherited from the former European great powers.

To say of a country that it is a great power is to imply that it is in the front rank of military powers; as Ranke said, a great power is one that can maintain itself against any other power without allies. But a definition merely in terms of military strength would fail to convey the special meaning the term has had in modern history. A country which is a great power is one that is recognised by other states to have a certain status in the international hierarchy. Such a state is entitled to have a voice in the resolution of issues that are not its immediate concern; it is expected to take a leading part in the affairs of the international system as a whole; it is, in other words, not merely the depository of a certain degree of armed strength, but the bearer of certain special rights and duties. To speak of great powers (or, in present day terms, of super powers) is already to presuppose the existence of an international society in which these states are 'great responsibles'.

It is sometimes considered that the great powers or super powers, far from being the guardians or custodians of international order, are the chief source of international disorder. In the post-war world, for example, it has often been contended that the Cold War, or the arms race, or the widening gap between the rich nations and the poor, is the work chiefly of the United States and the Soviet Union. It is held that the super powers are responsible for the disorder (and the injustice) that exists in the world, to a degree to which small states are not; and indeed that what chiefly obstructs the achievement of international order is that those who have the power to promote it do not have the will, whereas those who have the will do not have the power. There are many who believe that if the power wielded by the United States and the Soviet Union were available to Sweden, or Switzerland, or the non-aligned states of Asia and Africa we could expect to look forward to a more orderly or at least to a more just world system.

It is easy to see why this line of thought should seem persuasive. The history of international relations is in fact chiefly made by the great powers, and since it includes disorder and injustice this lends to the great powers the appearance of being the chief troublemakers. The notion that if power

had been exercised by others, this disorder and injustice might have been
avoided appeals to our progressive instincts, our will to believe that things
might have been and might be 'better' than they are.

To take this view, however, would be to overlook the possibility that
things might have been 'worse' than they have been; that while the history
of modern international society conforms to a pattern of war, insecurity,
and confusion, there are woven into this pattern elements of peace, security,
and stability; that this part of history has also been made by the great
powers, and that but for the role they have been able to play it might not
have been present.

Moreover, the idea that it is the great powers or super powers and not
small or weak states that are responsible for disorder and injustice in the
world, overlooks the fact that it is the states with superior power that
have superior opportunities. In order to establish that Sweden or Switzerland or India or Abyssinia was more virtuous than America or Russia we
should need to consider not merely what their record has been as states
whose opportunities for managing the world's affairs are in any case minimal, but how they would be likely to have acted if the temptations of great
power had actually been placed in their way. Many small states are in fact
troublemakers on the small stages on which they play a role; and while
there are others which, like Switzerland, enjoy a reputation for keeping out
of trouble or, like Sweden, one for espousing innocuous causes and promoting good works, theirs is a virtue deriving essentially from innocence of high
politics, not one tested by experience of it.

The contribution of the super powers to international order (like that of
other great powers in previous epochs) derives in the first instance from the
sheer facts of inequality of power as between the states that make up the
international system. If states were equal in power as they are in law, and
every state could assert its claims with the same degree of force as every
other, then it is difficult to see how, apart from resort to alliances that may
introduce a contrived element of inequality, international conflicts could
ever be settled and laid to rest, or the claims of any one state definitely
granted or denied.

Because states are grossly unequal in power certain international issues
are as a consequence settled, the demands of certain states (weak ones)
can in practice be left out of account, the demands of certain other states
(strong ones) recognised to be the only ones relevant to the issue in hand.
Because the United States is not merely one of a number of equal powers
within the Western alliance, but enjoys a position of leadership or primacy,
certain conflicts within this alliance are kept within bounds or prevented
from reaching the surface of conscious political activity. Because the Soviet
Union enjoys a hegemonial position in Eastern Europe, which it is willing

to defend by force, certain conflicts of interest in Eastern Europe are for this reason resolved, certain claims that Poland, Czechoslovakia, the German Democratic Republic, Hungary, Bulgaria, and Rumania might make of Russia or of each other are known to have no prospect of being met and are in some cases not even raised. When the two alliances negotiate over European political questions or the arms balance in central Europe it is known that the views of the United States and the Soviet Union have a significance which the views, for example, of Belgium or of Bulgaria do not have, and for this reason a structure is imparted to the negotiation which otherwise would not be present.

The inequality of states in terms of power has the effect, in other words, of simplifying the pattern of international relations, of ensuring that some states will prevail while others will go under, that certain conflicts will form the essential theme of international politics while others will be submerged. Thus it is possible for Ranke to tell the story of European international history (though with some distortion) as the history of relations among the great powers, and for the contemporary student or practitioner of international politics contemplating the vast and amorphous world body politic, to distinguish the relations among the great powers as its essential skeleton.

This effect the great powers have of simplifying the pattern of international politics, of reducing the vast agenda of world affairs to the smaller number of issues that arise between the 'essential actors', follows from the sheer facts of inequality of power, independently of what particular policies the great powers are pursuing. Even a great power whose policy was one of systematic aggrandisement, which sought only to override the rights and interests of other states, would by its very existence serve this end of simplification or reduction.

But over and above this contribution great powers make by virtue simply of the position they occupy in the tables of relative strength, they may play a role in the promotion of international order as the consequence of policies they pursue that work for it rather than against it. In some cases these policies will affect the preservation of order only in some area of the world or some segment of international society; in other cases they will relate to the maintenance of order throughout international society as a whole. In some cases these policies will be carried through without any conscious perception of the ordering role they fulfil, without any sense of a burden assumed or a trust fulfilled; in other cases some sense of the special mission of a great power as a custodian or trustee of the interests of international society at large may be found to have entered into the carrying out of the task. In some cases a great power may act so as to promote international order in a way that is wholly unilateral, independent of any reciprocal action on the part of other great powers; in other cases the action may be part of some structure of agreement among the great powers, or certain of them, to shape their policies in relation to objectives held in common.

The super powers may be said to shape their policies so as to contribute to world order in two main ways: by managing the balance of power between them, and by exploiting their joint predominance in relation to the rest of the world.

The Soviet-American or central balance of power vitally affects the prospects of order in international society as a whole. If the balance of power were to be decisively upset in the sense that one of the super powers became predominant over the other this would undermine the general balance of power within the international system as a whole, and place one state in a position of dominance from which it might threaten not only the independence of some states but the survival of the system of sovereign states itself. If the Soviet-American balance, even though it remained intact, were to issue in nuclear conflict between the super powers, this would be a catastrophe in which international society as a whole would be engulfed.

A decisive element in the Soviet-American balance is the situation of mutual deterrence brought about by the belief among decision makers on each side that the opposing super power, if subject to a direct attack, has the ability and the will to retaliate so as to cause an unacceptable degree of damage or destruction to the civil society of the attacking power. If this situation were to be undermined and one of the super powers came to believe it could attack the other with impunity, there might result a threat not only to the balance of power but also to the nuclear peace, which now rests on (among other things) the belief that nuclear war between the super powers cannot serve as a rational instrument of policy.

In principle the relationship of mutual deterrence as between the United States and the Soviet Union could be undermined either by changes in military technology or by changes in the way in which the military situation is perceived by the decision makers. The objective situation might be changed either by the development by one side or both of a disarming capacity, in the sense of a capacity to eliminate or cripple the other side's strategic retaliatory forces before they are brought into action, or by the development of an effective means of defending cities and populations against nuclear attack. Recent developments in strategic nuclear technology, such as the MIRV and the ABM, discussed by Dr Bellany above, pose the question whether such upsets are not now in sight, but it is likely that this question should be answered in the negative. Even in the presence of an objective Soviet-American strategic nuclear stalemate, however, there could be an erosion of the subjective factors on which the stalemate depends: the assessments made on each side about the strength and will of the other, and about the acceptability or otherwise of the likely damage that would result from an encounter. These factors are harder to assess but it is on them rather than on the objective stalemate (which, in strict logic, is not necessary to the situation of mutual deterrence at all) that the persistence of the stalemate depends.

The United States and the Soviet Union are still very far from having accepted a balance of power as the relationship between them for which each should strive, except in the field of strategic nuclear armaments, and even here the issue is very much in doubt: the balance that has obtained in their relationship is chiefly the fortuitous product of efforts on both sides to achieve preponderance. But the super powers have avoided war with one another, and beyond this they have gone to considerable lengths to provide safeguards or firebreaks against the possibility that a central nuclear war might break out, some of which are described above by Dr Coral Bell under the headings 'the exchange of hostages', 'surveillance', 'a common strategic ideology', and 'the convention of crisis management'.

These terms perhaps suggest a degree of conscious co-operation in the working of common institutions that is more an aspiration than a reality in the Soviet-American relationship. Mutual deterrence (or the exchange of hostages) is a fact, but it is not universally accepted as a goal of policy even in the West. Mutual surveillance is a fact, and so is a degree of tolerance of one another's surveillance, but the co-operation involved is subterranean; in official policy there is no agreed system of mutual inspection but only espionage and counter-espionage. There is some common understanding about the characteristics of strategic weapons and the meaning of their use, but 'a common strategic ideology' (in the sense, for example, of a common doctrine as to which weapons are stabilising and which de-stabilising, as to what levels and kinds of weapons are required for deterrence, as to what are the conditions under which limitations might be preserved in a central war) is something which might one day emerge as the consequence of protracted arms control negotiations, but which does not exist yet: in the meantime the problem of the strategic arms limitation talks is to reach accords in the absence of any such common strategic doctrine. An understanding does now exist that the super powers will consult so as to decouple their relationship from local crises; but 'crisis management' should be understood as the art of conducting policy in a crisis not merely so as to avoid the nuclear catastrophe which both sides wish to avoid, but also so as to inflict a diplomatic defeat on the adversary; this certainly is the sort of crisis management in which the super powers engage. But there is no doubt that the super powers, especially in the period since 1963, have taken important steps towards achieving a measure of security against a Soviet-American nuclear war, and that many outside Russia and America share Dr Bell's view that this is what provides 'the adverse partnership' with its chief justification.

M

Apart from managing the balance of power between one another the super powers may be thought to contribute to international order by exploiting their predominance in relation to the rest of international society. It is at first sight inconsistent to argue that whereas international order is served by balance or equilibrium between the super powers it is also served by a lack of balance in the relationships between these states and others. What reason is there to think that the super powers, when uniting to impose their will on other states, will be any less subject to the temptations of overweening power, any more capable of acting as the universal policeman, than either would be separately if it were not checked by the other? Is the idea of a super power concert or condominium anything more than a formula of collective aggrandisement at the expense of weak states? Yet the idea of the collective preponderance of the great powers is just as deeply embedded in traditional notions of world order as is the idea of a balance of power among them.

One way in which great powers act so as to promote international order is by maintaining dominance, hegemony, or primacy over particular areas of the globe or among particular groups of states. The preponderance of a great power in relation to a given area or group of states comprehends a great variety of relationships. There are some, like the relationship of imperial Britain to the Indian princely states and to 'protected' states in various parts of the world, where there is a habitual resort to force and where it is proper to speak of *dominance*. There are others, like the relationship of the United States to the states of Central America or the relationship of the Soviet Union to the states of Eastern Europe at the present time, where resort to force takes place only intermittently and the normal expression of preponderance takes an economic or an ideological form, where it is more appropriate to speak of *hegemony*. There are other relationships, like that of the United States to its NATO allies, where the special position of the great power does not appear to rest on explicit coercion but on acceptance of the fact that a more powerful ally makes a disproportionately large contribution to the common cause and is entitled to special rights and privileges in return, where it may seem best to speak of *primacy*.

The effect of all these kinds of preponderance is to establish order of a sort within the area or among the group of powers concerned. Soviet policy in Eastern Europe in the post-1945 period has prevented the eruption of any of the traditional national and territorial disputes among the powers of the area, and it has in addition through its interventions in Hungary in 1956 and in Czechoslovakia in 1968 maintained a broad ideological conformity in the area. The American primacy in NATO has provided the background against which France and West Germany have come to terms, West Germany has been restored as a military power without being regarded as a threat by her neighbours, the European community has grown up and the Greco-Turkish dispute over Cyprus has been contained.

The local dominance, hegemony, or primacy of a great power may be entirely unilateral; but it is sometimes reinforced by a spheres of influence agreement, in which two or more great powers exchange acknowledgments of one another's special rights in particular areas. A spheres of influence agreement is sometimes essentially predatory in purpose—as when the European great powers, together with the United States and Japan, staked out their respective claims in Imperial China. On the other hand it may sometimes reflect the conviction that burdens are being assumed on behalf of the areas in which influence is being exercised, as when Britain, France, and the United States decided on the distribution of their zones of occupation of Germany. In the former case as well as the latter, however, the interests of order may be served, for aggrandisement by the great powers is more tolerable to the international order when it is carried out within the framework of an agreement about the division of the spoils than when it is not.

A spheres of influence agreement may sometimes have the essentially negative purpose of avoiding friction among the great powers that concluded it: the agreements arrived at by the European powers during the partition of Africa, for example, had this purpose of allowing imperial expansion to take place while minimising the friction in Europe that was bound to result. However, a spheres of influence agreement may also have the positive purpose of establishing a division of labour in the execution of some common task. The notions entertained by Churchill and others in 1944-5 of establishing a world system based on the predominance of each of the several great powers in a particular regional bloc, such that each was the local agent of an agreed policy, represents the extreme case of a spheres of influence agreement that is positive in purpose as well as negative.

It is difficult to find evidence that spheres of influence agreements even of a tacit kind have yet come to play any important part in Soviet-American relations. The United States and the Soviet Union certainly recognise the fact of each other's predominant influence in certain parts of the world, but this is not the same as recognition of a right to predominant influence. It might be said that the two super powers, at least since the Soviet Union's abortive intervention in Cuba in 1962, have come to respect one another's rights on grounds of national security to predominant influence in Eastern Europe and Central America, even though they have not explicitly recognised any such rights, and are clearly unwilling to concede each other what used to be described 'a free hand', as witness American protests over Czechoslovakia and Soviet protests over Santo Domingo. But the idea of spheres of influence agreements that are positive in purpose and not merely negative, the idea that the United States and the Soviet Union should divide the world into spheres of responsibility as distinct from spheres of interest, does not yet appear to play any part in their thinking.

In addition to the unilateral dominance of particular areas or particular groups of states, and the dominance of these areas or groups in fulfilment of an agreement assigning spheres of interest or responsibility, great powers may exploit their preponderance so as to promote order by establishing a system of condominium or coimperium throughout the international system as a whole, of the sort discussed above by Dr Holbraad. Such a system was often advocated in the 1960s, when the United States and the Soviet Union were evolving methods of coping with the dangers of nuclear weapons but their efforts seemed likely to be frustrated by the rise of new nuclear powers, especially China and France. John Strachey, for example, advocated a form of super power condominium that would be restricted to two objectives, stabilisation of the nuclear balance between the super powers and prevention of the spread of nuclear weapons.[2]

There is no evidence that the United States and the Soviet Union have moved towards such a condominium, even one of the limited kind suggested by Strachey. It is true that the two super powers co-operate with each other against other powers over a number of issues. As co-sponsors of the Non-Proliferation Treaty they co-operate as nuclear haves against have-nots. In the debate about trade and aid they both act, despite strong conflicts of policy, as economic haves confronting have-nots. There is a form of tacit co-operation between them to contain China, especially in relation to the Indian sub-continent. Their policies in central Europe, so apparently in conflict, reflect the common interests they perceive in opposing any move by West Germany to acquire control of nuclear weapons or to alter the territorial *status quo* by force.

But there is no attempt to concert their policies *vis-à-vis* other states by regular discussions of the sort that take place within NATO and the Warsaw Treaty Organisation. There has been no attempt to enunciate any theory of world order, comparable with that of the Holy Alliance, that would state what their objectives were and assign to each its role in carrying them out. Such a theory of world order lies to hand in the provisions of the UN Charter concerning peace and security, which provide the great powers with the authority to keep the peace against disturbances of it by lesser powers, but recognise that they cannot deal with disturbances by one another; but the Soviet-American détente has not brought with it any revival of these provisions.

[2] John Strachey, *On the Prevention of War*. London: Macmillan, 1962. He did, however, argue that if the spread of nuclear weapons beyond the two super powers could not be arrested, a combination should be formed among the five or six nuclear powers. (See also Dr Holbraad's references to Strachey's ideas on pp. 12 and 22 above.)

To view the Non-Proliferation Treaty, discussed above by Dr Millar, as an instrument of super power hegemony would be to overlook the fact that the special privileges afforded to the 'nuclear weapon states' under the treaty apply to Britain as well as the United States and the Soviet Union, and would apply also to France and China if they acceded to it. Moreover, the actual division of states in relation to the Non-Proliferation Treaty is not one in which the super powers confront the rest, but rather one in which the super powers and Britain are aligned with the great majority of non-nuclear states, for whom the acquisition of nuclear weapons appears either unattainable or very remote, against the smaller number of non-nuclear states that are potential nuclear powers, supported for diplomatic reasons by China and France.

The policy which Strachey had in mind, that the super powers should actually prevent the spread of nuclear weapons, could be accomplished only by force and the threat of force, and it could even then be effective only for a limited period. Such a policy would in itself represent a considerable step in the direction of super power condominium. But the United States and the Soviet Union have never seemed likely to embark upon such a policy, separately or jointly. They have sought to combat the spread of nuclear weapons by promoting the Non-Proliferation Treaty, promoting safeguards against the military exploitation of civil nuclear aid projects, by providing their allies with guarantees of nuclear support, by persuasion and by a variety of political and economic pressures brought to bear upon potential nuclear powers. But they have shown no sign of being willing to resort to force, and in each case so far in which an additional nuclear weapon state has emerged, the super powers have come to terms with the situation soon enough.

Although the super powers both seek to contain China, each of them values China as a check upon the power of the other. Indeed the United States and the Soviet Union remain more concerned about each other than either is about its relations with any third party. In the 1960s the likelihood of war between America and Russia has seemed less than that of war between America and China, and in the late 1960s it has also seemed less than that of war between Russia and China. But it has been the Soviet-American relationship that has throughout been the relationship of major tension, in the sense that in allocating their political energy and attention, their military expenditures and deployments, the two super powers have been concerned primarily with each other.

The Soviet-American détente, then, has not given rise to any explicit condominium, nor is it easy to find evidence of an intention to move in that direction. But each of the super powers does have a preponderant position in certain parts of the world; in working out a *modus vivendi* with each other they necessarily impose a certain pattern or structure upon the international system as a whole; and in doing this they claim to be serving the interests of international society as a whole in security against nuclear war. The question we must now consider is whether this claim is valid.

As the détente became a reality during the 1960s it came to be perceived in some quarters not as a concert of the two leading powers forged to serve the interests of all nations in peace but simply as the beginnings of a new alliance serving the special interests of the United States and the Soviet Union. Professor FitzGerald has expounded the view of China that Soviet-American co-operation serves only to prop up the forces of imperialism and revisionism against just and inevitable revolution. Mr Richardson has discussed the differing and in some cases very negative reactions of 'the secondary powers' (Britain, France, West Germany, and Japan) to the emergence of the détente, and drawn attention to the ability these powers have to deter any tendency to arrogance on the part of the super powers. Professor Gupta has noted the disappointment of the Third World in the Soviet-American détente in which Nehru once placed such high hopes, a détente which for the poor countries of the world has brought with it not super power disarmament and an increased flow of foreign aid, but a new attitude of indifference towards poverty, anarchy, and violence in their midst.

It cannot be denied that the world order which is sustained by the co-operation of the super powers is one in which they have a special stake. International society as a whole may have a stake in the avoidance of a Soviet-American nuclear war. But states have conflicting ideas as to the objectives for which such a war may be risked, and the degree of risk that may be undertaken. The super powers themselves were prepared in the Cuban missile crisis to manipulate the risk of a central nuclear war for purposes of their own. Preservation of the nuclear peace between the super powers may be a primary interest of all countries, and may be assessed as such even in China, but it is not in any country's policy an objective which overrides all competing aims.

Where the super powers have been directly involved on opposite sides in a dispute, as in divided Germany, divided China, and divided Korea, the freezing of the *status quo* that has helped preserve the nuclear peace has resulted in the frustration in the demands of the super powers' allies. Where the United States and the Soviet Union have succeeded in 'de-coupling' their relationship from local conflicts, as has been the recent pattern of their policies in the Third World countries, this has produced a sense in these countries that they have been deserted and left to 'stew in their own juice'.

The super powers, moreover, in choosing the particular means that they will employ to preserve the nuclear peace, in choosing among competing doctrines of arms control and international security, always make choices that are self-interested, that are determined more by the special stake they have in the arms control doctrine in question than by the merits of the issue. In opting against radical disarmament and in favour of an attempt to stabilise the nuclear 'balance of terror' at high levels of strategic armaments, the United States and the Soviet Union have chosen a path for which compelling arguments may be given in terms of arms control, but which ensure the preservation of their own strategic pre-eminence. In espousing the doctrine that international security is endangered by the spread of nuclear weapons, as against the doctrines of some that the spread of nuclear weapons might positively enhance international security, or the views of some that nuclear proliferation may promote security in some cases and hinder it in others, the super powers have again espoused a line for which strong arguments may be made out in terms of the security of international society as a whole, but which reflect the fact that this particular arms control measure is one that calls for restrictions on others, not themselves.

The Soviet-American détente, then, promotes a world order that is super-power-preferred. International order in the sense defined at the beginning of this chapter, a pattern of activity that sustains the primary or elementary goals of the society of states, is in some sense a goal of all states. Allowing for the fact that statesmen from time to time adhere to the goal of overthrowing the society of states and establishing a world political system on some quite different basis, the policies of all major states now embody acceptance of the framework of international society. Even those states which wish to effect radical transformations in world politics—by eliminating capitalist economies or imperialist frontiers or unequal treaties or white racist régimes—still envisage international order as an important objective: they may see order as something to be temporarily subordinated until the transformations are made, but they see it also as something to be restored when this has been accomplished.

But international order is not an objective that any state regards as sacrosanct; and for states committed to radical change in international society as a whole or in some part of it, it is an objective that is bound to be subordinated. In so far as the lesser states of the world do value order as a goal, moreover, they are bound to perceive that a super-power-preferred world order is not the only route to it, that while disturbances might result in the transition from one system to another, a system in which for example China or Japan or a United Europe stood alongside America and Russia or in their place, would be capable of finding its own formula for the maintenance of order, and might embody a more congenial set of preferences.

It is not, however, a decisive argument against the Soviet-American world order that the two super powers have a special stake in its continuance. It is likely that any world order has to have its special custodians and guarantors, that no world order is possible that is not the preferred order of some group of states. The question the lesser states have to ask themselves is not whether they would prefer a world order in which no states had special privileges and responsibilities, but whether they would prefer that these privileges and responsibilities were exercised by a different or a wider group of states.

For the United States and the Soviet Union the problem is not how to eliminate their special stake in the system, but how to ensure that enough other states have enough of a stake in it also to produce that assent to or concurrence in the exercise of special responsibilities by the super powers that alone can give the system any prospects of enduring. The Soviet-American détente has in fact enjoyed a very wide measure of cautious and qualified support in international society at large, both within the opposing alliances and in the non-aligned world. There are some irreconcilable antagonists of the present system, but so are there in any political system.

In the long march of history the Soviet-American world order is bound to be swept aside. But it may last for some years yet if the United States and the Soviet Union are able to make the adjustments, hinted at in earlier contributions to this book, necessary to retain the consent they have so far enjoyed. In the case of the Third World this is bound to involve rejection of the doctrine, which applies Lin Piao's dictum in reverse, that the 'cities' of the world should pursue a life of isolated self-enrichment in disregard of the state of the 'countryside'. In the case of the secondary powers it will involve a willingness on the part of the super powers to treat Britain, France, Japan, China (and I should add India) as their equals in the affairs of Europe or Asia respectively. In the case of China there may be no way in which the super powers can win her co-operation except by treating her as an equal in every sense, and this would signify the transformation of the Soviet-American world order into something quite new.

INDEX